CARTERET AND NEWCASTLE

CARTERET AND NEWCASTLE

A Contrast in Contemporaries

BASIL WILLIAMS

FRANK CASS & CO. LTD.
1966

Published by Frank Cass & Co. Ltd.,
10 Woburn Walk, London W.C.1
by arrangement with Cambridge University Press.

First edition   1943
New impression   1966

Printed in Holland by
N. V. Grafische Industrie Haarlem

CONTENTS

PREFACE

When I had the honour, in 1921, to be appointed Ford Lecturer at Oxford, Professor Firth, that great historian, great teacher and generous counsellor to budding historians, explained to me that Ford Lecturers were expected to publish the gist of their lectures in book form; and he went through the list of past Lecturers, noting those who had complied with this condition and those who had not. I fear I have been slow in following his instructions; for my *Stanhope* did not appear till 1932, and this little sketch of my other two subjects, Carteret and Newcastle, makes its appearance over twenty years after the Lectures were delivered.

That I am enabled to publish this last instalment in difficult times such as these is due to the generosity of the sister University's great Press: for this and for the scholarly care with which it has been printed and illustrated I am deeply indebted.

I am also specially grateful, as usual, to my wife for her apt suggestions, and to my former colleague Dr D. B. Horn, of Edinburgh University, for his valuable criticisms of some of the chapters.

BASIL WILLIAMS

Christmas 1942

INTRODUCTION

CARTERET and NEWCASTLE were born within three years and died within five years of one another. Both went to school at Westminster and thence to the University; both started life with all the advantages of wealth, territorial possessions, powerful connexions and political traditions, advantages then almost essential for a political career. But here the likeness ends. No two men starting with almost equal advantages set themselves aims so different in public life, or attained positions so entirely contrasted in the estimation of contemporaries and succeeding generations.

Differing as they did in almost every respect—qualities and attainments, aims and ambitions in life—Carteret and Newcastle had this in common, that each, at the outset of his career, chose that part in the public life of the country in which he was most fitted to excel. For the organization of parties or the humouring of voters and members of the legislature Carteret had the utmost contempt; and for domestic politics he had no special bent, though even in that province, on a matter that interested him, he could show a master's touch. His chief ambition was to guide the fortunes of his country through the shoals and quicksands of foreign policy and to secure for England that predominance in the councils of Europe that he felt to be her due. To deal with kings and princes, then the arbiters of their countries' destinies, he regarded as his province, and conscious as he was of supreme ability in that sphere, he would brook no interference from colleagues whom he was too inclined to despise. Newcastle, with more limited vision, regarded the maintenance of a Whig majority in Parliament and the predominance of Whigs in every sphere of public life, lay and ecclesiastical, as essential for preserving the principles of the Glorious Revolution and the safety of the state. For his self-appointed role as fugleman of a pure Whig majority his wealth and territorial influence gave him immense advantages; and even before he came of age he had already started on his career of electioneer-in-chief to the Whig party. His marked success in that capacity brought him almost as soon as he came of age titles and dignities to which Carteret never attained and high office—eventually the highest—in the state, which his political intelligence by no means justified.

In the heyday of his power Carteret, when asked by his envoy to Berlin to procure for him the 'Green Riband' of the Thistle as a reward for services rendered, replied 'These are affairs I do not meddle with'; and to a pertinacious suppliant for some lucrative post, 'What is it to me who is a judge or a bishop? It is my business to make Kings and Emperors, and to maintain the balance of Europe.' Later, in the dark November days of 1756, when he himself, nearing seventy, had retired from executive office, he said to his favourite pupil Henry Fox, who had expressed his preference for the lucrative ease of the Pay Office to the post of danger as Secretary of State: 'I don't love to have you say such things. If you was my age, very well: I have put on my night-cap; there is no more daylight for me; —but you *should* be ambitious. I want to instil a noble ambition into you; to make you knock the heads of the Kings of Europe together, and jumble something out that may be of service to this country.'

Contrast with these outbursts of self-assurance and haughty in-difference to human weaknesses from Carteret Newcastle's feeble self-depreciation on which, almost at the outset of his career, his good friend the younger Craggs addresses to him these home truths: '[Do not] show that at the least difficultys made by some of your friends, you are ready to cry peccavi.... Men in your rank and credit, in order to keep up an interest, are to avoid making themselves cheap as much as they are to show no pride and insolence.... The noisy hot-headed people of your own friends, tho' much the majority of them, govern you and make you disoblige the rest. Don't let them see you so easily frighted.'[1] Contrast too the Duke's own timid out-pourings to his crony Lord Hardwicke later in life: 'I have done my best and think I have done well. I am afraid others are of a different mind:...If I err from *capacity*, it is not my fault'; his fretful com-plaints that he was 'not considered as much as he should be' by his colleagues; his admission that he was 'often uneasy and peevish, perhaps what may be called wrongheaded, to my best friends'; and his unwearying labours for half a century in 'obliging' suitors to him for bishoprics, pensions, sinecures and 'ribbands', and in practising all the arts of low political intrigue at elections, labours which stood him in no good stead on his fall from power, when, of all the twenty-six bishops he had created, only one attended his once thronged levée: 'Bishops', as he then said in the only witty remark recorded of him, 'Bishops, like other men, are apt to forget their Maker'.

Carteret never lacked a policy, but could never command a party

[1] Add. MSS. 32686, f. 143.

to carry it through: Newcastle, until the Patriot King found out the secret of his power and turned it against him, always had a party bound to him by self-interest, but never a policy on which to exercise the formidable instrument he had forged. For twenty years and more the two men, one with the grandiose ideas and the touch of genius, the other with the pedestrian talent, were rivals: and the victory at last rested, not with the brilliant statesman, but with the industrious politician, who, to make his triumph quite complete, swept his rival within his net. How came it about, it may be asked, that, where Carteret failed, Pitt, who admitted Carteret to be his master in all the upper departments of government, succeeded, not so much in beating Newcastle, as in using him for his own great purposes? It is the object of this study to find the answer to this problem, an answer which may be found not entirely discreditable, as might at first sight appear, to the English political sense of the eighteenth century.

The material available for an account of Newcastle's character and career is almost embarrassingly ample. After he came of age he seems to have preserved nearly every letter he received, and, not only the fair copies of those he sent, but also his own, almost illegible, first drafts, besides masses of memoranda and state papers, his rent rolls at various stages of his career, accounts of his expenses, especially on the banquets and electoral feasts (often with the menus) that he gave in such profusion, and above all full particulars of his own and his agents' activities at general elections. By the generosity of the late Earl Chichester all these documents are included in his gift of the Newcastle Papers (Add. MSS. 32684–33078) to the British Museum. Moreover, any conceivable gaps in this mass of self-revelation can be filled from the correspondence with and about him to be found in the 1000 volumes of his friend Lord Hardwicke's papers, acquired by the British Museum in 1899.

By contrast the records for the life of Carteret are disappointingly meagre. True, many of his despatches and official papers are to be found in the Record Office, and his own copies of them are conveniently collected in the volumes, Add. MSS. 22511–45, presented to the British Museum by his descendant, the Rev. Lord John Thynne. But there is a lamentable dearth of his more personal letters, except for stray remains in a few private collections. He himself wrote to the Duke of Newcastle, 'I never keep any copy of my private letters'; and what remained of his correspondence in the family archives was destroyed in comparatively recent times by one of his descendants, on the ground that 'In fifty years' time nobody will be interested in the old Carterets'. Still he was too forceful a personality to escape the attention of contemporary memoir- and letter-writers, such as Hervey, Horace Walpole, Mrs Delany, critical of him though they may have been; and even in his official correspondence he often indulges in an unconventional pungency of utterance, which gives a refreshingly personal touch to such usually arid documents. At any rate enough of him remains on record to tempt a veteran student and lover of the eighteenth century, long fascinated by Carteret's brilliant entrances and exits, to lay one more laurel at his feet.[1]

[1] Two biographies of Carteret have already been published, by Archibald Ballantyne in 1887 and by W. Baring Pemberton in 1936. So far, though much has been written about Newcastle, no full biography of him has been attempted.

Chapter I

CARTERETS & GRANVILLES;
PELHAMS & HOLLESES

§I. CARTERETS & GRANVILLES

In his person John, Lord Carteret, Earl Granville, first united the blood of the two Norman families Carteret and Granville,[1] who even before the Conquest appear as men of mark in the Cotentin peninsula facing the Channel Islands. Carterets had already obtained lordships and founded abbeys in the north of that peninsula, and also in Jersey, before two of them came over to England with William the Conqueror in 1066; Granvilles were lords of Corbeil, Thorigny and Granville farther south in the Cotentin when they obtained from the Conqueror lands at Kilkhampton in Cornwall. In John's reign, when the Norman barons had to opt between their English and French lands and allegiance, the Carteret Seigneur de St Ouen gave up his more valuable barony of Carteret and other domains in Normandy in order to remain a vassal of the English king in Jersey and for his English fiefs; the Granvilles likewise opted for their Cornish grants. During the next five centuries Carterets were always to the fore in defending the Channel Islands from French invaders and later against English rebels to the Stuart kings, not without reward from their sovereigns, from whom, as well as by prudent marriages, they acquired the lordship of Sark and great estates in Jersey and Guernsey. Of the Granvilles it is recorded that 'for at least Five Hundred years [they] never made any Alliance, Male or Female, out of the Western Counties', so that by the beginning of the eighteenth century 'there is hardly a Gentleman', writes a Granville to his kinsman, 'either in Cornwall or Devon but has some of your blood': in fact in the remoter parts of Cornwall the Granvilles exercised a sway more despotic than the King's. In Elizabeth's time a Carteret, Sir Philip, was knighted by the Queen for his family's support of the new religion and for services against the French; an even more notable

---

[1] The orthography of the family name was long unsettled. Besides Granville, the variants Greenvile, Grenvil, Grenville, and several others occur in old documents. John Lord Bath seems to have stabilized Granville as the spelling of his branch. The Bucks offshoot of the family, into which Chatham married, fixed on the spelling Grenville.

Grenville, Sir Richard of Flores in the Azores, had a like honour. Richard's grandson, Sir Bevil, was known in his Cornwall as the 'Father of his Country', while 'the vertuous actions' of his wife Grace, it was written after her death, 'do yet smell sweet, and blossom, and Preach very powerfully to all her living relations'. Sir Bevil himself was a dear friend of Eliot and, like so many of Charles I's best supporters, had many scruples before casting in his lot with the King; but, having chosen this side, became, says Clarendon, 'the Foundation of what had been done in Cornwall.... A brighter Courage, and a gentler Disposition were never married together to make the most cheerful, and innocent Conversation'—before he met a hero's death at Lansdown in 1643.[1]

Bevil's son John Granville[2] and Sir George Carteret, the maternal grandfather and paternal great-grandfather respectively of our John, Lord Carteret, Earl Granville, appear to have been the first of these two families to have been brought once more into close relationship since they left the Cotentin in King John's time. John Granville, after his father's death, made it his business to consolidate the royalists in Cornwall and hold the Scilly islands for the King, while George Carteret, bailiff and Lieutenant-Governor of Jersey and a daring naval officer, brought over supplies for the king's men in Cornwall, besides defending his own island as a place of refuge for Clarendon, and also for Charles II as Prince of Wales and later as king. But in June 1651 Granville was ordered by Charles to surrender the Scilly islands to Blake; and in December Carteret, after a desperate defence of Fort Elizabeth, Jersey's last stronghold, was forced to yield his island also to the parliamentary admiral. Thus both Granville and Carteret became fellow-exiles with their king on the continent. On the Restoration John Granville, who had taken a large part in the negotiations with his cousin Monck, was rewarded by the earldom of Bath, designed by Charles I for his father Sir Bevil before his untimely death: while George Carteret, besides obtaining a baronetcy, became Vice-Chamberlain and successively Treasurer of the Navy, Vice-Treasurer of Ireland and a Commissioner of the Navy; he also became one of the eight joint-proprietors of the new colony Carolina and was granted a large slice of New Jersey on its conquest from the Dutch. Sir George, after the death of his only son Philip, who was

---

[1] For these early Granvilles or Grenvilles see E. Handasyde, *Granville the Polite*, 1933.

[2] John seems to have been the first of the family to fix the spelling of the name of his branch as Granville instead of Grenville.

Portrait by William Hoare, R.A., in National Portrait Gallery

JOHN CARTERET, EARL GRANVILLE, K.G.

killed with his father-in-law Lord Sandwich at Southwold Bay in 1672, thinking it 'prudent to provide for keeping up the honour of his name and family; and there being the greatest friendship between him and the Right Honourable John Granville Earl of Bath...a marriage was agreed upon between his [Carteret's] eldest grandson George Carteret, with the Lady Grace Granville, the youngest daughter of the said Earl; which was solemnized on March 9th, 1674/5 when they were both very young'. In fact the bridegroom was only eight and the bride just ten; and the marriage was not consummated till eleven years later.[1] A year after Sir George's death this grandson, our Carteret's father, was created Baron Carteret of Hawnes in recognition of his grandfather's services and his father's gallantry. He died in 1695 leaving an elder son John, the second Lord Carteret, then only five years old, the subject of this memoir, another son Philip, a lad of great promise who died in 1711, and a daughter Jemima. Thus came it about that in Lord Carteret, the statesman, were united the two great pre-Conquest families of Carteret and Granville, equally notable in English history for their loyal services to the king, but hitherto mainly in their separate spheres of the Channel Islands and the West of England.

The first Lord Carteret's widow Grace, who survived her husband close upon fifty years, was created Countess Granville in her own right in 1715, four years after the death of her nephew the third and last Earl of Bath of the Granville family; and after several family law suits she and her sister Lady Jane Leveson-Gower were awarded most of their father's great estates in Cornwall and Devonshire. Grace, Lady Granville was a notable woman, hardly less shrewd in business than her contemporary Sarah, Duchess of Marlborough, and as formidable for plain-speaking to friends and enemies—'a pair of beldams' Horace Walpole calls them in recording their death on the same day. Known familiarly as 'The Dragon' or 'The Queen Mother' in the days of Carteret's power, Lady Granville was the terror of her cousin Mrs Delany and of that self-satisfied blue-stocking Mrs Montagu, notably on the day when 'she fell with all her violence on my complexion', though she was kind enough to attribute it to 'my lying-in': and perhaps the only person in whom she met her match in repartee was that saucy charmer Kitty, Duchess of Queensberry. But 'the pride that glowed in old Granville's heart', at which Mrs Montagu sneered, was chiefly concentrated on her son John.

[1] Collins, *Peerage* (1768), IV, 360–411; and *Remains of Denis Granville*, Surtees Society, 1865, p. 133.

She brought him up, after her husband's death, with the two other children, first at Hawnes, the Bedfordshire estate bought by Sir George Carteret with the help of Mr Pepys in 1667, with its park and noble trees, its lake and its historic house, where James I and his Queen had slept: there was also the town house in Arlington Street, 'the statesmen's row'. To his mother Carteret owed the care bestowed on his early upbringing and without doubt that 'noble ambition', of which he spoke to Fox in his old age, an ambition centred more on his country than himself. All the love and pride she felt for him overflows in one of the rare letters remaining from her. She was writing on his wife's illness to her son, then aged fifty, when he was in attendance upon the King in Germany, 'knocking the heads of emperors and kings together', the cynosure of all eyes in Europe.

My dear Son [the letter runs], you are infinitely kind and good to me in making me easy about Lady Carteret whose illness has lain very heavy upon my spirits....I am glad to hear you design to take your son under your protection [on his staff]....I am in great hopes he will turn out a man of bussiness for there is nothing I detest so much as an Idle Fellow.... The Dutchess of Marlborough has been lately told, and indeed yᵉ report is all over yᵉ Town, yᵗ there has been a Duel between you and a Foreign Minister, wᶜʰ report does not affect me in yᵉ least, tho' I can't help mentioning it....I beseech God to bless and preserve you in good health, and give you success in all your undertakings, for yᵉ honour and Glory of your King and Country. I am my Dearest son with gratitude and tenderness.

Intirely Yours

GRANVILLE[1]

At an early age Carteret was sent to school at Westminster, then the only rival of Eton for the training of great statesmen and of many of the princes of the Church. If Eton could boast of the two giants Walpole and Chatham, the Westminsters included—besides Carteret —Pulteney and Lord Hervey, Primate Stone, two archbishops of York and such notable bishops as Atterbury, Trelawney and Newton, Lord Chief Justice Mansfield, Lord Chancellor Northington, besides the Duke of Newcastle, his brother Henry Pelham and his faithful henchman Andrew Stone: Locke, the evangelist of the Whig party, had been of their number, Samuel Wesley overlapped Carteret at the school and his youngest brother Charles came later. The rivalry

[1] Add. MSS. 32416, f. 402.

between the two schools often survived the school age of Etonians and Westminsters. In spite of Locke, the Westminster of Atterbury and Freind had Tory leanings, and at any rate many of its pupils found in scholastic rivalry an additional incentive against Walpole. Not only did Pulteney vindicate the scholarship of his *alma mater* by his famous bet with Walpole on the correct reading of the line

Nil conscire sibi, nulla pallescere culpa;

but *The Craftsman* itself, the great opposition journal of George II's early years, posed as a Westminster opposition to the Etonian Sir Robert. Shelburne, Carteret's son-in-law, notes the strong *esprit de corps* of Westminsters, dating, he says, from Queen Elizabeth's reign, and explains thereby the fact that 'the Duke of Newcastle and the Newcastles were at the head of everything'. Newcastle himself, recommending Carteret's son going on the Grand Tour to the care of two of his ambassadors, picks out as the boy's chief merit that he 'issued from a place where you and I had our Education';[1] and Hervey records the scrape into which the Duke landed himself with Walpole, when he came back drunk from a Westminster dinner and urged Walpole to restore his school-fellow and fellow-diner Carteret to the Cabinet.

When Carteret went to Westminster, Thomas Knipe was wielding Busby's ferule, and Robert Freind was the undermaster. The curriculum was still practically unchanged from Busby's day. An exact training in Latin literature and composition was, as it still is, a glory of the Westminster education, finding expression, too, in the annual Latin play in the Dormitory. There Carteret acquired and retained to his dying day a taste for the Greek classics, and gained even a smattering of Hebrew and Arabic, English grammar and mathematics, while Busby's system of encouraging boys to read books extraneous to the normal curriculum bore fruit later in Carteret's omnivorous taste for good literature in most European languages. Knipe, a somewhat dim figure, is said to have been a good scholar; and Freind, though he took the wrong side in the Phalaris controversy, was a good Latinist with a happy turn for Latin verse. To him Carteret turned in 1711 for the Latin elegy inscribed on his brother Philip's monument in Westminster Abbey; Freind too was probably the author of the verses addressed to Carteret himself during his vice-royalty of Ireland:

[1] Add. MSS. 32693, f. 402. See also below, ch. v, p. 85.

Ad Dominum Carteret

Docte Baro, vocat ad partes te saepe Senatus,
  Poscit saepe tuam publica charta manum.
Te gnarum imperii turbata requirit Ierne,
  Tu noras solus conciliare Getas.
Quid sit scire vides; si mens foret inscia, possis
  Tu quoque securus luxuriare domi.[1]

The training at Westminster was undeniably rough and remained
so well into the Victorian era; not so rough though, but Cowper was
happy there. At any rate it did not deserve, relatively to other
schools, Chesterfield's scathing verdict on it as 'undoubtedly the seat
of illiberal manners and brutal behaviour'. Among its great attrac-
tions was, and still is, its proximity to and privileged connexion with
the Houses of Parliament and the Abbey, since the Westminster boys
have always had the right of attending debates in Parliament and
coronations etc. in the Abbey.[2] It was the custom too for members
of both Houses to stroll into the school yard to chat with the head-
master or any of the boys they knew,[3] or to listen to their declama-
tions and criticize their exercises. Thus Westminster justly earned its
reputation as a nursery for statesmen.

In January 1706 Carteret went up to Christ Church, with an
allowance for himself and servant of £200, which, though £300 less
than Commodore Trunnion allowed his nephew some forty years
later, was regarded as ample by the Christ Church don Dr Stratford;
while at Cambridge, even as late as 1774, the President of Queens'
told Lord Hardwicke that the usual allowance for a Fellow Commoner was '£300 p.a., keeping a servant and a horse, clothes and
pocket-money included'.[4] Little is known of Carteret's Oxford life,
save that he appears to have done some reading in the Bodleian, and
that he consorted with Edward Harley and his Tory friends, among
them being Dr Stratford and Bishop Trelawney's son: indeed it was
hard in those days to find any but Tories at Oxford; that he took no

---

[1] *Lusus Westmonasterienses*, 1730, p. 110: 'Learned lord, the Senate often calls thee
to debate, thy handiwork is needed in public business. Ireland, disturbed by civil
strife, needs thy skill in government; thou alone wast able to pacify the Swedes.
Thou seest what should be known; even though, hadst thou a vacant mind, thou
couldst live at ease at home' is a very rough translation of these couplets.

[2] My father, as a Westminster boy of ten, attended Queen Victoria's coronation.

[3] See the account of Stanhope's talk with Mar's son, Lord Erskine, a Westminster
boy, in 1716, in my *Stanhope*, pp. 195–6.

[4] D. A. Winstanley, *Cambridge in the 18th Century*, p. 23.

degree until 1756, when the D.C.L. was conferred on him by diploma; and that he imbibed there a lasting taste for good burgundy. But that his time at Oxford was not wholly ill-spent is attested by Swift's oft-quoted remark that, 'with a singularity scarce to be justified he carried away more Greek, Latin and Philosophy, than properly became a person of his rank; indeed much more than most who are forced to live by their learning will be at the unnecessary pains to load their heads with'; and also by Thomas Hearne's description of him at Oxford as 'morum suavissimorum et in primae classis scriptoribus, cum Graecis tum Latinis, supra annos versatus— (of courtly manners and precociously well-versed in the best Greek and Latin authors)'.

Carteret attained his majority in 1710, and, even before that, had begun to give evidence of the vigour and self-reliance that often disconcerted his rivals. An impetuous lover, then and later, he was already wooing Frances Worsley, a descendant of Elizabeth's Essex— with the blood of Seymours, Finches and Thynnes also in her veins— and, says Abigail Harley, 'a very pretty lady and £12000' to boot. In October he married her at Longleat, her mother's home; 'My Lord's matrimony sits very well upon him, as you'll easily guess', writes Robert Freind to Edward Harley, 'omnes decuit color et status'.[1] In the previous May, at almost the first possible moment, he had taken his seat in the House of Lords, and was soon deep in his own private concerns which were inextricably mixed up with affairs of state. For some time trouble had been brewing with the Granville relations, partly owing to their high-Tory, even Jacobite, proclivities, partly owing to property disputes with them. Of his great-uncle Denis, Dean of Durham, Archbishop Sancroft said 'he was not worthy of the least stall in Durham Church', to which the Bishop, Lord Crewe, had rejoined that he 'would rather have a gentleman than a silly fellow who knew nothing but books';[2] but he had become a non-juror and died in exile in 1703. Carteret's uncle John, Lord Granville of Potheridge, described by Mackay as a man 'of undaunted assurance, very hot for his Party, and Partial, jolly and of a fair complexion....inclining to be fat', was another high Tory and a high-flyer in ecclesiastical matters. During Carteret's minority he had represented his interests as one-eighth proprietor and Palatine of Carolina and had set the colonists by the ears by attempting, contrary to their constitution, to force upon them a Church of England

[1] H. MSS., Portland, v, 127.
[2] Surtees Society, 1861, p. 187.

establishment, and penalizing the numerous dissenters among them.[1] In Cornwall, where he managed the estates of Carteret's cousin the third and last Lord Bath of that creation, he was Lord-Lieutenant and used all his influence for the high Tories. But the most tiresome of all the relations was a cousin, the second-rate poet George, created Lord Lansdown in 1711, another high Tory. It was with him that Carteret's mother had the law-suit about her father Lord Bath's estates in the west. Besides personal reasons, Lansdown was especially anxious to secure these Cornish and Devonshire estates in order to consolidate the high-Tory interests in those counties, being himself a Jacobite and even joining the Pretender in 1715. Until the decision on the Bath estates was given in 1714, mainly in Lady Granville's favour, both sides were trying to establish themselves in key positions by putting forward their own candidates for vacant livings and higher posts. In 1711 Carteret, then no more than twenty-two years old, even went so far as to put himself forward for the influential post of Lord-Lieutenant of Cornwall, which so much alarmed Lansdown that he persuaded Harley, failing himself, to appoint Rochester.[2] It is hardly surprising, after these family bickerings, that in after years Mrs Delany, Lansdown's niece and for a time his ward, hardly ever mentions her formidable cousin Carteret without a sneer or a depreciatory innuendo. But in the main Carteret and his mother had carried the day; and Carteret's Olympian self-assurance was never much troubled by the tittle-tattle either of rival politicians or of relatives with a grievance.[3]

One of Carteret's first tasks on attaining his majority was to attend to the difficulties of colonial administration falling to him as Palatine of the Carolinas, the romantic title invented by Locke and well-suited to this brilliant and masterful young man. Nominally at least it implied quasi-sovereign rights over a vast province independent of the Crown. As Palatine he appointed governors, issued orders and approved of laws, for his seven co-proprietors took little interest in these distant possessions. He took his duties seriously; himself paid and housed the secretary who took the proprietors' orders; and, by his sympathetic dealings with the colonists and choice of officials,

[1] See B. R. Carroll, *Historical Collections of S. Carolina*, 2 vols. N.Y. 1836, II, 131–3, 145–57.

[2] *H. MSS. Portland*, iv, 693. For Lansdown's operations in the west and his law-suit with Carteret's mother see Handasyde, *l.c.* pp. 112–49. Later Lansdown was also concerned in the Atterbury plot, *ib.* pp. 188–217.

[3] For the Carteret and Granville family connexions see the genealogical tree at the end of this book.

tried to efface the grievances provoked by Lord Granville of Potheridge's tactless innovations. But it was a hopeless task he had undertaken. Neither he nor any of his co-proprietors had been to Carolina
to see for themselves the difficulties with which the settler had to
contend, nor were they 'inclined to involve their English estates in
debts for supporting their property in Carolina'. Matters came to
a head early in George I's reign, when the colonists, besides the
restrictions imposed on their trade and religious liberties by previous
Palatines, were suffering from the depredations of Indians and pirates
without adequate resources for defence. They sent over a deputation
to England in 1715 to demand help from the proprietors or, failing
them, from the Crown; and Carteret himself was forced to admit
that, since the proprietors could not provide adequate assistance 'on
this melancholy occasion', the King should be asked to provide the
money and, if it were not repaid within a reasonable time, should
have an 'equitable right to take the government within his immediate care and protection'. However, the danger passed off for the
time being and Carteret sent out a more sympathetic governor.
But four years later another deputation came over with a fresh sheaf
of complaints to lay before Carteret, in whose fair dealing the
settlers expressed confidence. Unfortunately he had just been sent
off as ambassador to Sweden, and his colleagues in England were
quite unable to settle the grievances, with the result that it became
necessary for the Crown to resume the grant of the Carolinas.[1]

The final settlements about Carolina still took many years to conclude, but they may be conveniently summarized here. It was not
till 1729 that an act was passed whereby Carteret's seven co-proprietors, for £3000 apiece, resigned to the Crown all their interests
and rights in Carolina. But Carteret himself stood out of this
arrangement. 'My interest in it', he wrote to the Secretary of State,
'is more considerable than that of any one of the other Proprietors....
I had much rather remain as I am under the Charter than surrender
the same'; so he remained with his undivided eighth, 'still Palatine
of Carolina, and the only subject', as he boasted, 'who has the
honour of being joint Proprietor with the Crown'. But, as might
have been foreseen, this anomalous arrangement did not work:
Carteret never received the £4800 annual income he considered his
due from the undivided eighth and his office of Palatine, and was glad
enough in September 1744, by an indenture signed by himself and

[1] See *Calendar of Treasury Books and Papers*, 1729-30, p. 122 and Carroll, *l.c.*
I, 200.

King George, to give up his eighth with all his powers of law-making and administration, in exchange for 'one full eighth part of the provinces of Carolina, in one entire separate district in the province of North Carolina', in absolute ownership; and in return to pay the King the sum of £1. 13s. 4d. annually on the Feast of All Saints.[1]

'A fine person, of commanding beauty, the best Greek scholar of the age, overflowing with wit...whose imagination never failed him, and was joined to great natural elegance'; such even in old age he appeared to his future son-in-law Shelburne. Small wonder that in the heyday of his brilliant youth it was a source of speculation to the political *quidnuncs* on which side in the last critical days of Queen Anne Carteret would bestow his great gifts. His only Carteret relation of any account, his uncle Edward, a joint Postmaster-General, was a Whig, but his Granville relations were all more or less deep-dyed Tories, and so were most of his Oxford friends. He was on good terms with the Treasurer Oxford, who commissioned him to find out if his wife's grandfather Weymouth could be tempted by an earldom, and still more so with Oxford's rival St John, to whose dining club he and Swift were invited: so it was on the Tory side that he first reckoned.[2] But he soon showed signs of independence, voting on the Hanoverian issue with Weymouth and Nottingham in December 1711; and by 1714 with Anglesey and a few other peers was regarded as the 'heart of a flying squadron' which inclined the scales in favour of the 'Whimsicals' or 'Hanover Tories'.[3] By the time George I arrived in England his loyalty to the Hanoverians and his political value were so marked that he was made a Lord of the Bedchamber and Bailiff of Jersey. At the outbreak of the 1715 rebellion he was even made Lord-Lieutenant of Devonshire and sent down to watch Jacobite activities in the west, his cousin George, Lord Lansdown, who had coveted the post, sourly noting that 'Carteret and Boscawen are gone Post into Cornwall, upon what Arrand the Lord knowes, for if we are to believe what we are told all prospect of disturbance

---

[1] See P.R.O., S.P. 63, f. 390 (15 March 1727/8), Add. MSS. 32693, f. 37 (21 Jan. 1739/40) and for Carteret's final renunciation Collins, *l.c.* IV, 406–9. It may here be noted that Carteret had with five other proprietors similar rights in the Bahamas. In 1735 Carteret and his fellow-proprietors transferred these rights to the Crown for 1000 guineas apiece. See *Acts of Privy Council (Colonial)*, III, 1720–45, pp. 370–6.

[2] *H. MSS. Portland*, v, 33; *Swift's Works* (Scott), II, 135, 184; III, 37.

[3] Bodleian MSS. Bullard, vol. 21, f. 175; Rawlinson, vol. 92, f. 627; see too K. Feiling, *History of the Tory Party*, pp. 443, 466.

is over'.[1] Lansdown himself was safely lodged in the Tower four days later; and Carteret, serene as ever, wrote to a friend from Stowe, his grandfather's palace near Kilkhampton, 'I am now 200 long miles from you situated on a cliff overlooking ye sea, and every tide have fresh prospects of ships coming home....Most of ye neighbouring Gentlemen have been wth me and I am satisfied y^t ye king will have no reason to expect any Disturbances from ye West....I will do all I can to improve their thoughts of ye ministry'.[2]

'His species of oratory', again says Shelburne, 'was more calculated for the Senate than the people'. But to this grandiloquent style the House of Lords of the day was specially attuned. There his speeches found favour from the outset, notably that of February 1719, in which he defended Stanhope's Quadruple Alliance and the policy which led to the destruction of the Spanish fleet at Passaro. It had even been hinted before that he might be brought in to supplant Stanhope himself as Secretary of State.[3] But he would certainly not have lent himself to such an intrigue. When Walpole and Townshend seceded from the ministry in 1717, he had stuck to Stanhope and Sunderland; and shortly afterwards Stanhope picked him out for the delicate and difficult negotiations he was setting in train to secure the peace of the North. For this task no better ambassador could have been chosen. Though barely thirty years of age, he had all the equipment needed by a finished diplomat for making himself at home in any society: he not only could speak French and German, but had, for an Englishman, a unique knowledge of the constitution and complicated politics of the Holy Roman Empire, bound to be involved in the consideration of Sweden's German possessions; above all he had such consummate self-confidence that he would never flinch from rapid decisions involving serious responsibility. On 11 July 1719 Carteret arrived in Stockholm and forthwith plunged into the most notable and successful negotiations which he ever undertook.

§II. PELHAMS & HOLLESES

Of Newcastle's forbears there is less of public interest to say than of Carteret's, for their importance lies not so much in service to the state as in amassing the great wealth and vast estates, which proved

---

[1] Handasyde, *l.c.* p. 149.　　　　　[2] Stowe MSS. 228, f. 126.
[3] See Paston, *Lady M. W. Montagu*, p. 289.

the foundation of Newcastle's influence and importance during the reigns of the first two Hanoverians.

Two families, as in the case of Carteret, mainly contributed to the Duke of Newcastle's eminence—the Pelhams and the Holleses. The earliest Pelham to attain renown was John de Pelham, who made good his claim to have been one of the knights who captured King John of France at Poitiers in 1356, earning thereby the right of quartering a buckle and a broken belt in the Pelham coat of arms. His son Sir John was made Constable of Pevensey Castle by John of Gaunt and was the first to settle in Sussex, thereafter the stronghold of the family. The Sir Nicholas of Henry VIII's reign distinguished himself in 1545, as recorded on his monument in St Michael's Church at Lewes:

> What time the French sought to have sackt Sea Foord
> This Pelham did repel 'em back aboard.

Otherwise in Tudor and Stuart times the Pelhams did not throw up any men of great distinction, but carefully built up the family fortunes by good marriages, by their influence as county members and by acquiring broad acres in Sussex and the neighbouring counties. The Sir Thomas, of James I's reign, who had married a niece of Walsingham, obtained a baronetcy; Newcastle's grandfather, Sir John, voted for the restoration of Charles II and married a Sidney, sister of Algernon and Sacharissa; and his father Sir Thomas, for his ardent support of the Revolution, was rewarded by a place on Godolphin's Treasury Board and by the barony of Pelham of Laughton. It was this Pelham who by his two marriages secured for Newcastle those great aristocratic connexions and that vast wealth which were the foundations of his political power. Sir Thomas's first wife Elizabeth, daughter of Sir William Jones, 'Bull-faced Jones', brought him a large fortune and a daughter Elizabeth, the first wife of Lord Townshend; his second wife Lady Grace Holles, daughter of the third Earl of Clare and sister of the Duke of Newcastle of the second creation, was the mother of Thomas Pelham, our Newcastle, who was of the third creation, of Henry Pelham and of four well-married daughters.

The Holleses had much the same history as the Pelhams, amassing large fortunes by good marriages and careful attention to their own interests. In the Tudor period the first of the name on record, Sir William, a Warwickshire man, is said to have acquired estates in seven counties, and became Lord Mayor of London. His grandson,

Portrait by William Hoare, R.A., in National Portrait Gallery

THOMAS PELHAM-HOLLES, DUKE OF NEWCASTLE, K.G.

John, bought from James I for £15,000 the barony of Laughton in Sussex and a revival in his favour of the great Earldom of Clare, which went back to the days of the conquest of Ireland. The second Earl, brother-in-law of Strafford and brother of Denzil Holles, had none of the public spirit of his brother or of the contemporary Carterets and Granvilles of the Rebellion days. 'A man of honour and courage', says Clarendon, 'if his heart had not been set too much upon the keeping and improving his Estates'; while Colonel Hutchinson dismisses him more curtly as one 'who was very often of both parties and never advantaged either'. The third Earl of Clare seems to have been a nonentity, but two of his children made marriages notable for their influence on the Pelham family fortunes. His second daughter was the Lady Grace who married Newcastle's father; his son John Holles, fourth Earl of Clare, married Lady Margaret Cavendish, the daughter and heiress of the last Cavendish Duke of Newcastle-upon-Tyne, on whose death he inherited Welbeck and most of the Cavendish estates. Three years later he was created Marquess of Clare and Duke of Newcastle-upon-Tyne (second creation). The richest man in England, he lived in princely style at Welbeck, where he entertained King William at vast expense for five days: his electoral and political importance was assured by his great estates in five counties, in four of which he was Lord-Lieutenant, a position then specially useful at election times. For this reason, no doubt, though a convinced Whig, he was allowed by the Tories to retain the Privy Seal, originally conferred on him by Godolphin, till his death in 1711.

By his will this first and last Duke of Newcastle of the second creation, having no direct male heir, and passing over his own daughter Henrietta, left all his property to Thomas Pelham (Newcastle), the eldest son of his sister Grace, Lady Pelham. This will led to litigation, as in the case of Carteret, between the Pelhams and Carteret's friend Edward Harley (second earl of Oxford), who had married Lady Henrietta Holles. This litigation was not concluded till 1719, when the Harleys obtained the Cavendish estates, but all the other property of the Holles duke was awarded to Thomas Pelham, by that time himself Duke of Newcastle of the third creation, with the proviso that, according to the last Duke's wishes, he should always retain Holles as part of his title.[1]

[1] This complicated litigation is well summarized in A. S. Turberville's *Welbeck Abbey*, I, 302–27. Newcastle always signed himself 'Holles-Newcastle'. For Newcastle's family connexions see the genealogical tree at the end of this book.

Thomas Pelham-Holles was born in 1693 and did not attain his majority till a few days before George I's accession, two years after he had succeeded his father as Baron Pelham of Laughton. Like Carteret he had been to Westminster and also, like Carteret, had Latin verses addressed to him in later life by Freind. He went on to neither of the Westminster colleges, Christ Church or Trinity, Cambridge, but to Clare, one of the smaller Cambridge colleges, no doubt because it was founded by one of the Clare family. Here the teaching was certainly better than Carteret is likely to have found at Oxford, especially that given by Newcastle's tutor Richard Laughton. But he profited little by it, and never thereafter showed any interest in scholarship or literature. None the less, he became Chancellor of his university in 1748, a dignity Carteret never attained. Scholarship indeed was hardly to be looked for in the owner of the richest and most extensive estates in England, estates covering large tracts of Sussex, Lincolnshire, Nottinghamshire, Yorkshire, besides smaller properties in Derbyshire, Dorset, Wiltshire, Hertfordshire, Suffolk, Kent and London, where he owned, and was nicknamed the 'King of', Clare Market, estates bringing in a rent roll of some £40,000 p.a.[1] Besides Newcastle House, his stately residence at the north-west corner of Lincoln's Inn Fields, he had three houses in Sussex—Laughton Place, Halland, his favourite seat in the county, and Bishopstone, chiefly used as a hunting lodge. He also owned Nottingham Castle, where, says Defoe, he laid out 'the finest gardens in all that part of England'. Not satisfied with all these mansions, when he was still Earl of Clare he bought, for a week-end retreat, an estate of 1500 acres at Weybridge, and got Vanbrugh to build him a 'castellated prospect house', with gardens laid out by Kent, naming it Claremont.[2]

In 1717 he added to his important political connexions by his marriage to the Lady Harriot, daughter of Lord Godolphin and granddaughter of the great Duke of Marlborough. He seems at first to have wavered about taking this step, but once married he found in his Duchess the most faithful and loving of all his numerous

---

[1] See *English Historical Review*, XII, 195; and S. H. Nulle, *Thomas Pelham-Holles, D. of Newcastle*, p. 17.

[2] On Newcastle's death in 1768 his duchess sold Claremont to Clive, who built another house designed by Capability Brown; Clive's coat of arms is still to be seen on the Corinthian portico of this edifice. It was bought for £66,000 for Princess Charlotte on her marriage, and then was given to the Duke of Kent on his marriage to the mother of Queen Victoria. (See D. M. Stuart, *The Mother of Queen Victoria*, pp. 17-18.)

confidants. She never took any public part in his affairs, but he confided to her all his troubles, his state-secrets and even his peccadilloes, such as occasional excesses at electoral feasts: at times too he even entrusted to her the transcription into legible form of his almost indecipherable scrawls to such faithful friends as Hardwicke about his grievances against other colleagues. His almost life-long correspondence with his 'dearest' is preserved in six bulky volumes of the Newcastle correspondence at the British Museum.[1]

Another faithful coadjutor during most of the Duke's official career was his secretary Andrew Stone, also an old Westminster. Shortly after taking his M.A. degree from Oxford in 1728, Stone entered Newcastle's service as private secretary, a post he held till the death of Frederick, Prince of Wales, in 1751, when he was made sub-governor to the young prince George, but for ten years longer remained a trusted confidant of the Duke. A touching illustration of Newcastle's and Stone's kindly relations occurred on Stone's marriage in July 1743: Newcastle writes to ask if he can still attend to his secretarial duties at Claremont or in the London office, adding that though he would miss his help very much he would not stand in his way, to which Stone replies thanking him for his considerate letter but that he had no wish to quit the Duke's service.[2] It must have been one of the bitterest blows to the Duke after the accession of George III that Stone attached himself to his enemy Bute.

On the accession of the Hanoverian dynasty in 1714 the electoral influence and the wealth of such a young man as Newcastle were indispensable to the new King, by no means yet secure on the throne. He was, it is true, unlike Carteret, of unimpeachable Whig connexions on both sides, but obviously his affections must be riveted by the methods best understood in that age. Ministerial office or even a Bedchamber appointment, as in the case of Carteret, could hardly be given at first to a youth barely out of his teens, but honours could be, and were, lavished upon him. At the coronation he was raised two steps in the peerage as Viscount Haughton of Notts and Earl of Clare in Suffolk; a year later, after some useful work in the election of 1715, he obtained his uncle's titles, Marquis of Clare and Duke of Newcastle-upon-Tyne, the Wardenship of Sherwood Forest, the Vice-Admiralty of Sussex and the Lord-Lieutenancies of Notts and Middlesex, with the City of Westminster. It was not till 1717, after the rift between Stanhope and Sunderland on the one side and Walpole and Townshend on the other, that he attained office as Lord

[1] Add. MSS. 30373-8.   [2] Add. MSS. 32700, ff. 211, 232.

Chamberlain and was sworn of the Privy Council. In the following year he was created a Knight of the Garter, a distinction not granted to Carteret till thirty years later. This event was also celebrated in a poem addressed *Ad Ducem Novi Castri*, presumably by Freind, who bade him, in an atrocious couplet:

> Sume Periscelidem meritam, dum candida gaudet
> Virgula munificam nobilitare manum.[1]

'Assume the well-earned Garter, while the Chamberlain's white staff gladly ennobles thy munificent hand.'

Newcastle had two ruling passions, devotion to the Hanoverian succession and its instrument the Whig party, and a love of power, which to satisfy him, must be amply recognized, for it was not enough for him to pull the strings, if the puppets were not consciously dancing to his tune. True, he rarely knew how to make the best use of what power he attained: the flattering unction that came from power over others was to him an object in itself. Failure to control colleagues abler than himself led in after life to his perpetual jealousy of them, to shrill complaints that he was not enough considered and in the end generally to successful attempts to jockey them. There were, however, two spheres in which he was ultimately allowed to be supreme: the management of elections and the distribution of places to peers, members of parliament, clerics and even down to tide-waiters, the lowest grade of customs officers, whose co-operation was thought necessary in Parliament or at the hustings. In those two connected spheres of political activity during most of his life his preeminence was hardly questioned.

* *
*

With these preliminary indications of their origins and dispositions, we may now trace the very different results attained by these two almost exact contemporaries, each in his own way characteristic of eighteenth-century political life. Both endowed with every advantage that wealth and family connexions could afford, and both, though in very different ways, with the country's interests at heart, neither of them, owing to some kink in his composition, succeeded in attaining the supreme distinction of the giants of their day, Walpole and Pitt.

[1] *Lusus Westmonasterienses*, p. 74.

Chapter II

CARTERET IN SWEDEN; NEWCASTLE AS LORD CHAMBERLAIN & GRAND ELECTOR

§I. THE PERFECT AMBASSADOR: CARTERET IN SWEDEN

In December 1718 Charles XII of Sweden was killed by a stray cannon-ball at the siege of Frederikshald. Charles, as Carteret said fifteen years later in the House of Lords, was 'so much the darling both of his nobles and commons that every one of his subjects was ready to sacrifice his life for him'. For twenty years the Swedes, fascinated by their heroic King, had endured without a murmur, even with enthusiasm, a state of war, first as victorious invaders of Denmark, Poland and Russia, and then, after Poltava, as desperate defenders of their own country, where they were gradually reduced to a state of semi-starvation. Now with the death of their King, their only desire was for peace and rest. The unanswered complaints of our merchants, excluded by Charles from their Baltic trade, which for four years running had brought a hostile British navy to their shores, suddenly found a hearing from the new Queen Ulrica, Charles's sister, who sent George I 'very respectful and obliging letters'. These overtures were eagerly welcomed by Stanhope, our great peace-minister. He wanted peace for our Baltic merchants to pursue their lawful avocations, but saw that no peace would be secure unless the unsatisfied claims of Poland, Denmark, Prussia and our own King George's Hanover were also settled. Above all he was alarmed at the growing might of Russia under Peter the Great, who after conquering Swedish provinces on the east of the Baltic was now attacking Sweden itself and seemed to aim at making the Baltic a Russian lake. As early as January 1719, in response to the Queen's obliging letters, Stanhope appointed an ambassador charged with renewing the old alliance with Sweden and with negotiating peace treaties between Sweden and Prussia, Denmark and Hanover, and also, failing a satisfactory arrangement with Russia, to promise aid to Sweden against that baleful cloud of power in the North.

The ambassador chosen for this exacting task was Carteret, a young man under thirty and with no previous experience of diplomacy. But Carteret had already shown many of the qualifications needed. An ardent supporter of Stanhope, after the formidable Whig brothers-in-law, Walpole and Townshend, had left the ministry, he had shown readiness in debate by eloquent and well-informed speeches in the Lords in favour of the Septennial Bill and in moving the address of congratulation on the completion of Stanhope's Triple Alliance and on the victory of Passaro; his pre-cocious knowledge of the Empire's constitution and of northern politics generally was a notable asset; and above all, with his buoyant self-confidence, he was not a man to decline responsibility when prompt action was called for in circumstances not foreseen in his instructions. For, as he wrote to his friend Craggs from Sweden, 'I am in a station where I can't stand still, but must do something; and to act without positive orders occasions, at least, anxiety. I hope I shall do nothing wrong in publick matters.'

Though appointed in January 1719, Carteret did not receive his instructions till May, nor was he able to start till June. After a fourteen days' journey by sea he landed at Gothenburg, where he found a Swedish army ready to repel a Danish invasion, and had to wait three days before he could get horses to take him to Stockholm. When he reached the capital it was already threatened by a Russian flotilla with an army of 30,000 ready to ravage the country. The Queen and her husband Prince Frederick of Hesse, shortly after-wards made joint King with her, were all for a brave front to the Russian invaders; but their power was very restricted, since one of the first results of Charles XII's death had been a revolution which transferred most of the authority of the state from the King to the Senate: and the Senate was for peace at almost any price with Russia. Carteret's first difficulty was to be admitted to present his letters of credence to the Queen, since the chancery pundits dis-covered that some of the Queen's titles had been omitted in them. But he was not to be put off by such trifles and, failing a public audience, secured a private and informal interview, at which he entirely won her heart by a well-turned compliment to the effect that, while her late brother Charles, of glorious memory, possessed all the military virtues, her own accomplishments proved that the Swedish house was no less endowed with the remaining virtues in their highest perfection. But there was not much time for pretty speeches with the Russians almost at the gates of Stockholm; and Carteret came at once to business. The only hope of salvation for the Swedes was the arrival of a British fleet sent to eastern waters under Admiral Sir John Norris. But that fleet was waiting at the Skaw at the north of Denmark, and Sir John's and Carteret's instructions were that it was not to move through the sound into the Baltic until satisfactory treaties had been made by Sweden with England and Hanover. As Carteret tersely put it, 'If the Muscovites land and beat the Swedish troops, there is an end of Sweden; if the Muscovites should be beat, which is most likely, Sweden will then be so elated, that there is an end of the King's business that way; but if she make a peace, which is the most likely of all, Europe, especially the trading countries, will feel the consequences of the Muscovite power in the Baltic'.

Unfortunately Carteret had to negotiate, not with the Queen and the soldiers, headed by their gallant old marshal Dücker, who were all for a renewal of the English alliance, but with representatives of the Senate headed by the Chancellor Cronhielm, a timid old man chiefly anxious to appease the Russian enemy at the gate, and also, as Carteret complained, 'an eloquent man, which has cost me much labour and time'. However, he finally induced the negotiators to agree, subject to the Senate's approval, to treaties with England restoring our trading rights in the Baltic and with Hanover for the formal surrender of Bremen and Verden, on condition that Norris should forthwith bring his fleet to the Baltic and cut off the Russians. But two evenings later the eloquent Chancellor and his deputation came to tell Carteret that the Senate would never accept the treaties without further modifications. To these new proposals Carteret could not agree, but offered a further compromise and gave them till 6 o'clock next morning to accept it. Six o'clock came, but no Senators; so Carteret prepared his master-stroke, an appeal to the Queen's consort Prince Frederick and the old marshal Dücker, encamped a six hours' journey away in front of the Russian invading army. Driving post-haste to the camp, where he found a Russian envoy presenting his ultimatum, he nevertheless obtained an order from the Prince and the marshal insisting on the acceptance by the Senate of Carteret's terms; he would rather, the Prince told Carteret later, serve in England than consent to the Tsar's conditions. The same evening Carteret, with the Prince's order in his pocket, drove back to Stockholm: 'As I came back', he wrote, 'I saw the Russian fires; he burns all upon the islands and takes the men prisoners.' After this the Senate made no further objection and agreed to the proposed treaties with England and Hanover, subject, of course, to the prompt arrival of Norris to deal with the Russian fleet. 'Our success is chiefly owing to the Tsar; he at the gates of Stockholm has reasoned best for us', as Carteret, ignoring his own prompt action, modestly observed; or rather, as his Hanoverian colleague more truthfully remarked: 'It is certain that if Lord Carteret had not been here, Sweden would at this moment be under the yoke of the Tsar.'

But he was not yet out of the wood. For, in spite of Carteret's urgent appeals, Norris did not appear in the Baltic for another month. This delay was due partly to Stanhope's orders to Norris not to move till he was certain that the Danes would not oppose his passage through the Sound, partly also to Norris's slow progress when he did start. During this month 'my house is full of Senators enquiring about the fleet', wrote Carteret; and in a private letter to his friend Craggs, 'no public minister was ever, for a month together upon so bad, nor upon so dangerous a situation as I have been. The common people looked upon me as the author of their misery by preventing the peace with the Czar, while no succour came'. In fact by 30 August the Swedes were on the point of breaking away from the provisional agreement, when at that very moment Carteret was able to show a letter from Norris saying he was on the way to Stockholm. To Norris Carteret wrote: 'I went immediately to Court, but Her Majesty was abed. I called up His Royal Highness, who received the news with the utmost pleasure.... You have a glorious scene of action open to you in which you will show the world what the English nation can do....Cut off the Czar's retreat and we are sure of him....God bless you, Sir John Norris. All honest men will give you just applause....I now thank God that I have prevented their making peace with the Czar. It lay heavy on my conscience whilst I saw their misery and heard of no succour coming.' In fact, as soon as news of Norris's approach came, the Russians precipitately re-embarked for Reval. 'At present', wrote Carteret to his friend Craggs, Stanhope's co-secretary, 'no ambassador was upon a better footing in this country'; while the Prince Consort said to him, 'Mon ami, ne me regardez pas comme prince, mais comme gentilhomme et officier anglais.'

Although the Swedes were glad enough to be rid of the Russian menace, their negotiators required tangible advantages in the shape of bribes before finally agreeing to any of the treaties Carteret had to negotiate; 'were it not for that money [already entrusted to his Hanoverian colleague Bassewitz] he and I should pass our time very ill in this country', he wrote to Stanhope; and he was accordingly allowed to draw up to £10,000 from the English treasury for similar purposes. His negotiations were even more eased by the gold ingots valued at £300,000 brought over in his luggage by his French colleague Campredon, whose instructions were similar to his own. Moreover, the English treaty with Sweden was only part of his task, for he was also charged with negotiating Swedish treaties with Prussia and with Denmark. 'One business at a time', he remarked at one stage of his negotiations, 'is enough for anybody, but I have always had the misfortune to have several on my hands at once.'

The treaty between Sweden and Prussia was chiefly concerned with Sweden's formal recognition, for a sum to be paid by Frederick William, of that King's conquest of Stettin. Carteret, helped by Campredon and the Prussian envoy Kniphausen, took the leading part in the negotiation which seemed on the eve of success, when Frederick William suddenly had 'a little start of passion', and forbade Kniphausen to sign the treaty. Carteret was in a quandary, for he knew this treaty was essential to Stanhope's great scheme of a general peace for the North, and that, if it were not signed forthwith, the whole question would be referred to the dilatory proceedings of a congress at Brunswick. So once more he assumed responsibility and decided to sign it alone for Prussia, *ad referendum*. 'I would give a good sum of money out of my own pocket to be well out of these circumstances', he wrote to Whitworth, the English minister at Berlin, 'I don't care for bold strokes and yet I have lived by nothing else here. Since I must venture I must do what is honestest, finish my treaty and keep my word to the Queen and Prince,...who will suffer extremely if I don't keep my word.' So on 1 February 1720 Carteret signed both the English and Prussian treaties; 'By experience [I have learned]', he wrote to Lord Polwarth at Copenhagen, 'one can do on a push and on a sudden what a long train of arguments and great skill and capacity in a minister cannot effect.' Fortunately Frederick William accepted the treaty and sent to Stockholm the 2,000,000 crowns agreed upon as the price for Stettin, after characteristically deducting the cost of the waggons used to convey the treasure.

There still remained a treaty to be negotiated between Sweden and Denmark. This proved to be one of Carteret's hardest tasks, owing to the bitterness engendered between the two peoples during the northern war. The Danes had driven the Duke of Holstein, Sweden's ally and a possible successor to the Swedish throne, from his province of Sleswig; they had captured Stralsund and Rügen in Swedish Pomerania and Marstrand on the Swedish border; and they showed no inclination to abandon these conquests. In addition they claimed dues, from which they had hitherto been exempt, from Swedish ships passing through the Sound. To these 'exorbitant and absurd' claims, as Carteret called them, the only concession the Swedes were at first willing to make was the recognition of the Danish conquest of Sleswig; all the other Danish conquests must be returned without any compensation. However, in October 1719 Carteret in Stockholm and Lord Polwarth at Copenhagen with difficulty had persuaded the Swedes and Danes to declare a six months' truce during which it was hoped that a permanent peace might be achieved. One happy result, at least, in English eyes, from this armistice was that Denmark was now definitely separated from Russia, with which our relations were becoming steadily worse.

But, though Carteret was supported in his attempt to secure a final settlement between Sweden and Denmark by the French envoy Campredon, no direct contact between the two nations could be made till the six months' truce had nearly elapsed. Then at last the Danes sent as negotiator to Stockholm Count Lövernörn, described by Carteret as 'the most disagreeable minister to this court that could have been chose'. What at last brought King Frederick IV of Denmark to consider concessions was the support secured by the dispossessed Duke of Holstein in a tour he made to Vienna, Berlin, and St Petersburg as well as Stockholm, and the fear that Denmark might even lose Sleswig. Finally Carteret with Campredon drew up a treaty whereby Denmark restored to Sweden Stralsund, Rügen, Marstrand and her claims to Wismar, while Sweden gave up her opposition to the cession of Sleswig to Denmark, and agreed to pay 600,000 crowns, about half the Danes' original demand, and to give up her exemption from the Sound dues. Thus Carteret had obtained unexpectedly good terms for his friends the Swedes, who accepted the treaty forthwith. But the Danes still stood out. So Carteret, ten days after he had finished his business in Stockholm, in June 1720 crossed over to Copenhagen to strengthen Polwarth's hands with the Danes. Before arriving he had written to Polwarth to meet him as soon as he landed to concert measures before he saw the Danish ministers, 'who desire to talk to me before I meet your lordship. I let them think I will fall into those traps, but I am older than to be so caught.' When he did meet the Danish ministers, for four days they kept raising objections which led nowhere, but on the fourth Carteret dined with the King, who then took him over to see his stud. During this jaunt the two men went through the difficulties raised, and Carteret was so successful in meeting objections that on returning to Copenhagen the King called in his ministers and told them, to their stupefaction, that there was nothing more for them to say, as he had accepted the treaty. Some days later the King, taking Carteret aside, handed him his sword, valued at 20,000 crowns, with the words: 'Milord, comme par votre entremise j'ai fait la paix, et qu'à cette heure mes armes me sont inutiles, permettez-moi que je vous fasse présent de mon épée.'

By this time Carteret, who had been over a year in northern capitals, was fretting to go home to his family in England, but still had to wait in Copenhagen with little to do till the end of October. For one of the conditions of the Swedish-Danish treaty was that the Regent of France should guarantee to Frederick of Denmark the undisturbed possession of Sleswig, and it was not till October that Carteret at last extracted this guarantee from Campredon: in fact the French had made so many difficulties about honouring their obligation that Stanhope said Carteret had done wonders in finally securing it. Then at last, at the beginning of November, Carteret was able to start, but, owing to vile roads on the continent and contrary winds in the Channel, did not reach London till 13 December 1720. He had expected his mission to last three months: in fact it had lasted over a year and a half.

He might well have felt satisfied at the completion of one of the most arduous and complicated peace negotiations in the eighteenth century. It is true that, though he had made peace between Sweden and Hanover, Prussia, Denmark and England, he had not been able to round it off by bringing Russia also to terms. But that was not his fault. Conciliatory letters which he and Norris wrote to Peter the Great, when Norris first appeared in the Baltic, were contumeliously returned unopened by the Tsar; and indeed Stanhope himself does not appear to have wished for any serious effort to be made for a complete understanding with Russia. He seems to have thought that, with all the other northern powers at peace and with the annual despatch of Norris with a fleet to the Baltic, he would be able to bring Peter to terms and recover for Sweden her Baltic provinces, a fatal miscalculation, as was proved after his death by the treaty of Nystad imposed by Peter on Sweden in 1721 with a studiously contemptuous neglect of England's influence. But, as far as his instructions went, Carteret amply justified Stanhope's selection of so young and inexperienced a negotiator. His frank, easy-going manners, without a trace of the ordinary diplomatist's morgue, put him on the best of terms with kings, queens, ministers, soldiers and sailors with whom he had to deal; and by that frankness he won their regard and trust. The Queen of Sweden and her husband and the King of Denmark treated him, as we have seen, as an equal; the French ambassador Campredon, prejudiced at first against his policy, was soon won over. He hated that common refuge of weak diplomats, punctilio on trifles. 'Little points', he wrote, 'must ever be overlooked in transacting great business in such a ticklish conjuncture as we have here.' And he was as good as his word. After his 'pitched battle' with his 'eloquent' foe, the Chancellor Cronhielm, when the Chancellor had been beaten, and even severely reprimanded by the Queen for his behaviour, Carteret was not so ill-advised as to triumph over him. On the contrary, 'I now make my court to him', he reports, 'and by this incident shall finish the treaty sooner. I am never for pushing a victory too far.' In the same spirit he writes to Finch, his successor at Stockholm, not to treat Campredon with reserve, just because he happened then to be out of favour with the Swedes; he may come to the top again, and his support might at any time prove useful. 'The reason why', continues the wise young ambassador, 'the concurrence of so many people is wanted in negotiations is because it is not always to the interest of one's own court to exert itself so as to arrive at its end by the quickest way.'

His relations with Norris were a signal example of his tact. Norris was a 'rough admiral', as Newcastle called him, a man of little education to judge from his atrocious spelling, nor was he remarkable, as appeared on a later occasion, for his powers of co-operation in a delicate diplomatic mission. But Carteret soon understood his man and earned his goodwill by appearing always to defer to his opinion. He consulted him even on matters that could not be within the sailor's province. 'Send me your opinion on this', he writes when it is a question of bribing certain senators, and adds cheerfully, 'I have a working brain and will be an adventurer with you'. Nine months later he is just as tactful in representing himself to be anxious for the admiral's advice and just as full of that adventurous spirit calculated to attract the sailor's temper. 'I am in a station', he writes to him in June 1720, this finished diplomat of thirty, 'where I can't stand still, but must do something; and to act without positive orders occasions, at least, anxiety. I hope I shall do nothing wrong in publick matters. I am sure that I shall always make it my study to do right with relation to you, Dear Sir, for ever yours, Carteret.' By such tactful methods he secured the hearty co-operation of Norris, and no wonder the bluff sailor was completely won over.

Throughout his long and difficult mission he showed, not only tact and patience with his colleagues and opponents, but a large generosity in recognizing their merits. Not long before his return to England he well sums up, in a private letter to his friend the younger Craggs, his trials and this essential magnanimity: 'I have been in the *avant-garde*, almost an *enfant perdu*; but I have been well sustained by my friends. I have made no retreat, but maintained my post till the enemy left me. Sir John Norris has done very well. Don't be surprised at his backwardness at first. 'Twas for want both of strength and orders. I was uneasy at it once; but since I have talked with him am perfectly satisfied that his conduct from the beginning has been right....Love me, dear Craggs, as I love you. Yours for ever.'

The most engaging characteristics in his correspondence during this mission are a puckish humour in his descriptions of the tiresome people with whom he had to deal, and an almost schoolboyish zest in taking risks and tackling the sudden difficulties with which he was confronted without waiting for detailed orders from home, orders which would have taken weeks, if not months, to reach him. Under a chief such as Stanhope, of the same courage and power of initiative as himself, he could be assured of support for those independent actions and those risks which he had the rare courage to take. Later in life, unfortunately, he was to find colleagues less understanding of his audacious methods and less amenable to his proudly self-dependent ways.[1]

§II. NEWCASTLE AS LORD CHAMBERLAIN AND GRAND ELECTOR

Even before Carteret, by his brilliant diplomacy at Stockholm, had proved that he had in him the makings of a great statesman, his younger contemporary Newcastle had already, as he would have expressed it, 'chalked out' for himself the place in political life for which he was most fitted and in which he proved a supreme master: as grand elector and caucus-leader to the Whig party both in and out of Parliament. Unlike Carteret, he had no Tory connexions to hamper him, no doubts about pinning his faith to the pure doctrine of Hanoverian Whiggism; and, unlike Bubb Dodington, who expressed his disgust at having to spend three days 'in infamous and

---

[1] Carteret's correspondence about his northern negotiations is to be found partly in Add. MSS. 22511, 22513, and 28156 (correspondence with Norris) and also in *H. MSS. Polwarth*, vol. II.

disagreeable compliance with the low habits of venal wretches', he delighted in the gargantuan feasts and oceans of liquor with which he rewarded supporters or tried to conciliate adverse voters at election times. With few political ideas beyond that of carrying on the affairs of the country through Whig majorities, but with an intense pertinacity in securing for himself a commanding position in the party councils, he had all the means and characteristics necessary for his self-imposed task. With an inborn taste for the intrigues and shifts of electioneering contests and for the lavish expense and ceremonial display calculated to seduce or impress the electors, he started his career as the owner of no negligible number of pocket boroughs,[1] where his wishes were law, and with a fortune seemingly adequate even for the profuse entertainments and wholesale bribery then thought necessary to convince the voters in constituencies not so entirely dependent upon him. Above all he realized that success for the party depended not merely on the results of elections, but also on the constant refreshment of elected members by a judicious distribution of favours, and by an equally careful attention to the recruitment of the other House by packing the episcopal bench with clergy of unimpeachable Whig sentiments and the lay benches with peers likely to be equally 'obliged' to their creator. There had of course been bribery in elections and the dispensation of refreshers to members of both Houses long before Newcastle's day; Newcastle's great achievement was to create a system which proved permanent and supremely effective as long as he retained his own influence, and which his successors, Bute and George III himself, at best could only imitate.

As early as 1711, when he was barely nineteen, he began to exercise his territorial influence in Nottinghamshire, for the benefit of his Whig friends in the county; and two years later, while still under age, he took part in the general election, in which the Whigs had some success from their stand against the commercial clauses of the Treaty of Utrecht, helping to bring in the Whig candidate for Aldborough and exerting his territorial influence in Sussex.[2] In the same year, with his brothers-in-law, Lords Lincoln and Castlecomer,

---

[1] Professor Namier, in his *Structure of Politics*, I, 13, estimates the number of seats 'owned' by Newcastle as no more than twelve. His success as an electioneer was of course mainly due to his attention to the details, including lavish expenditure, of electoral campaigns throughout England.

[2] Bateson, *Changes in the Ministry*, p. 166; *H. MSS. Portland*, v, 377; H. Walpole, *Memoirs of George II*, I, 171 sqq.

the younger Craggs, Methuen, Pulteney, Steele and Addison, he helped to found the Hanover Club to promote demonstrations in favour of the Hanover Succession. In July 1714 he celebrated his coming of age by 'a noble entertainment' at one of his Sussex seats, the precursor of many such calculated to impress the Sussex electors: at this feast it is recorded that 7 oxen, 15 sheep, 8 bucks, a suitable accompaniment of dressed fowls, 80 stands of sweetmeats at the first table and a proportionate amount at the other tables were provided, and all this food was washed down with 49 hogsheads of strong beer, 7 of claret, besides champagne and burgundy and 4 hogsheads of punch, at a total cost of £2000[1]—a fitting foretaste of his habitual expenditure at election feasts throughout his life. Even in his old age he was almost as lavish, relatively, at his own table. In the *Register of bills of fare in the Duke of Newcastle's Household*, 1761–2,[2] the Christmas Day, 1762, bill of fare at Claremont with an abstract of the week's expenses, 'not including game sent from Sussex', is set down at £36. os. 1d. Nor in his early days was he afraid of enforcing his political opinions by more violent methods. In the last year of Queen Anne's reign, even at the risk of his life, he organized Hanoverian mobs; and during the Jacobite alarm of 1715–16 led storming parties against Tory and Jacobite strongholds in London. On the Pretender's birthday June 11/22, 1716, according to the Jacobites, 'the soldiers were ordered to fire upon Tories...and to support the Whig mob, or my Lord Pelham's, who distinguished themselves yesterday by wearing farthing warming pans;[3] his Grace's cunning contrivance, which aggravated the people like fire'. Of these exploits Newcastle retained a tender memory up to the very year of his death, when he declared: 'I love a mob, I headed a mob myself. We owe the Hanoverian succession to a mob.'[4] As a result of these activities he was able, at the general election of 1715, to claim victories in no less than eighteen seats, including one of those for which Stanhope himself was returned. By the next general election in 1722 he was already in office as Lord Chamberlain, which gave him some patronage and increased prestige. Two years before the actual contest he had begun laying groundbait for the Nottinghamshire electors in the form of 'Country entertainments', as a result of which he was

---

[1] *H. MSS. Portland*, v, 476.   [2] Add. MSS. 33256.

[3] In allusion, of course, to the supposed introduction in a warming pan of the Young Pretender into Queen Mary of Modena's bed in 1688.

[4] S. H. Nulle, *Thomas Pelham Holles, D. of Newcastle*, 1693–1724, pp. 73–5; *H. MSS. Stuart*, II, 227.

fain to confess to his friend Craggs: 'I have scarce been sober since I came, and did not go to bed till six this morning': but he no doubt thought the aftermath of victories in all the contested elections in the county was well worth a few splitting headaches. In Sussex, his chief electoral stronghold, where he had three country seats of his own, and where Pelhams and other relations, such as Shelleys and Ashburn-hams, were thick on the ground, he got all his candidates save one returned: and in the Yorkshire boroughs under his influence he also made 'a Sweep'. As a result of this general election the Whigs had a majority of over 200, largely due to Newcastle's exertions. At the election of 1727 on George II's accession he was even more successful: for the first time he secured the two county seats in Nottinghamshire for the Whigs, and brought five Pelhams besides six other relations into the House of Commons.[1]

No better example of Newcastle's electioneering methods can be found than in the general election of 1734. That was the only election in which, during the plenitude of his powers as grand elector, every exertion was needed to secure a victory for the government. For it was held in the year following Walpole's introduction of his Excise Bill, and though, owing to the intense opposition it aroused, Walpole had been forced to withdraw it, the agitation it caused and the sus-picion that it might be reintroduced had led to widespread alarm and indignation against the ministry. The loyalty of some of his most faithful adherents was shaken, and he found himself compelled to part with not a few office-holders, of whom the most conspicuous was Lord Chesterfield; while the passions of the country were in-flamed against him by the unscrupulous ability of the political writers in *The Craftsman*. On this occasion Newcastle remained entirely loyal to his chief, and prepared for and conducted the elections with conspicuous ability in the many constituencies where he had special interests as well as others in which his influence was less direct. Two bulky volumes of his MSS.[2] are entirely filled with his correspondence on this election—reports from agents, letters from voters and others asking for favours as the price of a vote, his own directions to his agents and others, and prompt replies to the most unblushing requests for favours. The magnitude of his operations may be judged from the fact indicated in these volumes that, either directly or indirectly, he had something to do with the election of nearly all the twenty

[1] Accounts of 1715, 1722 and 1727 elections are to be found in Nulle, *l.c.* and Id. *The D. of Newcastle and the Election of* 1727 (pamphlet), 1937.
[2] Add. MSS. 32688-9.

members for Sussex, of at least eight of the barons of the Cinque Ports, and with elections in Cumberland, Westmorland, Durham, Cheshire and Chester, Derbyshire and Derby, Nottinghamshire and its three boroughs, Yorkshire and at least two Yorkshire boroughs, Cambridgeshire and its University, Shropshire, Montgomery, Denbigh, Flintshire, Somerset, Hampshire, Monmouthshire and Dorchester: probably, too, though the fact is not evident from this correspondence, he had much to do with the election of the five government supporters out of the eight members elected in Lincolnshire, where his estates were large. It would certainly be no exaggeration to estimate him as responsible directly or indirectly for a round hundred members of parliament in this election alone, including a compact company of his own relations. Thus his brother Henry Pelham was elected one of the knights of the shire for Sussex;[1] two Pelham cousins came in for Lewes; one brother-in-law represented Shoreham, another Rochester; W. Hay, a cousin by marriage, sat for Seaford; and Pelhams were elected at Newark-on-Trent and Hastings.

For these favourable results Newcastle's own exertions and lavish largesses were principally responsible, especially in his own county of Sussex. In the eastern half of the county he was the chief local magnate, with his three seats, Halland, Bishopstone and Laughton, and estates extending over the parishes of Seaford, Laughton, East Hoathly, Ripe, the rape of Hastings and Lewes; he also had a brother-in-law, Sir John Shelley, at Arundel, and allies in the Ashburnhams, Sir William Gage, Lord Wilmington, the Duke of Dorset and Lord Abergavenny. In the western half of the county also, Lords Tankerville and Scarborough and the Duke of Richmond were in his interest, and even the Duke of Norfolk, though, as a Roman Catholic, unwilling to take an active part in the election, let it be known that he favoured Newcastle's candidates. In Sussex he had his best agents, notably one Richard Burnett, in charge of the Lewes district, whose quaintly spelt reports to the Duke about his Grace's 'pirtickerlor Commands' are of almost daily occurrence during the heat of the contest: in fact the poor man by his exertions developed 'a scurbitick humour' in his leg, but 'aughter a little recovering' resumed his labours until after the election was well over, when he was able to 'live very Regulor' and follow his doctor's directions. But the Duke did not depend solely on his own official agents; his correspondents during this election include bishops and clergy, peers, custom-house

---

[1] *Ex abundanti cautela* H. Pelham had also been put up for Aldborough, where also he was elected.

officials, inn-keepers, estate-agents, lawyers, tradespeople and even smugglers, a class of delinquent especially popular in Sussex, one of their happiest hunting-grounds. Thus a Major Battine, apparently a high police or customs official, wrote to the Duke that 'about 40 or 50 Freeholders that live on the sea coast between Chichester and Arundell' have sent the Duke of Richmond word that they will 'vote for Your Grace's brother and Mr Butler if one Tho⁸ Newman a notorious smuggler be released out of Horsham Gaol, but if he be not they will vote the other way'; and even Pelham himself wrote to his brother urging Newman's release on the eve of the poll, which the Duke accordingly secured, though not on such favourable terms as Newman had expected.[1] On the other side of the picture was the great use made of posts as tidesmen and other preventive officers bestowed on voters as an inducement to support the government. The people of Shoreham petition the Duke to appoint a Mr Clarke as collector of customs on the ground that 'he will make an agreeable neighbour' and presumably will vote straight. Such posts were safe investments for the government, as their holders were bound, on pain of dismissal, to vote as directed by the authorities. As early as 1715 Newcastle obtained the dismissal of John Daw, a tidesman in the port of London, for having incurred the Duke's 'displeasure at an election in Sussex'; and the poor man had to wait till 1729 before he was reinstated.[2] In most of the ports, indeed, a government candidate was bound to succeed owing to the predominance of such officers on the voters' roll. The clergy also, by their influence over their flocks, were found useful as fuglemen for the government. Accordingly the Duke not only exercised pressure on them, but also invited his friend the Bishop of Chichester, and even the Archbishop of Canterbury, to exercise their powers of patronage or of disciplinary monitions to secure a docile clergy. The Primate duly appointed a good Whig to the vacant living at Ringmer, and the bishop says he will 'do wᵗ he can if it does not appear to bee by way of a jobb'. The Bishop of Chichester, indeed, was a whole-hearted supporter, and had no hesitation in proclaiming his views, drinking the Duke's health immediately after the King's at a visitation banquet, and urging the Duke, with his numerous company and equipages, to

[1] He was required to obtain two bonds of £500 each to surrender again if called upon and not to smuggle again; and Newman complains that thus he would not be properly discharged, and might be falsely sworn against as a smuggler and be sent to prison again.

[2] *Calendar of Treasury Books and Papers, 1729-30*, pp. 156, 239.

put up at the episcopal palace during his final progress through the county on the eve of the election, promising him ample refreshment for himself and his suite, and making a special note of the Duke's desire to have his own bed well-aired and well-warmed.[1]

Such elections involved vast expense. During the long months taken up in preparation for the polling the amount of drink consumed, mainly at the Duke's cost, by his partisans, or wobblers whom it was hoped to enlist, was prodigious. When one of the opposing party treats the people of Burwash to a revel at which the candidate declares he would 'shake every freeholder by the hand and kiss their wives before Christmas', the indefatigable Mr Burnett responds with an entertainment of punch ushered in by the ringing of the church bells. The Duke's friend Sir William Gage, alarmed at the enemy's activity in his village of Firle, 'immediately secured every voter in Firle within his walls and talked to them so much last night over a bowl of punch, that I believe £10,000 would not purchase one of them'. Some of the Duke's supporters were so enthusiastic that they even 'got drunk...at their own cost and Huzza'd Pelham and Butler [the other Whig candidate for the county]'. But such spontaneous enthusiasm was rare. On the King's birthday, 30 October 1733, bonfires—with drink—were the favourite method of celebrating the occasion; and Burnett, wishing these festivities to be 'done with as much frewgalatry as possible', and finding that each bonfire cost 20 guineas, tried to group several villages at one bonfire; but Collier, the Duke's agent at Hastings, sent in a bill for £82. 16s. 9d. for his bonfire which Burnett paid, though with reluctance: while an innkeeper of Chichester sent in a bill for £65, on which, says a correspondent of the Duke, 'I am grieved when I think of ye Unreasonable and Exorbitant bills that have been brought in on acct of our General Election, and 'tis the Admiration of all to Observe wth what honour they have been paid, even without reasonable abatements'. There seems to be no actual statement of the Duke's expenses in this election, but those for that of 1741, which was not so hotly contested, paid by Burnett alone, amounted to £4257. 16s. 7d.;[2] so that in 1734 the total expenses incurred by all the Duke's agents can hardly have amounted to less than some £20,000.[3] Some, indeed, of the money

[1] The Duke was always very particular about this precaution, and expected his own bed in any of his various houses to be slept in by a servant on the night before he arrived.   [2] Add. MSS. 32321, ff. 30–7.

[3] Professor Namier, *Structure of Politics*, I, 205, makes a rough estimate of the cost of a seat at £1500 in 1754, and by that date it had been progressively growing. Of course Newcastle did not spend anything like so much on most of the other

spent on elections came from the Secret Service Fund, but probably very little of this came to Newcastle.

Perhaps the Duke's three progresses through Sussex during this election impressed the electors most. He set out in a coach drawn by six horses—for the Sussex roads were notoriously atrocious—with a crowd of retainers, while, in each district he went through, the local noblemen and gentry came out to greet him as he passed. These he entertained in regal style—he had specially sent down 'ye French cook and yᵉ silver covers' to Bishopstone for his feast at that seat; and, as he could not invite all the voters to dinner, 'for their wives and families and all the Rabble would come with them, which would run the thing to a monstrous expense', his agent was ordered to tell the populace 'that his Grace had given me leave to say that since he could not have their Company at dinner, there would be half a guinea for every man to spend when his Grace came to Bishopstone'. In the villages, as he drove through, the yokels stood openmouthed to see the great man pass, and even the gentry thought it an honour to be spoken to by such a mighty lord, as appears, for example, in a letter from Sir Thomas Wilson of Uckfield, lamenting that he was sitting in his study when his Grace drove past, as he would like to have had the honour of greeting him.[1]

The election of 1741 was on much the same lines as that of 1734, for, though Newcastle was then actively intriguing against Walpole, he had no desire to break up the Whig majority in Parliament, and was as eager as ever to maintain his own personal following.[2] His part in the elections of 1747 and 1754 is chiefly memorable for his provision of seats for Pitt, then Paymaster, at Seaford and at Aldborough. Seaford was generally considered a safe seat for his nominees, as the electors were nearly all revenue officers or otherwise dependent on the government. But in 1747 the Gages, former allies of Newcastle, put up an opposition candidate, so Newcastle

constituencies in which he had an interest as on those in his own county of Sussex. According to the same authority, I, 238 sqq., the average amount provided from the Secret Service Fund to help government candidates at a general election barely exceeded £20,000; so that Newcastle's share must have been very meagre. In fact he himself steadily reduced his patrimony at each general election.

[1] In the *English Historical Review*, XII, pp. 448–88 (1897), I have given a more detailed account of the Duke's activities, especially in Sussex, during the 1734 election.

[2] Clarence Perkins has published a short account of this election in *Electioneering in 18th-Century England*, a pamphlet reprinted from the *Quarterly Journal of University of N. Dakota*, 1923.

thought it advisable to go down himself with Pitt, accompanied by his nephew Lord Lincoln and Lord Ashburnham, to overawe the electors, only to find another opposition candidate, Lord Middlesex in the Prince of Wales's service, proposing to stand against his other nominee, Hay. Accordingly, besides the usual dinner to the corporation, and personal talks with most of the electors, and, in spite of standing orders of the Commons, he took his seat on the hustings next to the returning officer, to overawe any voters still recalcitrant. Pitt and Hay were of course elected. In 1754 there was no such trouble, for Aldborough was one of the Duke's own pocket boroughs, and, though Pitt himself was too ill to appear on the day of election, he was duly returned at the Duke's behest. How personal was the tie between the member and the owner of a pocket borough may be seen from Pitt's resignation of his seat for Aldborough on his leaving the ministry, and finding another seat at Bath.

Game to the end, Newcastle took some part in the first two elections of George III's reign, in 1761 and 1768; but even in 1761, though still in the ministry, he was much shorn of his power. In that year no help was forthcoming to needy candidates from the Secret Service Fund, owing to Pitt's declaration that the vast sums spent openly on voters and members through offices, sinecures and contracts 'will be sufficient to carry a Parliament, with some perhaps immaterial alterations, without giving a farthing of the King's money': Newcastle for his part feared that 'the expense of several places I know will be so very great, that it will be very difficult to find private persons, able to be at it, and therefore we shall not have great choice'. In the event Pitt, not Newcastle, proved right, for no great change was apparent in the composition of the House of Commons elected in 1761.[1] For the election of 1768, Newcastle, though finally out of office, was busy making preparations in 1767, for though at the end of that year he was stricken with paralysis, as late as October Lord Dartmouth found 'your friend and my cousin the Duke of Newcastle, who is no bad electioneer' engaging all the Kent freeholders living at Lewes to vote for Sackville.[2] But his power had gone and even his nearest relations and friends in the Midlands, as he complained in some of his last letters, were deserting him to pay their court to George III and his party.

It cannot be denied that Newcastle thoroughly enjoyed all the hurry and bustle of elections and the admiration of gaping electors when he appeared before them in all his ducal magnificence. Nor

[1] Namier, l.c. pp. 258–62.   [2] H. MSS. Sackville, XI, v.

were his bustling energy, vast expenditure and pompous display mere bravado. He was essentially a kindly soul and generous to a fault with his wealth; and he regarded his electoral activities as necessary in the public interest for the preservation of the Revolution settlement. On at least three occasions he refused to be recouped from public funds for losses due largely to his electoral profusion, against which even his vast wealth was not proof. In 1723, when Townshend offered to have electoral expenses of some £7000 repaid to him out of the civil list, he told the Bishop of Chichester how 'backward I have allways been to ask or secure any summ of money of ye King, how I detest it in others and consequently how unwilling I shall be to do ye like myself'.[1] Even when his princely income had dwindled to a paltry £7000 in the last years of his life, he twice refused a pension from George III in 1762 and 1765. But at least he had the satisfaction from all his electoral expenses to have become master of the game. In 1719 he modestly told Stanhope that he himself could 'make the difference of 16 votes' in the House of Commons, certainly an understatement: at any rate by 1734, when he could exercise ministerial as well as personal influence, some 80 members of the House of Commons owed, as we have seen, their seats largely to him; while in 1760 some 101 members of the House could, in euphemistic language, be 'spoken to' by the Duke of Newcastle, or in other words were, owing to favours received or expected, accessible to his influence.

Already in 1717, two years before Carteret was given his first important mission, Newcastle's claim to high office, if only for his value as an organizer of elections, had been recognized. On the reconstruction of the ministry by Stanhope and Sunderland, after their quarrel with Townshend, and Walpole, Newcastle began his ministerial career, which lasted almost uninterruptedly till 1762, with the court appointment of Lord Chamberlain. In this office his specific duty was to control the household servants 'above stairs', the Lord Steward being responsible for those 'below stairs', the Groom of the Stole for those of the Bedchamber and the Master of the Horse for the royal stables.[2] The Lord Chamberlain also had some more important places to dispose of; and he took care to exercise his patronage with a single eye to the interests of the ministry. A characteristic example of his methods is to be seen in his dealings with Richard Steele, who in 1717 held the patent office of supervisor of the Theatre Royal, Drury Lane, worth £1000 a year. In the last

[1] Add. MSS. 32686, f. 251. [2] Add. MSS. 32699, f. 66.

critical days of Anne's reign and the first years of George I Newcastle and Steele had been close allies, Newcastle even providing his friend with a seat in Parliament for his pocket borough of Boroughbridge. But when, in 1717, Steele adhered to the Townshend-Walpole party, Newcastle's friendliness cooled off; and three years later, after Steele had voted against Stanhope's Peerage Bill, the Duke deprived him of his patent and did not restore it to him till the spring of 1721, when Stanhope was dead, and Walpole and Townshend had returned to power.

Limited as Newcastle's direct means of patronage were in this his first office of state, he found it useful as a stepping-stone to greater powers. As one of the chief household officials, he had access to the Closet and full scope for whispering and receiving state secrets from ministers and from the King himself, then still a power in the land. He may have been 'very silly', as Lady Mary Wortley Montagu said of him in 1714,[1] 'but', as she added, 'very goodnatured', and so not likely to arouse jealousies. Old Horace Walpole, indeed, once said of him: The Duke of Newcastle is like the children in the wood..., not knowing what is proper to be said or omitted according to whom he talks to.'[2] He was perhaps too fussy and hardly dignified enough for a post which calls for sublimity of demeanour, such as his successor Grafton, in spite of a cloudy understanding, displayed to perfection. At any rate George II said he was not fit to be a Chamberlain in a second-rate German court. But George II was not an unbiased judge; for, when Prince of Wales, he had a notable quarrel with the Duke. At the baptism of his second son in 1717 the King was the chief godfather, and for the other godfather the Prince wanted his uncle the Duke of York, Prince Bishop of Osnaburg: but, instead of the Duke of York, the King insisted on naming the Duke of Newcastle, an insult deeply resented by the peppery Prince. So, as soon as the King had left the Princess's bed-chamber after the christening, the Prince ran round the bed and, going up to the Duke, shook his fist in his face and shouted to him: 'You are von rascal, but I shall find you.' Newcastle thinking he had said 'fight you', in great trepidation reported the incident to the King, who ordered his son to leave St James's Palace forthwith, took away his guards, forbade the courtiers to visit him, and even took away his children from his custody, with the result that the infant prince, deprived of its mother's milk, pined away, and died within a few days. No wonder it took George II a long time to overcome his dislike and contempt for the unfortunate Duke.

[1] In her *Letters*, I, 211.　　　　[2] *H. MSS. Buckinghamshire*, p. 3.

Otherwise Newcastle found his court office useful as a stepping-stone to more important functions. Then, and throughout his life, he loved whispering scandal and exchanging confidences with court ladies and members of the royal family, his deferential attitude to whom earned him the nickname of 'Permis'. In the next reign indeed there was a considerable amount of flirting between him and George II's daughter the Princess Amelia, until, as so often occurred in his relations with others, he imagined himself neglected by her and chattered about this grievance to other confidants. But, as proved even more important for his advancement, Newcastle soon found himself not only the recipient of state secrets but even consulted by Stanhope and Sunderland on matters of policy. This was especially the case in reference to the Peerage Bill of 1719, when he and those two ministers exchanged a lively correspondence as to the prospects of that and other measures in contemplation for the security of the dynasty.[1] Such confidences were indeed justly earned, for no minister had the time or opportunity, seized by Newcastle, for feeling the pulse of the public and reporting what measures would help or hinder success at elections. No one, too, in his century understood so well as Newcastle how important it was for the smooth working of government to fill places of profit and power in the state with devoted adherents of the ministry. Later, as Secretary of State from 1724 to 1754 and as First Lord of the Treasury from 1754 to 1760,[2] his opportunities for patronage were enormously increased; and, though George II did not always accept his nominations to peerages, garters, red ribbons and ministerial posts, he got a far larger share of them than any other minister could claim. But of one class of patronage, the ecclesiastical, he made a speciality.

Newcastle's attitude to the Church is interesting. In his way he was a deeply religious man, and regularly attended divine service conducted twice a day in one of his private chapels by his own domestic chaplain, Thomas Hurdis. He was willing, too, to accept advice and even reproof from bishops whom he trusted, such as Bishop Hare of Chichester, who in 1724 sent him solemn warnings against his extravagant way of living,[3] and in his last years from Hume, Bishop of Salisbury. Newcastle had consulted Hume as to the state of mind he should be in to take Holy Communion in a fitting spirit, and Hume gave him sensible encouragement to over-

[1] See my *Stanhope*, pp. 410–12, 459–63.
[2] After George III's accession in 1760 Newcastle, though still First Lord till 1762, was no longer the chief dispenser of patronage.
[3] Add. MSS. 32687, ff. 42, 46.

come his scruples and even wrote for him special prayers for daily use and before partaking of the Eucharist.[1] But, though a devout churchman according to his lights, Newcastle regarded the hierarchy of the English Church mainly as a bulwark for the Hanoverian Succession or in other words the Whig government.

The twenty-six bishops of the English Church, each with a seat in the House of Lords, were no negligible factor in that assembly; moreover their influence in their dioceses was useful at elections, and so to a less degree was that of deans, prebendaries and even humble parish clergy. Walpole accordingly paid special attention to church patronage, employing Bishop Gibson of London for many years as his chief adviser in that sphere, even though at times he found the bishop's domineering attitude in ecclesiastical affairs unduly irksome. As early as 1723 Walpole remarked to Newcastle that 'His Lordship seemed in very good humour, and as long as we continue such good boys, and obey our orders so punctually, I should hope our spiritual governours will not be much dissatisfied'.[2] But by 1736 Walpole and the bishop had quarrelled so fundamentally about the Quakers' Relief Bill that Walpole was only too glad to hand over ecclesiastical recommendations to Newcastle. From that date until the end of George II's reign Newcastle in turn became the almost undisputed dispenser of church patronage. By 1743, as the poet Young told the Duchess of Portland, 'The Duke of Newcastle is our Pope. Ecclesiasticals are under his thumb, and he is as fixed as St Paul's by his own weight in spite of all the revolutions of the little court buildings round about him.'[3] It is true the King on some rare occasions jibbed at Newcastle's nominations; but by 1762, when Newcastle was turned out of office, there was hardly a bishop on the bench who did not owe his sacred office, or his translation to a richer see, to the Duke.

Nor indeed was Newcastle content with the nomination to English bishoprics. He was wont to trench on the former privilege of Lords-Lieutenants of Ireland to nominate to Irish bishoprics; and the creation of three successive Primates of Ireland—Boulter, Hoadly and Stone, the last the brother of his own private secretary—was largely due to him. Again, according to the royal chaplain Pyle, he was a persistent begger to the bishops for the nomination to benefices in their gift. Writing to the antiquarian Kerrich, Pyle complains that, 'The Minister himself is Fac Totum in ecclesiastic affairs, and a sweet manager he is; for what with the last election and his pitiful passion

---

[1] See N. Sykes, *Church and State in 18th Century*, pp. 278–82, 437–9.
[2] Add. MSS. 32686, f. 312.   [3] H. MSS. *Bath*, p. 280.

for the Chancellorship of Cambridge, he has involved himself in promises of Church preferment to the greatest degree of perplexity....He torments the poor Archbishop of Canterbury for everything that falls in his gift, so that if a thing drops, he is forced to give it away the moment he is informed of it for fear of the Duke of Newcastle. He is as great a plague to the other bishops, asking even for their small livings. Ely gives him everything (they say by bargain); Chichester, Peterborough, Durham, Gloucester, Salisbury etc. are slaves to him in this respect. Only London and Winchester give him flat denials, unless we are to add York, which is a point problematical. As to the Lord Chancellor, it is a kind of bargain made with everyone that enters upon that high office "that the Minister shall dispose of most of the Church preferments in his gift".'[1] Newcastle indeed was sometimes hard put to it to fulfil the promises he had rashly made. To quote Young again, 'The Duke received me with great complaisance, ministerially kind, took me by the thumb so cordially, as if he designed it should go for payment in full,...but would certainly do what he could so that, if nothing is done, he has kindly prepared me for it'.[2] At times, too, he would quite frankly explain to his nominees the reasons for their ecclesiastical promotions. When, for example, Newcome, Master of St John's College, Cambridge, was offered the deanery of Peterborough, he was given to understand that 'firm attachment to Lord Fitzwilliam's interest' at elections was expected of him.[3]

Another valuable source of politico-ecclesiastical influence to Newcastle was the post of Chancellor of Cambridge University. The former undergraduate of Clare had always retained a great love of Cambridge and particularly of his old college, and when in 1737 the post of High Steward of the University became vacant, he offered himself for it as a step to becoming its Chancellor on the death of the existing Chancellor, the Duke of Somerset. He was accordingly elected High Steward without opposition, after a careful packing of the electoral body by his friends at Clare. But by 1747, when Somerset was reported to be dying, a formidable opponent for the Chancellorship had appeared in the person of Frederick, Prince of Wales, who, 'after professing great regard to the University of Cambridge, said he should take it as a favour and honour to stand in a nearer relation to it whenever a vacancy...should happen'. Somerset did not actually die till December 1748, a year during several months of which Newcastle was in Hanover with the King, so that pre-

---

[1] Quoted in Sykes, *Edmund Gibson*, p. 396.
[2] *H. MSS. Bath*, p. 288.　　　　[3] *H. MSS. Weston-Under-Wood*, p. 278.

parations for the contest had to be made by his brother Pelham and other friends in London and Cambridge. Indeed it looked as if the election would be a contest between the ministry and the opposition, of which the Prince of Wales was the avowed patron. Fortunately, however, for Newcastle, the King, who detested his son and his son's supporters, made it known that 'it would be disagreeable to his Majesty to have any of his family elected without his consent and approbation': so in the end the Prince withdrew from the contest, and Newcastle was duly elected without opposition. In the following July he was solemnly installed as Chancellor amid banquets and festivities which lasted four days; and to complete his personal and political triumphs his friend Hardwicke succeeded him as High Steward.

Rarely has a Chancellor of either Oxford or Cambridge taken his duties, as he interpreted them, so seriously as Newcastle. His object was to make Cambridge a stronghold of the Whiggery he professed, and to that end he kept in touch with the university by frequent personal visits and by means of successive agents drawn from heads of colleges and others, with whom he corresponded freely. Through these agents, whose good will he stimulated as occasion arose by bishoprics, deaneries and other ecclesiastical plums, he busied himself with elections to professorships, masterships or fellowships of colleges; and, though he met with some rebuffs, especially from such a powerful college as Trinity, he on the whole succeeded in his campaigns.[1] Certainly, at the end of his twenty years as Chancellor, Cambridge contrasted favourably with the sister university in genuine loyalty to the Hanover succession and incidentally, though that was not specially due to the Duke, in learning and scholarship.

Thus at the outset of his long career Newcastle had 'chalked out' for himself that department in government in which he proved unrivalled: to secure, by the means most agreeable to the temper of the times, a compact body of supporters for what seemed to him essential for the security of the Revolution settlement—Whig predominance in Parliament and in all influential spheres of the body politic and ecclesiastical. Had he been content with this comparatively modest part in securing the dynasty, it would have been well for him and the country. Unfortunately he also aimed at directing the policy of the organization he created, a province for which he was unfitted by temperament and intelligence.

[1] An illuminating account of Newcastle's dealings with the University is given by D. A. Winstanley, *Cambridge in the 18th Century*.

Chapter III

CARTERET SECRETARY OF STATE:
NEWCASTLE'S INTRIGUES

When Carteret returned to England at the end of 1720 the South Sea Bubble had burst[1] and the whole political world was in a turmoil. The ministers most deeply implicated in the shady business were Aislabie, Chancellor of the Exchequer, the elder Craggs, Postmaster-General, and his son, Carteret's special friend, the Secretary of State for the South. Sunderland himself was acquitted by the Committee of Enquiry of any irregular dealings, but, as promoter of the original scheme for incorporating the national debt in the capital of the South Sea Company, which started the wild speculation in the Company's shares, he felt bound to resign the Treasury, though he remained in the Ministry as Groom of the Stole.[2] But Aislabie was expelled from the House and sent to the Tower; the elder Craggs committed suicide; and his son died suddenly of small pox. Against Carteret's friend Stanhope, Secretary for the North, there was not even a suspicion of underhand dealings; but, when answering a venomous attack in the Lords by the Duke of Wharton, he was seized by an apoplectic fit and died next day, 5 February 1721. In the previous year Stanhope and Sunderland had become reconciled with Walpole and Townshend, but they had been given only subordinate posts in the ministry. Now Walpole, as the only man capable of restoring the country's credit, had become indispensable, and in April 1721 once more became First Lord of the Treasury and Chancellor of the Exchequer, bringing with him his brother-in-law Townshend to resume his office of Secretary for the North. Carteret, who in January had been appointed by Stanhope ambassador to the Congress of Cambrai, on the younger Craggs's death succeeded him as Secretary for the South.

[1] Carteret himself, being in Sweden, had taken no part in the South Sea speculation; but his wife and his mother, Lady Granville, had invested £12,000 in the stock, and lost it all in the crash. *H. MSS. Polwarth*, II, 582; III, 25.

[2] Since the Revolution the only other notable holders of this purely honorary post were Portland in William III's time, the Duchess of Marlborough in Anne's and Bute in George III's first year. The office, which gave the holder easy access to the royal ear, was abolished in 1837.

It was unfortunate for Carteret that in this, his first experience of high office, he had to deal with countries such as France, Spain, Italy and Turkey, of which he had no special knowledge, instead of those in the northern department, Sweden, Denmark and Russia, of which his recent embassy had given him first-hand knowledge, and the Empire, with the complicated interests and politics of which he was already familiar. He was unfortunate, too, in having been deprived, at this critical moment of his career, of his great friend and patron, Stanhope, to whose memory some twenty years later he paid this glowing tribute: 'Few ages and few countries produce such a man as he.... My Lords, where he spoke there was no occasion for counsel; he talked, my Lords, like a statesman, a lawyer and a merchant at once; I do not know, my Lords, if we ever had a greater man in his way.'[1] Moreover, though strongly supported by Sunderland, he laboured under the disadvantage, as the pupil of Stanhope, of being suspect to his powerful colleagues Townshend and Walpole, even though at first they are said to have accepted his appointment 'with good grace'. For the time being, indeed, they were quite content to have him as a colleague, if only as a pledge to the Regent Orleans and his Minister Cardinal Dubois, that Stanhope's and Sunderland's policy of close union with France would not be abandoned. In fact, even after Sunderland's death a year later, Carteret with the full approval of Walpole and Townshend sent a despatch to Paris stating frankly, 'que les ministres du Roy sont entièrement d'accord; et que nonobstant les disputes et contrarietez qu'il y a eu entre nous, c'est la ferme intention de tous de suivre les maximes des Comtes de Sunderland et Stanhope par rapport à la France et au Cardinal, et que le Roy ne veut jamais s'en départir'.[2]

In his dealings with France, Carteret was not happy in his representatives at Paris—Sir Robert Sutton, appointed by Stanhope in 1720, and Sir Lukas Schaub, sent over to assist him in February 1721. Schaub, of Swiss origin, was well enough for the temporary missions with drafts of treaties etc. on which Stanhope used to employ him, but as an ambassador he was of very light weight: while Sutton, a better man, appears to have got into the black books of Dubois, who accused him of being a Jacobite—so his colleague Schaub wrote to Carteret. Carteret indeed was not the man to countenance such vague accusations. In his reply to Schaub he admits that since Dubois objects to Sutton, he must be recalled and Schaub remain alone at

[1] *P.H.* x, 1047.
[2] Add. MSS. 22517, f. 48; and *H. MSS. Polwarth*, III, 86.

Paris: but he adds that it is quite false that Sutton is a Jacobite and gives Schaub this stinging reproof: 'vous ne devriez pas répéter dans vos lettres ce que Sa (the Cardinal's) mauvaise humeur lui fait dire contre lui. Le Roy et ses ministres ne soupçonnent pas la fidélité de M. Sutton; et pour moi je ne puis souffrir qu'on réitère des coups fourrez contre un homme de sa qualité et de son mérite.'[1] Even earlier Carteret had found it necessary to reprove Schaub severely for taking it upon himself not to present a despatch sent to him for delivery to the Cardinal. Telling him that he must get òut of the mess as he can, he adds: 'Les grands négociateurs sont au dessus des règles communes. Mais je ne connais point de moyen plus sur pour gagner de la réputation et de la conserver que de se borner à ses ordres, et de tempérer l'ardeur de l'imagination en se conformant à ce qui est prescrit. Vous aurez la bonté de rendre la lettre en question à l'Archévêque.'[2] Such difficulties with Schaub no doubt confirmed this masterful young minister in the opinion he had expressed to Stanhope from Stockholm: 'It is really my opinion that to doe great business in a foreign country a Prince should rather chuse new men than one that has lived in it a great while: For by long habitude one contracts partialities, enmities and friendships, all which, carried too far, are equally destructive of the well conducting great matters in this place.'[3]

Throughout this, his first, short term as foreign secretary, Carteret illuminates his despatches with these and other shrewd sayings, some of which are worth pondering by our diplomats and their masters at the Foreign Office even to-day. Thus he tells Sutton to favour a request from the Duke of Parma, who is supporting our views, for 'though out of a principle of his own interest, yet it carries its obligation along with it. For it is very happy for all that are concerned with Princes [or Peoples to-day] to have them act pursuant to their own interests; and then we know where to have them for the good of the whole.'[4] Again, when England and France had signed a separate treaty with Spain conveying general support of the Spanish case as against the Emperor, Dubois, a foxy intriguer, if ever there was one, had suggested to Schaub that the treaty should be secretly shown to the Imperial ambassador as a warning against excessive claims from the Emperor. Carteret at once, and unhesitatingly, rejected such underhand double-crossing: 'Des finesses de cette sorte', he wrote, 'sont dangereuses à être pratiquées, et ne

---

[1] Add. MSS. 22515, f. 267. [2] Ib. f. 80.
[3] Add. MSS. 22511, f. 65. [4] Add. MSS. 22515, f. 56.

peuvent durer longtemps quand on s'en serve. Je ne suis jamais pour ces coups de politique qui ruinent toute confiance et tout crédit personnel. Le silence, l'honnêteté et une prudente discrétion font aller aussi loin qu'il le faut, et personne ne se récrie contre ces finesses.'[1] In another despatch on the same secret treaty, which he contends is as much in the Emperor's interest as in that of France and England, he gives a further reason for not making it known to him, since 'Telle est la délicatesse des grands Princes, qu'ils rejettent souvent ce qui est convenable à leurs propres intérêts, s'ils croient qu'on ait formé sans eux des concerts, dans la conséquence desquels ils doivent être compris. Ils regardent de tels mesures comme une espèce de contrainte, ou tout au mieux comme une amitié officieuse....Et c'est pourquoi, quand d'autres arguments leur manquent, ils s'en tiennent souvent à ce seul prétexte.'[2] To cap his remark about 'la délicatesse des grands Princes' here is another on a subject which was not Carteret's best effort in diplomacy. He is speaking of a projected marriage between the daughter of the King's mistress and a French nobleman, and adds this warning: 'Le cardinal connaît la délicatesse des affaires dans lesquelles les dames sont intéressées...qui difficilement peuvent être tenues secrètes longtemps, et qui ne doivent pourtant jamais être rendues publiques, qu'après qu'elles sont sûres.'[3]

When, in April 1721, Carteret took up his duties as Secretary of State, the halcyon days of Stanhope's alliance with France seemed to be passing away. In March, only a month after Stanhope's death, France and Spain had made a secret treaty whereby, *inter alia*, France agreed to use her good offices in obtaining the restoration of Gibraltar to Spain. The fact was that Orleans and Dubois believed that the South Sea scandal had so much weakened England that they could resume the leadership of Europe which Stanhope in his lifetime had secured, all the more as they were well aware of the antagonism between the Sunderland-Carteret and the Walpole-Townshend sections of the ministry. None the less, the French ministers had no wish to see England veering towards the Emperor, and welcomed the idea that she might enter into a tripartite agreement with France and Spain. Accordingly, in June, England signed a treaty with Spain, whereby it was agreed that England, France and Spain should have a common policy at the Congress of Cambrai, where details of the differences between Spain and the Emperor arising from the terms of the Quadruple Alliance were to be settled. The difficulty about Spain's demand for the return of Gibraltar was overcome by a letter

[1] Add. MSS. 22515, f. 167.　　[2] *Ib.* f. 118.　　[3] Add. MSS. 22519, f. 71.

from Carteret, stating that King George would be willing to do so if he could obtain the consent of Parliament, a proviso which in effect postponed the return to the Greek Calends.[1] On another point of difference as to the terms of the treaty Carteret was less successful. He had demanded of France that if, as a result of the treaty, the Emperor began hostilities, France would not carry the war into the Low Countries, which by the Barrier Treaty of 1715 England was bound to defend; a demand which Dubois rejected with indignation and threats; and Carteret was forced to content himself with the vague promise that the Anglo-French-Dutch Triple Alliance of 1717 would be respected.[2]

After these preliminary skirmishes, and as long as Dubois and the Regent were alive, relations between Carteret and the French government became increasingly cordial. In fact Dubois more than once had cause for gratitude to Carteret in supporting him against his enemies at the French court—'enemies', wrote Schaub, 'who never sleep, seeking to embroil him with the Regent'. Thus, in answer to a despatch from Carteret stating that some pro-Imperial views uttered by Cadogan, Marlborough's successor as Master-General of the Ordnance, were quite irresponsible and had no backing in the country, Schaub writes that 'just as the uneasiness of the Cardinal had reached its height...your letter written with such cleverness, solidity and ingenuity [carried] complete conviction...and he said to me, he speaks like a man and a friend; and, referring to the ties between the King of Great Britain and France, said they would be the security of future tranquillity'.[3] On their side the Regent and Dubois did service to England when in 1722 they warned Carteret of a Jacobite plot for the invasion of England and of the precautions they had themselves taken against such an attempt; for they had not only refused permission to the Duke of Ormonde to pass through France to a Channel port, but had even removed their own Irish Brigade from too close proximity to England at Dunkirk, stipulating only that Carteret should not allow the source of his information to leak out in England.[4] On the other hand, when Walpole passed an act imposing a tax of £100,000 on the English Roman Catholic

[1] See my Stanhope, p. 350.

[2] See British Diplomatic Instructions, France, 1721-7, pp. x, 9, 11-16.

[3] Carteret's despatch of 28 Dec. 1722 is in Add. MSS. 22517; Schaub's answer in H. MSS. Polwarth, III, 227-8. Unfortunately the editor of this volume thought it necessary to translate the French despatches into English—not always correctly.

[4] Add. MSS. 22517, ff. 148, 159, 184. Carteret was able to reassure them on this point, as he had obtained the same information from another source.

community, on suspicion of their being concerned in the plot, Dubois sent over a strong protest against so unfair a discrimination against a whole religious body; and Carteret was hard put to it to make a case for the act, which he maintained was justified not by religious but by political considerations; adding, as an instance of the King's clemency and tolerance that in the first year of his reign he had remitted two-thirds of the confiscations incurred by the Roman Catholics up to that date.[1]

The Congress of Cambrai did not actually meet for business till the end of January 1724, only two months before Carteret resigned office; but he had plenty to do before that in removing obstacles, chiefly from the Emperor, to its meeting at all, and settling the programme of its future proceedings. In both these respects the policy he laid down for Schaub at Paris and for our plenipotentiaries at the Congress was to 'leave the first step to be taken by France and commit ourselves as little as possible';[2] no doubt because France was in closer touch than we were with Philip V of Spain, to whose views England and France had agreed to give general support. He fully realized, in fact, that 'unless the union between the King and the Regent were as sincere as it is...it would be difficult, if not impossible' to keep a check on the Emperor's and Philip V's opposing views. Most of the trouble in settling the preliminaries of the Congress came from Vienna, where the Imperial ministers, especially the Vice-Chancellor, made every difficulty about transmitting the 'expectatives' promised by the Emperor in the Quadruple Alliance treaty to Don Carlos for his eventual succession to Parma and Tuscany. Finally Carteret forwards to France a copy of a stiff despatch from Townshend to Vienna complaining about 'the Vice-Chancellor's tricks', and entirely agreeing with Carteret's and Dubois's proposal that there should be no further dealings with that shifty and arrogant minister.[3] Meanwhile the ambassadors, envoys, secretaries of missions from the various states concerned in the proceedings, accompanied in some cases by their wives, together with an 'introductor of ambassadors', who gave some trouble by his claim to sit at the head of the ambassadors' bench, and a whole army of major-domos, cooks, heyducks, footmen, etc. etc. had been assembling at Cambrai with nothing whatever to do except to settle the minutest details of procedure, to entertain one another at banquets, which made Lord Whitworth so ill that he had to retire to the 'Spaw' for

[1] Polwarth, l.c. pp. 199–202; Brit. Dipl. Instr. France, 1721–7, p. 36.
[2] Add. MSS. 22517, f. 10.   [3] H. MSS. Polwarth, III, 290–3.

three months, and to assert their dignity against the magistrates of Cambrai for meddling in diplomatic affairs that did not concern them. When the Congress did actually get to work, it spent so much time in procrastinating discussions that, after fifteen months engaged in such futilities, Spain and the Emperor settled their differences by a private treaty and the Congress came to its inglorious end in May 1725.[1]

The death of Sunderland, Carteret's only powerful supporter in the ministry, in April 1722 was a serious blow to him for private as well as public reasons, since he was personally attached to him, quite apart from politics. On hearing that the Regent had remarked in Schaub's presence that 'Lord Sunderland's death was no loss to the King, and that he had told the Cardinal so long ago', he at once wrote a fiery letter demanding an explanation, for, 'I will sooner dye', he said, 'than give up my friend's character, which I will contend for at the hazard of everything'; and on receiving an assurance from Schaub that Dubois had never believed Sunderland guilty of intriguing with the Jacobites, as the Regent had implied, he replied with heartfelt relief: 'A thousand thanks for your private letter which enables me to refute every kind of calumny against the memory of a man who will always be dear to me. I have shown it to the King, who is entirely satisfied with it....Adieu, Carteret.'[2]

In spite of Carteret's reassuring message to the French court in April 1722 about the union of the ministry after Sunderland's death, from that time his own position was becoming more and more precarious: 'the only two of note that are reckoned to his account', it was stated by a correspondent of Polwarth,[3] were Roxburgh, the Secretary for Scotland, and Cadogan, the commander-in-chief, neither of whom had much influence. Carteret himself seems to have had an inkling of the truth and about this time made approaches to some of the Hanover Tories, who had repudiated the Pretender. On the failure of this negotiation, according to Chesterfield, Carteret 'applied to the King to support him, as he was surrounded by his enemies; the King promised it him but told him the necessity of the time forced him to temporize; thereupon Lord Carteret spoke to the Duchess of Kendal, who bid him have patience and told him the King hated his other ministers'.[4]

---

[1] Full accounts of all these trivialities are to be found in *H. MSS. Polwarth*, III *passim*. See also my article on the Congress in *E.H.R.* xv, 479–94.

[2] Add. MSS. 35837, ff. 496–7.

[3] *H. MSS. Polwarth*, II, 184.

[4] *Marchmont Papers*, I, 3.

But in spite of the King's dislike of his other ministers, the extent to which Carteret was losing ground soon became apparent from the change of attitude towards him of that barometer of political feeling, the Duke of Newcastle. On the split of the Whig party in 1717 Newcastle had, as we have seen, opted for the then more powerful section led by Stanhope and Sunderland, and, largely owing to his precocious understanding of the trend of opinion in the constituencies, was taken into their confidence and even consulted on the measures they proposed. Writing to Stanhope in 1719 Newcastle went so far as to predict that, at the next general election, 'Mr Walpole, and the few friends his party will be able to bring in, will be so incorporated with the Jacobites that we shall have little difficulty with them'.[1] On Stanhope's death in 1721, he still adhered to Sunderland and included Carteret in his effusive embraces. In a characteristic letter to Sunderland, to rebut the charge of having ratted to Walpole, he unctuously expresses his satisfaction that Sunderland and Carteret had not lost the King's favour; and, when he hears from Carteret that Walpole and Townshend made great professions of friendship, he writes, 'You know I neither love their persons nor court their interests'; but it would be dangerous to break with them; and they may 'at last begin to think it their Interest to behave themselves as they ought'. Carteret in his reply to Newcastle is less optimistic. 'The reconciliation', he writes, 'proceeded from Lord Townshend, which we embraced for many reasons....If he can govern Mr Walpole, all will answer to his engagements.... The King is resolved that Walpole shall not govern, but it is hard to be prevented.'[2] In fact Walpole proved himself so dexterous in clearing up the confusion caused by the bursting of the South Sea Bubble and in providing the King with adequate supplies that he very soon made himself indispensable, and convinced the King that 'the Whig Party was the only security he had to depend on'; in which, says Newcastle, 'he was most certainly right'.[3]

One of the first results of Sunderland's death was the transfer of Newcastle's affections to those whose 'persons he never loved nor courted their interests'; and from that time forward, until circumstances had again altered, he flattered and served these same persons. To begin with, as an earnest of his new loyalty, he entered wholeheartedly into their plans for getting rid of Carteret. Carteret suffered under one serious handicap, that, though by this time as convinced

[1] Add. MSS. 32686, f. 153. [2] Ib. ff. 179–97.
[3] M. Torrens, History of Cabinets, I, 304.

a Whig as Walpole himself, he could plausibly be represented as suspect from his many Tory connexions. He had even had some dealings with Bolingbroke in exile and encouraged his hopes of obtaining the King's pardon and returning to England.[1] Walpole himself was hardly qualified to cast a stone at him for such approaches, as he himself had been willing to work with the Tories during his years in the wilderness out of office; and he still had no objections to Bolingbroke's return to England, as long as he was kept out of Parliament; whereupon Bolingbroke had also thought it more prudent to switch over from Carteret to Walpole. But Walpole, when in office, was above all a strong party-man, in the sense that he was determined to admit none but the most obedient Whigs to share with him the power and emoluments of government. Carteret, on the other hand, was never disposed blindly to follow a fugleman; nor was he ever gifted with the power of forming a party for himself. As he rather pathetically explained to Newcastle, in the days of their mutual confidences, 'I am sometimes uneasy to have no one near to whom I can open my thoughts; for writing does by no means supply this. Still I will let no opportunity slip of acquainting you with what passes, since you are so well acquainted with what my Lord Sunderland and I propose that you will understand hints without explanation.'[2] He was also possessed by an incurable optimism, as when he told Newcastle of the King's remark to him in 1721: 'Je veux qu'ils sachent que j'aurai toujours une particulière distinction pour Lord Sunderland et vous',[2] a 'distinction' somewhat dimmed by Walpole's financial successes. But though Walpole had obviously made up his mind to get rid of Carteret as soon as the opportunity offered, he was unwilling to do so as long as the Regent and Cardinal Dubois were in power in France, since they attached the greatest importance to Carteret as a link with Stanhope, the founder of the close entente between the two governments. But unfortunately Dubois died in August 1723 and Orleans followed him only three months later, so that by the end of that year the need for Carteret as a link with the French government had passed.

Even before these French supporters of Stanhope's policy had passed away Carteret had been made to feel the insecurity of his position. The King, like his son George II, infinitely preferred his Electorate to his Kingdom, and was always eager to spend as much of the year as was possible at Hanover. These sojourns were highly inconvenient to his ministers, for not only were the meetings of

[1] *Marchmont Papers*, II, 185.   [2] Quoted by Torrens, *l.c.* I, 305.

Parliament often unduly delayed thereby, but also the conduct of current business of state, which had to be referred by the Regency Council to the minister in attendance at Hanover for the King's approval, was seriously hampered. These Hanover jaunts also afforded unrivalled opportunities for intrigue by the minister in attendance against his less fortunate colleagues at home, deprived as they were of access to the royal ear; and Townshend no doubt remembered that it was during George's absence in Hanover that he was summarily dismissed from the secretaryship in 1717. At any rate in 1723 it was decided that both Secretaries, Townshend and Carteret, should accompany the King when he went to Hanover early in June, while Walpole was to act for them both as Secretary *ad interim* at home. Carteret, with his accustomed buoyancy, seems to have been quite satisfied with this arrangement, in the fond confidence that his familiarity with the King's mother-tongue and with the northern politics in which George was most interested, besides his friendly relations with the Regent and Dubois, would easily retain for him the favour of the court.

The chief public business which the two Secretaries of State had in hand during their sojourn in Hanover concerned Russia. Carteret's valiant efforts, during his embassy to Sweden in 1719, to bolster up Sweden, exhausted by Charles XII's wars, had proved unavailing; for by the Treaty of Nystad of 1721 Russia had forced her to give up all her eastern Baltic possessions, while the King, Frederick of Hesse, had been obliged to surrender all the royal power to a defeatist council of ministers and Senate. Thus Peter the Great was supreme in the Baltic and had further plans, either to regain for his intended son-in-law, the Duke of Holstein, the duchy of which he had been dispossessed by Denmark, or to secure for him the succession to the throne of Sweden. For the first time France began to realize that Sweden, her traditional ally in the north, had become useless for her purpose and turned her eyes to Peter the Great as a better counterweight to the Emperor. Accordingly in 1723 the French ambassador in St Petersburg was busied in exploring the ground for an alliance. But one of the main difficulties was England. Both George I and the Regent were agreed that both their countries should be included in any alliance with Russia, but in the case of England there were serious obstacles to be surmounted. George I had been much piqued at being studiously ignored in the Treaty of Nystad, while the Tsar had never forgiven the summary expulsion from England of his ambassador Bestuzhef in Stanhope's time, and not only talked of demanding an indemnity from George I for prolonging Swedish resistance to his advances in 1719, but also required an apology for the Bestuzhef affair. In deep suspicion of Russian designs and a consequent unwillingness to enter blindly into an alliance in the wake of France, Carteret and Townshend were for once in agreement. At the beginning of the year, when Peter was engaged on a punitive expedition on the borders of Persia, Carteret had sent a despatch to Stanyan at Constantinople ordering him to stir up the Turks to take up arms against Russia. In July, on the mere report of the Tsar having put to sea with his fleet in order to intimidate Denmark and Sweden, both Carteret and Townshend supported George I in requiring Walpole to set aside £150,000 or £200,000 to provide for counter-measures by an English fleet. Townshend, who, as Secretary for the North, wrote the despatch to Walpole, drew a blood-curdling picture' of Peter the Great's designs on Sweden and Denmark, which, if successful, 'would make Russia able to terrify and distress all the coasts of Britain'. But Walpole was not to be alarmed. As a concession to the King's express request he agreed—'as a courtier, to please His Majesty'— to set aside £150,000 for the King's purposes, but if George decided to stay in Hanover beyond Christmas that sum would have to serve for his expenses over there and no more could be provided without a vote of Parliament: 'My politics', he added, 'are in a narrow compass, to keep free from all engagements as long as we possibly can. If we keep perfectly well with France and the Czar I am under no alarm of foreign disturbance, which alone can confound us here.' As a matter of fact Walpole, with his horse common sense, proved right in not being unduly alarmed. The story retailed by Townshend as to Peter's sinister designs on Sweden and Denmark, in the immediate future at any rate, proved to be a mare's nest. He had simply been exercising a small squadron of his fleet, as he frequently did, without any ulterior object.[1]

On the other hand both Carteret and Townshend took part in a negotiation which appeared much more calculated to avert danger from Russia. In spite, or because, of Frederick William of Prussia's marriage with George's daughter, there had long been antagonism between the two kings, fostered largely by a clique headed by Bernstorff at the Hanoverian court and not entirely extinguished by Stanhope's treaty between them in 1719. Now again a common

[1] A well-documented account of the alarms about Russian designs is in *E.H.R.* **XXVI**, pp. 278–309, by J. F. Chance.

antagonism to the Emperor's policy in Germany and a common apprehension of Russia's growing power drew the two Kings together. A better understanding between them was brought about by family visits of George's daughter and son-in-law to Hanover and of George I to Berlin in October. On his visit to Berlin George went accompanied by both Secretaries of State, Carteret and Townshend, who were furnished with full powers to sign another treaty at Charlottenburg. This treaty made no explicit mention of possible enemies but bound each King to support the other if attacked, whereby, as Townshend explained to Walpole, 'this alliance must inspire more respect towards the King, both in the Emperour and the Czar, since His Majesty is now at the head of a mighty force by land [including 18–20,000 of Frederick William's excellent troops], as well as Master of the most powerfull fleet in Europe'. It was important too in weaning France from the idea of a separate treaty with Russia, for, as Carteret wrote to Schaub, 'ce traité nous fournira un argument très-solide pour faire revenir la Cour de France de tout empressement à se lier avec la Czar, si ce n'est en signant conjointement avec le Roy le Traité avec Sa Majesté Czarienne'. In fact the Regent expressed great satisfaction at the conclusion of this treaty and abandoned the idea of a separate treaty with Russia without England's co-operation.[1] This visit to Berlin was also notable, since here, for the only time in his life, Carteret saw Frederic II, then Crown Prince and a boy of fifteen, marching at the head of his regiment of Cadets, and had speech with him.

But this was almost the only occasion, during their prolonged stay at Hanover, that Carteret and Townshend saw eye to eye with one another. Walpole and Townshend had long made up their minds to make Carteret's position impossible; and in their correspondence during this period were fertile in suggestions to one another for setting the King against him and driving him to resignation. The only third person to be entrusted with the tale of these secret machinations was Newcastle, who was flattered to the top of his bent by the other two conspirators' confidences and by being allowed, during Walpole's absences at his place in Norfolk, to deal with the Secretary of State's business. This arrangement suited them both well enough, for as Walpole said, 'your messenger gave me your letter in ye field a-hunting, which indeed I did not vouchsafe to open till I came home. That any man could think Politicks should take place

[1] See *E.H.R.* xxvII, pp. 52–7 for J. F. Chance's account of the Treaty of Charlottenburg.

with a hare a fool!' while Newcastle told him, 'you know I'm
a great dabbler in foreign politics', the *mot juste* to express his
capacity in that line.[1]

The lion's share of the work in making Carteret's position impossible fell to his colleague Townshend at Hanover. He had been
there hardly over a month when he began complaining to Walpole
about 'the false and vain accounts which our friend thinks proper
to send over of his superior interest at this place', but assured him
that 'the King is determined to be on his guard against taking any
step, which may carry the least appearance of turning the balance
in favour of those who wish us ill'. He then makes suggestions for
ministerial changes to strengthen still further their own friends in
the ministry, such as transferring the Secretary-at-War to Ireland and
putting in his place Newcastle's brother Pelham, 'which would have
been a most sensible and indisputable mortification to your general',
Carteret's ally Cadogan. Although this re-shuffling of the ministry
was for the time being postponed, it was contrived by Walpole
and Townshend that Carteret should be the Secretary charged with
the duty of rebuking Cadogan for exceeding his powers as Commander-in-Chief and Master-General of the Ordnance in a way
objected to by Walpole.[2] Then Townshend reports to Walpole that
Carteret is paying court to those like Bernstorff, whose influence at
Hanover had been destroyed by Stanhope, and other 'little emissaries
and intelligencers, brought up to lying and intrigue', and later has
the satisfaction of telling his brother-in-law that Carteret 'has gone
a-shooting for some days, he seems pretty much at a stand, what
course to steer next, having no great reason hitherto to be satisfied
with his negotiations'. As for himself, writes Townshend unctuously,
'I make it my chief business to pay my court to our master; and to
preserve the confidence of our old friends'; but such private matters
should be 'imparted to no one living but the Duke of Newcastle',
while Walpole responds with malicious tittle-tattle against Carteret
obtained from Bolingbroke, and rumours from the continent that
Carteret is soon returning to form a new ministry. Finally Townshend
presents a scheme which ultimately proved successful in ridding the
brothers-in-law entirely of Carteret.[3]

Carteret was not by nature an intriguer: his main interest was in
conceiving bold strokes of policy. But he was a bad judge of the

[1] Add. MSS. 32686, ff. 286 and 440.   [2] Torrens, *l.c.* I, 522–3.
[3] The correspondence between Townshend and Walpole during this period is
in Coxe, *Walpole*, II, 251–95.

men to be employed in carrying out his schemes. His ambassador at Paris, for example, Sir Lukas Schaub, though useful enough, as we have seen, as a messenger to explain treaties or settle passing diplomatic difficulties, was not of the calibre to be the sole representative of the English court at Paris, and needed to be reinforced by a colleague of heavier metal. Again, when confronted by the intrigues of men like Walpole, Townshend and Newcastle, who were much better at the business than he himself could ever hope to be, Carteret attempted a counter-intrigue with the help of people vastly inferior in credit and accomplishments in that sphere. Of George I's two mistresses at this period the Duchess of Kendal was easily the first in political insight and also in influence on the King. She it was who had obtained from Walpole the patent for the notorious 'Wood's Halfpence' contract in Ireland by which she netted £10,000: by this and other means Walpole and Townshend had been far-seeing enough to secure the favour of the 'good Duchess' as they called her. The other mistress, the Countess of Darlington, was perhaps more attractive personally but had little political influence. Carteret, always of a sanguine temperament, paid his court to her and thought, by seconding an ambitious scheme of hers, to gain not only her favour but also that of the King and so confound his adversaries. The Countess had a daughter by the King, known by her mother's original title of Comtesse de Platen, and was anxious to forward a marriage between this daughter and a French nobleman the Comte de St Florentin. At the same time she professed that it was beneath the dignity of a King's daughter, even though left-handed, to marry anybody of a lower rank than a duke, so the Regent Orleans was to be approached to create the Comte a Duc et Pair de France. Carteret entered enthusiastically into the scheme, and with the King's full approval instructed Schaub to press for the coveted dignity. That he should have lent himself to such an intrigue, and indeed persisted in it with unusual pertinacity, is a melancholy instance of *corruptio optimi pessima*. It was all the more unfortunate, since the Regent was much embarrassed by the request, as it would offend the old nobility, many of whom, he said, were more deserving of the coveted dignity. To add to Carteret's difficulties, his chief ally at the French court, Dubois, died in August 1723 and the Regent himself in the following December; and Orleans's successor, the Duc de Bourbon, who had no such close ties with the English court, finally rejected the proposal to confer a dukedom on St Florentin. So the whole stupid intrigue fell to the ground. It would have been better if Carteret had remembered his own proud saying: 'What is it to me who is a judge or a bishop? It is my business to make Kings and Emperors, to maintain the balance of Europe.'

This unfortunate incursion into French court intrigues gave Walpole and Townshend just the excuse they wanted for interfering with Carteret's own province in foreign affairs. Their excuse was that it was difficult to gather from Schaub's reports the exact state of the St Florentin negotiation, especially after Dubois's death, when the Regent himself, during his last months, seemed more and more averse to it: and they made great use of a report from that busybody Peterborough that Orleans had expressed a great contempt for our ambassador in Paris. But even so it was almost unprecedented for one Secretary to meddle with the business of his colleague. Nevertheless it was proposed by the brothers-in-law that Walpole's brother Horace,[1] who had been on a mission to Holland, should go as a 'tourist' to Paris and report confidentially to the brothers on Schaub's proceedings and as to the amount of credit attached to him by the French ministers. This suggestion, when submitted to the King by Townshend, was approved of; and Horace soon reported in accordance with the brothers' expectation. Thereupon Townshend went a step further and convinced the King that it would be useful to give Horace some official status at Paris, the subterfuge adopted being that he should be given full powers as an envoy plenipotentiary to sign the accession of Portugal to the Quadruple Alliance in the French capital; and, to make the rebuff to his colleague more patent, Carteret was ordered to sign Horace's full powers and instructions. 'This indisputable mark of confidence towards us', writes Townshend exultingly to Robert, 'and neglect towards Carteret and Schaub cannot fail' to make Orleans and the French ministers 'open themselves to Horace and to court our friendship', and will 'show the world the superiority of our credit' over Carteret, who shows 'visible marks of despair' at this 'mortifying stroke [wounding him] in the most vital and sensible part', whereas the King shows 'daily civilities to me'. Newcastle alone, he adds in a postscript, is to be told the secret of Horace's mission.[2]

Meanwhile Newcastle, while left in charge of the Secretary's office during Walpole's absence at Houghton, was adding fuel to the fire

[1] This brother of Robert Walpole's was sometimes spoken of as Horatio, but more often as Horace. To distinguish him from his nephew, the memoirs- and letter-writer, I generally speak of him as 'old Horace'.

[2] This correspondence is in Coxe, *Walpole*, II.

by his letters to Townshend, reporting all the tittle-tattle he could gather from others about Carteret and adding venomous suggestions on his own account. One of his most detailed informants was Lord Lechmere, the holder of a minor office in the government, who expressed surprise that 'there could be any question about him [Carteret], one that was very abandon'd...as He was; that He knew the single hopes of the Tories were in him'; he may even, he added, have given Atterbury warning of his arrest. Then Carteret 'had a manner of setting forth his own credit to the World, that till very lately every Body thought he was the chief Favourite', talking of his 'universal interest' and that 'the Bench of Bishops were all at his devotion'. As his own suggestion Newcastle writes in another letter that Schaub may 'now be wise enough to see that you and Sir Robert have all influence and so he may be detached from Carteret...and attach himself to those who have more credit with the King and who can consequently serve him best: who they are, he must want the ability of a common courtier, if by this time he has not learnt.'[1]

Carteret himself, always buoyant and self-reliant, did not take Horace Walpole's appointment as tragically as Townshend had represented it to Sir Robert. Writing about it to Schaub, he said, 'Cette affaire ne me cause point de peine, quoique mes collègues ont certainement quelque chose en tête...qu'ils ne m'ont pas expliqué, et peut-être pas même au Roi. Vous serez fort attentif à voir si Horatio Walpole tâche de me mettre mal dans l'esprit du Duc d'Orléans et du Comte de Morville. Mais vous vous garderez bien de lui laisser entrevoir mes soupçons ou les vôtres.'[2] A month later he was equally optimistic. Referring to rumours as to the decline in his influence, he told Schaub once more that 'all the reports to which you allude are false. I have mentioned them to the King, who expressed as much kindness as ever, and the same approbation of my conduct, and of my zealous, though feeble, services....My colleagues, instead of attacking, have courted me for some time past.'[3] All the same it was an impossible position with Schaub and Horace Walpole both representing the King at Paris but each taking his directions from a different Secretary of State. Horace lost no opportunity of depreciating his colleague to his brother in London, while Schaub, in turn, as ambassador nominally superior to Horace, tried

[1] Add. MSS. 32686, ff. 268, 304.
[2] Quoted by Ballantyne, p. 97, from Sloane MSS. 4204, f. 93.
[3] Ballantyne, p. 98.

on every occasion to prevent his colleague from doing any business with the French ministers. Finally each found his position so irksome that he clamoured for the other's recall; but it was not till April 1724 that Schaub was at last recalled, leaving Horace Walpole in sole possession of the embassy. Carteret himself had then no alternative but to resign his post as Secretary of State, jockeyed out by Robert Walpole and Townshend with the help of their jackal Newcastle, who stepped into his place.

Thus Carteret's first term of office as Secretary of State came to a somewhat inglorious end. He had many handicaps, a province affording him little scope for his special knowledge in foreign politics, a powerful combination against him from his own colleagues, and insufficient political backing to enable him to triumph over his adversaries. But his own weaknesses partly account for his downfall—an inability to work well with others, bad judgment in the choice of subordinates, and a buoyant optimism which blinded him to the dangers besetting him. He was always at his best when working by himself as he was at Stockholm, as he was about to be in Dublin and as he very nearly succeeded in being in his second ministry.

Chapter IV

NEWCASTLE & TOWNSHEND

When the Duke of Newcastle in April 1724 was appointed to succeed Carteret as Secretary of State for the South, Chamorel, the
French envoy in London, wrote to his minister in Paris that, though
knowing little of foreign affairs, he had been promoted chiefly for
his wealth and political influence, useful for the Hanover succession:
'il leur suffit', he adds, 'qu'il ait de la docilité pour agir et parler
comme ils [Walpole and Townshend] lui dicteront',[1] and two years
later this view is confirmed by the Imperial Ambassador Palm, who
tells his master that 'it is known to everybody that Newcastle is
nothing but a figure of secretary of state, being obliged to conform
himself in everything to Lord Townshend, who is *proprié autor et
anima negotiorum*'.[2] That this was so seems to have been fully understood by the English representatives at Cambrai, Polwarth and
Whitworth, who disliked and despised Newcastle. Finding that
Newcastle's reiterated injunctions always to defer to the French
views in the conduct of affairs at the congress were especially
irritating to the Emperor, who in consequence vented his ill-humour
against England, they took it upon them to write 'in the greatest
confidence', not to their immediate chief Newcastle, but to Townshend, to remonstrate against these instructions. In this instance the
complaint was singularly ill-timed, for it was Townshend himself
who had initiated the policy and of course supported Newcastle's
directions. He therefore handed over the letter to Newcastle to
answer; and the only result for the peccant ambassadors was a stinging
reproof from Newcastle concluding with the words, 'His Majesty
doubts not but you will confine yourselves entirely to the business
that shall come before you...and punctually observe the directions
which he shall from time to time think proper to send you.'[3]

But though Townshend thus officially supported Newcastle, he
had no illusions about his competence. After working with him as
a colleague for some time he conceived, says old Horace Walpole,
'a strong aversion to him. He regarded his Grace as utterly un-

[1] Add. MSS. 32308, f. 171.   [2] Coxe, *Walpole*, II, 505.
[3] See *E.H.R.* L, pp. 113–19.

qualified and an intolerable incumbrance in public business',[1] a view entirely shared by Horace himself after a long experience of his despatches. It must be admitted that on first assuming office the Duke took an almost equally humble view of his own capacity. Writing to Horace in April 1724, he says: 'Though perhaps it may be unpolitick in a minister yet it is very pardonable in a friend freely to own to you that nothing but my dependence upon the friendship and great ability of my Lord Townshend at home and the information and advice that I shall receive from you abroad could have induced me to undertake an office which at present is so difficult to me.... I shall in everything act in concert with my Ld. Townshend and according to the advice and instructions that I shall have the pleasure of receiving from him.'[2] Finally, according to Hervey, Sir Robert Walpole, with the choice between Pulteney and Newcastle for the post of Secretary, rejected Pulteney, though obviously the abler, because he was more likely to take a line of his own and pitched upon Newcastle, because he 'thought His Grace's quality and estate, his popularity in the country, and the great influence he had in Parliament by the number of boroughs he commanded, were qualifications and appurtenances that would always make him a useful friend to any minister; and looked upon his understanding to be such as could never let him rise into a dangerous rival'.[3] In fact Walpole proved right about Newcastle for the next ten years at least; but subsequently, when Sir Robert was beginning to lose his grip of affairs, if Newcastle was not a 'dangerous rival', he became a dangerous intriguer against his chief.

During the first six years that Newcastle was Secretary of State with Townshend as his colleague, the policy initiated by Stanhope of close alliance with France and of guarded observation of the Emperor, was consistently followed by Townshend and obsequiously imitated by Newcastle. Walpole himself, freed to a large extent by the exile of Atterbury from the dread of a Jacobite revival, was mainly engrossed during these years by his fiscal reforms, and was quite content to leave the conduct of foreign affairs to his capable brother-in-law. Townshend indeed, and Robert Walpole himself, had no scruples about receiving letters on French affairs from Horace, the very departure from official routine so severely reprimanded in the case of Polwarth and Whitworth. For Newcastle had not been Secretary a year when he was complaining to Horace about such

<hr>

[1] Add. MSS. 9200, f. 54.   [2] Add. MSS. 32738, f. 178.
[3] Hervey, *Memoirs*, p. 657.

letters; to which Horace replies that no slight was intended and that he enjoyed writing to the Duke above all things.[1] But in general Newcastle was meek enough, as when he was reproved by Townshend for spending too much of his time at Claremont, to which he replied in a very humble school-boyish letter that he hoped his conduct in managing foreign affairs gave satisfaction.[2]

The main problems that occurred during this period were the establishment of the Ostend East India Company by the Emperor as a rival to the English East India and Associated Companies, and, while the Congress of Cambrai was actually sitting, the sudden volte-face of Spain and the Emperor from open antagonism to a close alliance. The Ostend Company received a comprehensive trading charter from the Emperor, as ruler of the Low Countries, in 1722, and at once the English companies were up in arms against what they regarded as poaching on their preserves. This move of the Emperor's indeed had a great deal to do with the English ministers' anxiety to retain the support of France, not so much interested in that dispute as England was, and so to allow their ally to take the lead in the Congress of Cambrai. The sudden change in Spanish policy was precipitated by the Duc de Bourbon, who took over the Duc d'Orléans's post as chief minister in 1724. Already by that time the Spanish King, disgusted at the inconclusive verbiage at Cambrai, had sent Ripperda, a plausible adventurer of Dutch parentage, to sound the Emperor about coming to some secret agreement on the points at issue between them. This negotiation hung fire till March 1725, when a crowning insult from the French court determined the Spanish monarchs to secure another ally at any cost.

In 1721 after the first resumption of friendly relations between Paris and Madrid a marriage had been arranged between Louis XV and the Infanta Marie Anne; but, as the Infanta was then only three years old, the marriage could not take place for many more years, and meanwhile she was sent to live in France as the King's affianced bride. But early in 1725 Louis XV, then a delicate youth, was seriously ill, and almost on the point of death. This disturbed Bourbon, not so much for the King's sake, but from the knowledge that, if he died childless, his successor on the throne would be one of the Orleans family, with which Bourbon had a deadly feud. So he determined to find for Louis a wife of marriageable age, and, without even a previous warning to Philip, packed off the little Infanta back to Madrid. Outraged at this insult, Philip broke off

[1] Add. MSS. 32742, f. 265.   [2] Add. MSS. 32687, ff. 101, 118.

all relations with France and ordered Ripperda to conclude a treaty with the Emperor with the least possible delay. At the same time he proposed to the English ministers, that, on condition of their disassociating themselves from France, they should undertake the sole mediation at the Congress of Cambrai.

At first sight there seemed to be a plausible case for accepting Philip's offer, as a settlement of our interminable trade disputes with Spain might well be expected as a return for our support of Spanish interests at the congress. This indeed was the view strongly urged on Newcastle by Horace Walpole from Paris, who argued that France could hardly blame us for taking advantage of a difficulty which was not of our own making, especially as one of our most important interests was in our Spanish trade.[1] But reports of Ripperda's secret negotiations with the Emperor had already reached London, reason enough for Townshend to reject Spain's offer; for he always distrusted the Emperor, all the more since the establishment of the Ostend East India Company, and therefore was determined to hold fast to the French alliance. Accordingly Newcastle, in a series of despatches to Horace Walpole and his secretary Robinson in Paris,[2] decisively rejected the proposal to leave France in the lurch, pointing out that her friendship was far more useful to us than that of Spain. If we supported Spain alone we should either have to make far higher demands for her than we cared to, or lose the credit of supporting her by not going far enough to meet her wishes, which would throw her back again on France; and we should thereby have estranged both powers; while if we made one step separately towards Spain, France would make twenty. So we had much better stick to the French alliance, a course which would considerably strengthen our claims on France's loyalty and compel her to depend more on our support. Lastly if, as might be hoped, the reconciliation of France and Spain were brought about by our good offices the gratitude of both countries would be secured. But, while thus remaining firm to the French alliance, Newcastle at the same time expressed the considered views of the King and his fellow-ministers in emphatically rejecting a proposal made by the Duc de Bourbon, at the suggestion, it was reported by Horace Walpole, of that unfortunate intriguer Lady Darlington, that George I's eldest daughter Ann should become the wife of Louis XV. Apart from the consideration, so well expressed by Carteret, that royal marriages afforded no certain security for national alliances, Louis's marriage

[1] Add. MSS. 32742, f. 515.   [2] Add. MSS. 32742, f. 307; 32743, ff. 1, 3, 340.

with a protestant princess would have been highly unpopular in France, while her necessary conversion to Roman Catholicism before marriage would, as Newcastle wrote in his despatches to Paris, be so strongly resented in England that the popularity of the French alliance and even of the Hanoverian dynasty might be imperilled.[1]

After England's refusal to accept the sole mediation at Cambrai, Philip, in desperation, ordered Ripperda to come to an agreement on almost any terms with the Emperor. Accordingly on 30 April 1725 three treaties, of peace, alliance and commerce with the Emperor, were signed at Vienna by Ripperda. By the peace treaty, the only one published to the world, Spain guaranteed the Pragmatic Sanction which aimed at securing the indivisibility of the Habsburg possessions in favour of the Emperor's heir, male or female, in return merely for a fresh confirmation by the Emperor of the Italian duchies for Don Carlos of Spain, already agreed to by the Quadruple Alliance. The terms of the other two treaties were to be kept secret, but soon leaked out owing to the calculated indiscretions of Ripperda, and aroused considerable alarm in France and England. The Emperor, it appeared, was to support Spain's demand for the return of Gibraltar and Minorca, while Spain was to recognize the Emperor's Ostend Company and give it trade facilities. There was also talk of marriage between the Infants of Spain, Don Carlos and Don Philip, with the two Archduchesses, daughters of the Emperor. Such talk was especially alarming to France, reviving as it did the prospect of a close family union between the Emperor and Spain, to prevent which she had exhausted herself in the War of the Spanish Succession. Ripperda also boasted that the Pretender was to be restored to the throne of England, and that France was to be shorn of her border provinces to the benefit of Spain and the Emperor. In fact the Emperor in all these treaties had the best of the bargain. He was to receive support for his shattered finances from the argosies of Spain; he was to give nothing in return for the trading privileges granted by Spain to his Ostend Company; and, though he offered his good offices for the return to Spain of Gibraltar and Minorca, he was not committed to giving Spain effective military aid for their forcible recovery. The immediate result of these treaties was the break-up of the Congress of Cambrai, which obviously had no further usefulness to serve. A secondary result was the division of Europe into two opposing camps—the Emperor and Spain on the one side, France and England on the other.

[1] Add. MSS. 32742, ff. 307, 332.

War seemed imminent, and the two opposing sides at once began arming and seeking allies for the expected struggle. In the diplomatic battles for alliances that ensued, on the Anglo-French side England took the lead. England was also more forward in taking military measures, such as the despatch of a fleet to the Baltic to overawe Catharine of Russia, who had joined the Hispano-Austrian alliance, and of another to watch the coasts of Spain and intercept the galleons as they came from the West Indies with treasure to pay for the Emperor's troops and alliances. It proved much more difficult for the French foreign office and its envoys abroad suddenly to abandon the policy of union between the two Bourbon powers and to enter whole-heartedly into the more vigorous measures proposed by the English ministers; but in the long run they usually had to acquiesce. During the next few years it was Townshend who entirely dictated the measures taken by the allies: he even dictated the policy to be urged upon France during the critical months of preparation in the latter half of 1725, though that was formally within Newcastle's province. For once more George I spent those months in Hanover, and this time Townshend was in sole attendance upon him and wrote the despatches to Horace Walpole and his secretary of legation Robinson in Paris without interference from Newcastle, who had little to do in London except to receive copies of his colleague's despatches. Townshend was undoubtedly in the circumstances the right man to take the lead; for he was a consistent opponent of the Emperor, then the more important factor in the Hispano-Austrian alliance. The first-fruits of his activity was another treaty for mutual support with Frederick William of Prussia signed at Hanover on 3 September 1725; and for the next two years French and English on the one side, Spain and the Emperor on the other, were bidding against each other for allies all over Europe. On the whole Spain and the Emperor were more successful in the bidding, beginning with Frederick William himself who, barely a year after signing the Treaty of Hanover, was induced by more alluring promises from the Emperor to change sides. But though by 1727 the Emperor and Spain could reckon their own and their allies' land forces at close on 400,000, as compared with only 315,000 under the banners of England and France, this deficiency in land forces was more than made good by the activity of the English fleet, the only force actually called into action.[1]

But meanwhile important changes had been made in the French

[1] See *E.H.R.* xv, 696–8.

ministry resulting in a cooling off of relations with England. In June 1726 the Duc de Bourbon, the blundering first minister who had precipitated the breach with Spain, was summarily dismissed and replaced by Cardinal Fleury, who in August of the following year appointed Chauvelin as foreign minister. Both these ministers were set upon a reconciliation with Spain, and dreaded above all things a lasting renewal of the Austro-Hispano alliance which had for so long been the bugbear of French rulers—with this difference that Fleury, a cautious politician, was still set on also maintaining the Anglo-French entente, while Chauvelin's views from the outset were definitely Anglophobe. Already by the beginning of 1727 the Emperor, finding that, owing to the English blockade on the Spanish treasure fleets, he was not obtaining the subsidies promised him by Spain, was willing to listen to terms. Accordingly in May 1727 he agreed to a treaty with England, France and Holland, whereby he was to suspend the Ostend Company's trade and restore the *status quo ante*: a fortnight later Spain also adhered to this treaty, though characteristically delaying the settlement of various outstanding questions till March 1728 by the Convention of the Pardo.

In June 1727, before these arrangements had been completed, George I died suddenly on the last of his journeys to Hanover. The accession of George II seemed at first to bode ill for Newcastle, the man he had declared 'not fit to be a Chamberlain in a second-rate German court',[1] and even for Walpole himself, with whom he had also quarrelled: indeed his first action was to supersede Walpole by the Speaker, Spencer Compton. Fortunately his wise Queen, Caroline, realized that Walpole alone was capable of doing the King's business, especially in financial matters; so Compton was promoted to the House of Lords as Lord Wilmington, and Walpole confirmed in office, with his ministry unchanged, though both George II and Caroline always retained a mean opinion of Newcastle. Another result of the new reign was that Townshend's pretension to rival Walpole for leadership was finally scotched.

In the final struggle between Walpole and Townshend, Newcastle, with his instinctive flair for the winning horse, backed Walpole. He had indeed some excuse, for Townshend, though willing enough to conspire with Newcastle against Carteret, had soon taken his measure as a colleague, and played much the same game with him as they had played together against Carteret. It was not only in 1725 that, as minister in attendance on George I, he carried on all the

[1] See above, ch. II, p. 39.

negotiations for the alliance against Spain and the Emperor without consulting Newcastle; but once more in 1729, when he again accompanied George II to Hanover, he showed the same disregard of his colleague's opinions. In April of that year Newcastle complained bitterly that 'a negotiation that had been on foot since March 18th had been kept a secret in great measure from us all';[1] and in November of that year the French ambassador in London writes to Chauvelin in Paris, in regard to a secret negotiation with four of the Electors for a new coalition against the Emperor, that Townshend had given him 'la copie des articles secrets...dont il n'a fait aucune part à M. le Duc de Newcastle, non plus du projet du traité, qui par conséquent n'en a pu instruire M. Horace Walpole' at Paris.[2]

In fact by this time Townshend's 'aversion to Newcastle...as utterly unqualified and an intolerable incumbrance in public business' had become so confirmed that he had formed a scheme for treating him as they had both treated Carteret, by substituting Chesterfield for him as Secretary for the South. But Walpole, backed by the Queen, put an end to this intrigue,[3] the last in which Townshend was able to indulge. In 1729 the brothers-in-law, Walpole and Townshend, had had a violent personal quarrel and almost came to blows; they disagreed, too, fundamentally on foreign policy. Walpole had for some time been uneasy about growing differences between England and France—especially since Chauvelin, a declared Anglophobe, had become foreign minister—and was anxious to return to the Old System of alliance with the Emperor: Townshend, on the other hand, was as firmly opposed to the policy and methods of Vienna, and had no wish to entangle England by a guarantee of the Pragmatic Sanction, which he foresaw might lead to war on behalf of the Emperor's daughter. Walpole carried the day, with the support of Newcastle, who declared that 'the Cardinal [Fleury] is not dead, but dead to us' and that he 'had long been of the opinion that nothing could be so much for the interest of the King and Nation as a thorough reconciliation with the court of Vienna'.[4] At any rate, after ten years as practically sole director of English foreign policy, Townshend was a tired man, and anxious to retire and cultivate his turnips, which he accordingly did in May 1730. As his successor Newcastle already had his candidate ready in William

[1] Coxe, *Walpole*, II, 642.
[2] *Brit. Dipl. Instr. France*, 1727–44, p. xv note.
[3] Add. MSS. 9200, f. 54; Coxe, *Walpole*, I, 33.
[4] Add. MSS. 32769, f. 143; 32772, f. 179.

Stanhope, recently created Lord Harrington, who had been under him as ambassador to Madrid and had just concluded another treaty with Spain, whereby all outstanding differences, it was optimistically hoped, had been settled. Walpole's objections to Stanhope were overcome. So, on Townshend's definite resignation, Newcastle was able to secure him as his colleague in the northern department, the first of the many he chose as likely to be entirely docile to himself, but not destined to be as amenable as he hoped. He had already written to him on the conclusion of his mission to Madrid, congratulating him on his success, but taking care to prejudice him against Townshend, who had not yet resigned, and, as he told him, 'blames loudly your instructions, which, he says, were drawn up by yourself, and now has attacked you for even exceeding these instructions. Your joint despatch has made him outrageous; he says we have been wrong from the beginning.'[1] Later, when Stanhope was on his way back to receive the seals of office, he wrote him another letter overwhelming him with flattery on his appointment. 'My dear friend, you must now consider yourself in a quite different light from what you have ever been. We must now greatly depend upon you, for directing us (and we cannot have a better guide) and as we shall be jointly responsible for everything, we cannot be too earnest for the success of our affairs. We are all here full of doubts, though Lord Townshend, upon parting, said, all was as good as done, if we did not spoil it.'[2] These halcyon honeymoon days did not last long; for though Harrington was a lazy man, he was also obstinate, and not inclined to take his orders from Newcastle or anybody else.

[1] Coxe, *Walpole*, II, 678.　　　　[2] *Ib.* p. 696.

Chapter V

CARTERET IN DUBLIN AND IN PRIVATE LIFE

§I. DUBLIN

In 1724 Carteret had easily been got rid of and replaced by Newcastle. But the new triumvirate, Walpole, Townshend and Newcastle, were not quite easy in their minds. It would never do to have Carteret, still formidable for his power in debate and his profound knowledge of European affairs, as a 'disobliged' man to oppose them in the House of Lords. So a shelf of some dignity must be found for him: and where better than in the Irish vice-royalty? He would still be a member of the government, so with his lips sealed to some extent against his colleagues:[1] better still he would have to be in Ireland during most of the parliamentary sessions. There was another excellent reason why he should be chosen for this post. Ireland was then seething with discontent at the imposition of 'Wood's Halfpence',[2] a discontent with which the reigning viceroy, the Duke of Grafton, was quite unable to deal: and small wonder, since it was of him the wicked and witty Lord Hervey said that 'the natural cloud of his understanding, thickened by the artificial cloud of his mistaken court policy made his meaning always as unintelligible as his conversation was unentertaining'. Carteret, on the other hand, might prove able to allay the discontent and save the government from an awkward situation, or, as was almost hoped, he would fail, as Grafton had, and so a dangerous rival would be finally discredited. Walpole indeed was quite frank about this hope when he wrote to Newcastle, 'I should not be for sending him over now, if I did not think it would end in totally recalling him. We shall at least get rid of him here'.[3] The only difficulty was that Grafton had evinced no appreciation of his own futility or any desire to resign: so it fell to Townshend and Newcastle to write him two somewhat tactless letters[4] explaining that the ministry found it necessary to provide some post for Carteret and that none appeared more suitable than Grafton's, who accordingly

[1] There was, however, not the same sense of government solidarity then as there is to-day.
[2] For the 'Wood's Halfpence' affair see my *Whig Supremacy*, pp. 283–6.
[3] Add. MSS. 32687, f. 54.
[4] Coxe, *Walpole*, II, 295–6. Torrens also mentions Newcastle's letter.

had no option but to accept the office of Lord Chamberlain, just vacated by Newcastle.

Happily for the plotters Carteret made no difficulty in accepting the thankless office of Viceroy. As an Irish correspondent of Bishop Nicolson of Derry wrote, on hearing the news: 'It is said Lord Carteret is declared Lord-Lieutenant of Ireland....If this be true, Lord Townshend and Mr White may sing, *Hey boys, up go we!*'[1] Though banished to Ireland for half each year, Carteret consoled himself with the thought that he would still retain his seat on the English Council for the other half, and that, on the death of George I, he might with his friends Speaker Compton and Pulteney, who had also been dismissed from office by Walpole, return to power in England.[2] Moreover, he had powerful friends in Ireland, notably the Brodrick clan, headed by the Irish Chancellor Midleton, with whom, as Walpole already knew by intercepting his correspondence, he agreed in deploring the policy of introducing Wood's Halfpence. So gaily, as was his wont, he prepared for his new adventure. Making unusually rapid arrangements about his equipage and staff, he arrived at Kingstown on 12 October 1724 with his wife and a daughter, as if meditating a prolonged term of office. As he wrote to a friend on the eve of departure: 'Certainty of success is in nobody's power, however I'll do my best and it is not the first difficult commission that I have been employed in; often goes the pitcher etc. says the old proverb, but it frightens me not; and if I am to have the fate of the pitcher, people shall lament me and say I deserved better luck.'[3] This was a very different spirit to that in which his cynical contemporary Chesterfield embarked on the same undertaking twenty years later. For, when asked why he had accepted such a thankless task, Chesterfield replied, because 'it is a place wherein a man had business enough to prevent his falling asleep, and not so much as to keep him awake.'[4]

'The Lord-Lieutenant appeared to-day [12 October] off the Hill of Hoath', wrote Bishop Downes, 'and landed before eleven at George's Key; the same minute (as good luck would have it) that the Lords detached from the Privy Council, to compliment him upon his arrival and to let His Excellency know that the Lords Justices

---

[1] *Wm Nicolson, D.D., Letters etc.* 1683–1726/7, pp. 569–70.
[2] W. M. Torrens, *History of Cabinets*, I, 369.   [3] P.R.O., S.P. 63 (Ireland).
[4] Dobree, *Chesterfield*, I, 106. It must be admitted, however, that Chesterfield was better than his word and proved, next to Carteret, the best Viceroy in the eighteenth century.

and Council were sitting ready to receive him, got thither...[but] the Militia was not half gathered or put in order....He seems well and pleased; but how long he may continue so I know not. We seem here bent upon our ruin.'[1] In fact the 4th *Drapier's Letter* had just appeared, the first of the series openly to incite the Irish people to revolt against the imposition of Wood's Halfpence. Though anonymous, it was an open secret that the *Letters* came from the most formidable writer in Ireland, Swift, then Dean of St Patrick's and an old friend of Carteret since 1710. Carteret himself, indeed, had never concealed his disapproval of the way in which the Halfpence had been foisted on the Irish people. But ties of friendship and dislike of the government's policy could not for a moment stand before what Carteret felt to be his clear duty in dealing with an incitement to revolt: 'So long as I have the honour to be chief governor here', he wrote to Newcastle, 'the peace of the kingdom shall be kept.' His first action, therefore, after being sworn in at the Castle, was to summon the Irish Privy Council and cause them to issue a proclamation offering a reward for the name of the author of the *Drapier's Letters* and to have him prosecuted; and he told Archbishop King, inclined to dissent from such drastic measures, that 'the Libel contained such seditious, and in my opinion treasonable matter, as called upon a Chief Governor to exert his utmost power in bringing the author to justice.' And when, on the day after the proclamation appeared, Swift suddenly presented himself at Carteret's levée and addressed him on his 'glorious exploit...in issuing a proclamation against a poor shopkeeper, whose only crime is an honest endeavour to save his country from ruin', Carteret, without a moment's pause, replied:

> Res dura et regni novitas me talia cogunt
> Moliri.

But no reward could induce anybody to reveal Swift's authorship, well known as it was to everybody in Ireland, including Carteret himself, nor would any jury present a true bill even against the printer of the 4th *Letter*. But the sting of this defeat for the English government was much softened by Carteret's tact. At the outset he had made it plain to the Irish that nobody need accept Wood's coinage, in spite of the patent; and by the beginning of the Irish session of 1725 he had persuaded Walpole to cancel the patent

---

[1] *Wm Nicholson, D.D., Letters etc.* p. 586.

altogether and the Irish parliament to send dutiful thanks for this concession to the King.

Even before he had cleared away this formidable stumbling-block he initiated a much-needed series of reforms in Ireland, reforms which no doubt helped to divert attention from the major grievance of Wood's Halfpence. The Irish public accounts were more than three years in arrear, the Commissariat's and Barrack Master's were as bad, and no less than £12,000 was found to be due to the soldiers for pay; but only two months after Carteret's landing Lord Midleton was writing from Dublin to his brother: 'We are in a horrible hurricane by my Lord-Lieutenant's looking into the money matters of the Custom House and Treasury, and I hear all hands are at work to borrow money to powre into the treasury (the army and some other branches of the establishment being vastly in arrear, some say 20 months'...)....This unexpected looking into the management was suddain as a thunder clap on those who were not used in a late government to have their actions looked into, but everything was taken on trust to be as they represented.'[1] Carteret's investigations, as he told Newcastle, revealed an actual deficiency of £80,000 in the Treasury at Christmas 1724, due to bribable officials at the Customs and to a badly chosen appeal commission, which he forthwith put on a sounder basis: and not only was the soldiers' pay in arrears but the state of their barracks and hospitals was deplorable, while many of the officers were found to be absent from their posts. All such defects as could be remedied by executive action he at once remedied, those requiring money votes from the Irish parliament he induced it to pass. When in 1725 there was a prospect of war with Spain, he took energetic action for the security of the country, seeing that garrisons were up to strength, reviewing troops and inspiring them with his own ardent spirit. 'A Daniel come to judgment' was Bishop Nicolson's verdict on him.[2]

Nor was Carteret content merely with the removal of obvious abuses. A chronic cause of Ireland's poverty and discontent was the complete subordination not only of its economic system but also of its government to the supposed interests of Great Britain. Irish industries thought likely to compete successfully with those of England and Scotland were drastically restricted or even entirely prohibited: no legislation could be passed by the Irish parliament which had not

[1] Add. MSS. 9243, f. 53.
[2] See P.R.O., S.P. 63 (Ireland), f. 385 et passim, and Letters...by Hugh Boulter, 1724-38.

previously obtained the sanction of the English Privy Council. Carteret, indeed, was not prepared to attempt any radical changes in the system, which was then fully accepted by all sections of opinion in England; but he made serious efforts to modify some of its resulting abuses. He did his utmost, for example, to obtain a reduction of the almost prohibitive tax of 7s. 6d. a lb. levied in England on silk manufactured 'to such perfection' in Ireland. He also tried to lighten the burden on imported Irish woollens; 'I being a Devonshire squire', he writes, 'am fully versed in that matter, and it certainly is of great importance to England in general, and particularly to the west; but Ireland must be a little humoured to wean them from their way of reasoning on that head', especially as the high tax on Irish woollens in England encouraged the 'running' of Irish woollens to France. By 1728 the famine, which had been almost endemic in Ireland from the day Carteret landed, was at its height; and he pressed forward, besides temporary measures to re-lieve distress, a bill to encourage better land cultivation by the draining of bogs, improved methods of tillage, etc. This 'Bog Bill', as he called it, 'is at present our darling', he writes to his under-secretary in England; 'I hope I shall have no unnecessary difficulties lay'd upon me, I have got over some considerable ones, and sure it cannot be good policy entirely to disgust this country for nothing.'[1]

Another legitimate grievance of the Irish was the appointment of Englishmen to all the most lucrative posts in Church and State, many of whom were even content to draw their Irish salaries in England without ever visiting the country. Carteret himself was against this practice, but found determined opponents of his more enlightened policy not only in the English ministry, but also in Hugh Boulter, taken from an English bishopric to become Archbishop of Armagh and Primate of All Ireland in the same year that Carteret was himself appointed Viceroy. Boulter was in many ways an enlightened eccle-siastic, anxious to remove abuses in the Irish Church, to improve the position of the established clergy, and to promote education among the Irish; during the famine years, too, he spent freely from his own resources to relieve the widespread distress. But he was a fanatical supporter of the system of importing Englishmen to hold the key positions in Church and State: indeed, he appears to have been specially chosen by Newcastle to watch Carteret's proceedings and to put the brake on his more liberal policy. Shortly after his appoint-ment to the primacy he wrote to Newcastle demanding that all

[1] Add. MSS. 38016, f. 11.

nominations to Irish bishoprics should be in his hands, to enable him 'to carry on H.M.'s service here'; and, not content with the spiritual sphere, he freely pressed his advice on the Duke as to legal and other civil appointments. On the very day that West, the recently appointed Chancellor, died he wrote to Newcastle suggesting Wyndham, another Englishman, for the post; and though Carteret was actually in London at the time and asked to see Newcastle before the post was filled, Newcastle had already obtained the King's consent to Wyndham's appointment. Carteret indeed, under the powers given him by his first commission as Lord-Lieutenant, had made several appointments of Irishmen to Irish deaneries, but when, on the accession of George II in 1727, he received a new commission, he was specially excluded from the power of nominating deans, members of the Board of Exchequer, officers in the army or governors of forts without the sanction of the Secretary of State, who was much more disposed to accept Boulter's than Carteret's recommendations. A likely reason for this restriction was that Carteret was known to listen to the advice of his Tory friend Dean Swift, who told Carteret that 'as long as you are governor here, I shall expect the liberty of telling you my thoughts; and I hope you will consider these until you find I grow impertinent and have some bias of my own'. In 1725 he suggested to Carteret nine of his Dublin friends, including Dr Sheridan and Dr Delany, for Church preferment. Some of these, notably Dr Sheridan, were promoted by Carteret; but Boulter stopped the preferment of Dr Delany by reporting him to Newcastle as 'a great Tory' and 'a pupil monger' at the university. Still Swift was able to note that Carteret had 'paid attention to six of my recommendations for Church preferment', and later, during the viceroyalty of Carteret's successor, he wrote to Pulteney wishing that the Duke of Dorset 'would a little more consider that people here might have some small share in employments civil and ecclesiastical, wherein my Lord Carteret acted a more popular part'.[1]

Carteret's administrative reforms and his struggle to get Irishmen for Irish posts were only two of the many ways he identified himself with Irish interests, social, literary and historical, as well as political. Thereby he entirely won their hearts, especially those of the impressionable citizens of Dublin, who were made to feel, during his six years as Viceroy, that he was one with themselves. For one thing

---

[1] Boulter's activities are recorded in *Letters...by Hugh Boulter*, 1769, and P.R.O. S.P. 63 (Ireland); for Swift see his correspondence *passim*, especially his *Letter to Lord Carteret* of 3 July 1725, about his clerical recommendations.

he paid the Irish the compliment of spending far more of his time as Lord-Lieutenant in Ireland than was the custom of most of his predecessors and successors, who generally hurried back to England as soon as the Irish session was over and sometimes did not even return for the next session,[1] leaving their duties to be performed by Lords Justices. It was characteristic of him, too, that at the very height of the Drapier crisis he found time to carry off his Chancellor on a jaunt to visit the historic battlefield of the Boyne. Political differences were never allowed to interrupt his and his wife's intimate relations with their old friend, the formidable Dean of St Patrick's. Indeed he and Swift could cap verses at one another even during the turmoil occasioned by the 4th *Drapier's Letter*. Kept waiting for an audience of the Lord-Lieutenant, Swift dashed off to him the lines:

> My very good Lord, 'tis a very hard task,
> For a man to wait here who has nothing to ask,—

to which Carteret at once replied:

> My very good Dean, there are few who come here
> But have something to ask, or something to fear.

Already on the announcement of Carteret's appointment as Lord-Lieutenant Swift had welcomed him in his poem, *The Birth of Manly Virtue*, wherein his friend is described as:

> Completely form'd in every part
> To win the soul and glad the heart.
> The powerful voice, the graceful mien,
> Lovely alike, or heard or seen;...

[Then, after an allusion to the success of his Swedish mission, he continues:]

> Fame now reports, the Western Isle
> Is made his mansion for a while,
> Whose anxious natives, night and day,
> (Happy beneath his righteous sway)
> Weary the gods with ceaseless prayer,
> To bless him, and to keep him there;
> And claim it as a debt from Fate,
> Too lately found, to lose him late.

After the Wood's Halfpence grievance had been disposed of, Swift became a frequent guest at the Castle, welcomed alike by Lady

[1] Two of Carteret's predecessors, Sunderland and Townshend, never set foot in Ireland at all.

Carteret and the Lord-Lieutenant. An old friend of Lady Carteret's mother, Lady Worsley, Swift soon became an intimate friend of the lady at the Castle. Professing to be too deaf or too shy to accept one of her invitations to dine at the Castle, he begs her forgiveness in his charming *Apology to Lady Carteret,*

> Can it be strange, if I eschew
> A scene so glorious and so new?
> Or is he criminal that flies
> The living lustre of your eyes?

which with his jovial verses on *Hamilton's Bawn* were privately printed by Carteret's orders. So intimate were they in their friendly relations that the Viceroy's wife would chaff him when he came to visit her and even played tricks with his hat. These must have been the last of the great dean's bouts of care-free playfulness: within a few years after the Carterets left Dublin his deafness increased and the melancholia which clouded his last days finally settled on him.

With King, the saintly and none the less witty Archbishop of Dublin, Carteret had felt obliged to take a strong line on the question of the 4th *Drapier's Letter*; but this had proved no obstacle to a lasting and intimate friendship between him and the Carterets. In a letter from Lady Carteret to her friend Mrs Clayton, she wrote, 'I have great reason to be vain of having, as you say, the Archbishop of Dublin as my Lover.... H.R.H. can tell you there are few people that has his witt and spiritt or that is more difficult to be pleas'd. He realy is a Prodigy considering he is fourscore year old.... [I dont care] to be the Discourse of the Publick, but if it keeps my memory green among friends that is well.'[1] Mrs Clayton's husband, promoted to the bishopric of Killala on the eve of Carteret's departure, was another of those urbane Irish clerics in whom the Carterets delighted. It was he who wrote this quite polite but devastating retort to a piece of rudeness from Lord Perceval, son of Carteret's friend Lord Egmont: 'If I was as capable of being as rude to yr Lordship as you was to me...I should not have answered this letter. But I think it is a duty owing to myself to show that I cannot be provoked to be guilty of ill-manner. I therefore return you thanks for your letter and congratulate you sincerely on the birth of your son, both because it seems to give you pleasure and because I am very sure it will give great delight to Lord Egmont. But', he adds, to 'you who sett up for a hero in former times', there is nothing

[1] Add. MSS. 20102, f. 24.

specially heroic in begetting children, quoting Pope and Prior to enforce the view that heroes rarely get many children, while rascals often do.

Another episcopal friend of Carteret, H. E. Downes, then bishop of Meath, but later, thanks to the Viceroy's favour, promoted to the rich see of Derry, describes a dinner with the Lord-Lieutenant and others at Lord Chief Justice Whitshed's, the judge before whom the printer of Swift's 4th *Letter* was tried, at the very height of the Drapier agitation. 'It was a dismal day without doors, but', said the bishop, 'we made it as bright as we could within. We had no politicks; as not being of one mind in anything, unless in our public respect to our Lord-Lieutenant, who amazes me every day more and more. On Thursday night he took me with him to hear a Greek play at Mr Sheridan's school; his Excellency being disposed to encourage Learning, from the School to the College.'[1] Still more charming is Mrs Laetitia Pilkington's account of another dinner, at Dr Delany's, who later married one of Carteret's Granville cousins, authoress of the *Correspondence and Autobiography*. Carteret came 'unattended' to Delany's house, and, after walking in the garden, went into dinner with Delany's old mother as hostess, who told him, as they sat down to the simple but good fare:

> To stomachs cloyed with costly fare
> Simplicity alone was rare.

When the cloth was taken away, Carteret told Delany 'he always believed him to be a most well-bred gentleman, but never had so clear a demonstration of it as he had this day seen. Others whom I have tried the same experiment on have met me with as much confusion as if I came to arrest them for high treason; nay they would not give me a word of their conversation—which, and not their dinner, I sought—but hurry from me, and then, if I had any appetite, deprive me of it by their fulsome apology for defects'; capping his remarks with the tale of Swift and the apologetic hostess.[2] Another Irish blue-stocking, Mrs Grierson, described by Boswell as a handsome and learned woman, edited several classics including a Tacitus, which she dedicated to Carteret in elegant Latin. In return Carteret procured for her family the lucrative post of King's printer in Ireland.

Carteret succeeded in his viceroyalty more perhaps than he had hoped, and certainly more than the triumvirate, Walpole, Towns-

[1] *Wm Nicolson, D.D., Letters etc.* 2 vols. 1809, p. 590.
[2] L. Pilkington, *Memoirs*, ed. J. Isaacs, 1928, pp. 374-5.

hend and Newcastle, had expected or even wished, when they sent him on what seemed a forlorn hope. By his tact and courage he had averted the danger of rebellion aroused by Swift's 4th *Letter*, diverting anger by his calmness, combined with reforms in Irish finance and other beneficial measures; until at last he persuaded the home government that, as an Irish correspondent put it, even all Carteret's tact and reforming zeal 'shall not do; neither eating and drinking Civilities, nor good Words shall alter their minds as to that [the halfpence],'[1] and that Wood's patent must be withdrawn unconditionally. He had flattered Irish susceptibilities by his genuine appreciation of Irish culture and society and convinced the country generally that its interests held the foremost place in the Irish Viceroy's thoughts. The best proof of the enthusiasm aroused by his rule is to be found in the genuinely heartfelt expressions of the Irish Parliament's thanks passed in the customary addresses at the end of each session. At the end of his first session in September 1725 the King is thanked for 'the distinguishing mark of his Tender Care and Concern for us in sending His Excellency the Lord Carteret to be our Chief Governor', while Carteret himself is praised for his 'unwearied Application and the Exact Enquiries you have made into everything that relates to the state of this Kingdom...and the affectionate Concern you have shown for the Welfare of this Nation'. In later addresses he is thanked for his 'unwearied Application in settling the Publick Accounts, in securing the Publick Debts, in regulating the Forces on this Establishment... and in [uniting] Minds, Tempers and Inclinations', in the Kingdom; and above all he is told that his 'Application...Prudence and Justice have not rendered Your Government more acceptable than your Candour and Humanity have endeared your Person to the Nation'.[2]

Carteret's friend, Bishop Clayton of Killala, gives us a happy picture of the Lord-Lieutenant on his final departure from Ireland. Writing to his wife from the Lancashire port where Carteret disembarked, he says: 'When I came to the waterside I was oblig'd to wait there a few days for the arrivall of Lord Carteret, having obtained an order for the King's Yatch that brought his Lord[p] over to carry me back again. On his coming on shore I returned him thanks for his Recommendation from Ireland, he seem'd in high spirits and well pleased with his success in that kingdom.'[3] But

[1] P.R.O., S.P. 63 (Ireland), f. 385.
[2] These addresses are in P.R.O., S.P. 63 (Ireland), f. 385.
[3] Add. MSS. 20102, f. 135.

after all perhaps the best eulogy of Carteret's viceroyalty is Swift's mock complaint to him: 'What the vengeance brought you among us? Get you back, get you back; pray God Almighty send us our boobies again!'

§ II.   CARTERET IN PRIVATE LIFE

On his return from Ireland Carteret was offered the post of Lord Steward, vacated by the Duke of Dorset, his successor as Lord-Lieutenant. In spite of the remark attributed to him by Lord Hervey,[1] that 'any man who hoped to get power, or hurt those who possessed it, had better be a Gentleman Usher within the palace than leave it open to his rivals by retiring out of it', Carteret, as one might expect, refused this household appointment. He had no taste for the malicious tittle-tattle whereby Hervey secured the Queen's favour, nor any desire to obtain power by back-stairs intrigues. His main public interest was in foreign politics, which, after the Treaty of Vienna of 1731, seemed to promise some calm; and in the meantime he had no hankering for office which called forth none of his special gifts. For, unlike Newcastle, to whom the parade of official life and the self-importance it brought him were as the breath of his nostrils, Carteret had his own private interests to which he could always turn when he was not needed by the country: his family, his houses and his love of literature, good talk, and, it must be admitted, good burgundy wines.

His London house was in Arlington Street, the statesmen's row, where he had as a neighbour his great adversary Sir Robert Walpole, and later Walpole's youngest son Horace, and Henry Pelham. He also had a country seat, Hawnes, seven miles from Bedford and adjoining the little village of Haynes with its old church, where there is a Carteret mausoleum containing a tablet commemorating Carterets from Sir George, 'High Bailiff and Defender of Jersey', who died aged 80 in 1680, down to our Lord Granville, besides memorials to later descendants. Hawnes was bought by Sir George, according to Pepys,[2] for £3000 in May 1667 as a home for his son Philip and his bride Jemima Montagu, Carteret's grandparents. The manor with its 800 acres of parkland is noted in Domesday Book as held of the King in chief and was owned from the Middle Ages by

---

[1] *Memoirs*, p. 120.   [2] *Diary*, 17 May 1667.

Beauchamps and Mowbrays and in Elizabeth's reign by Newdigates, who there entertained James I's Queen, Anne, whose bedroom is still shown to visitors. When Carteret inherited the house it still had remains of the medieval and Tudor buildings, but, as was usual at that time, he undertook large re-building schemes, employing as his architect Thomas Ripley, who worked for Sir Robert Walpole and his brother Horace, and built the Admiralty in Whitehall. The West front, noble in its simplicity and fine proportions, and the spacious rooms inside, with their massive doors and splendid brass fittings, and a notable oak staircase were designed by Ripley and completed about 1725, when Carteret was still in Ireland.[1] At Hawnes Carteret had his well-stocked library, his family portraits, including those of Sir Bevil Grenville, Sir George Carteret and others, and the celebrated ring traditionally said to have been sent to Elizabeth by Essex before his execution, brought to him by his wife, who was a lineal descendant of Essex. At Hawnes he usually spent the summer months with his large family, friends and dependants. It is only within living memory that the library and family portraits have been dispersed in the auction room; the ring was secured for the Abbey where it now rests on Queen Elizabeth's tomb. The house itself is a girls' school.

To his family Carteret was devoted, and especially to his first wife, Frances Worsley, with whom he made a love-match in his twentieth year. By her he had eight children, two sons and a daughter who died in infancy, besides four other daughters and another son Robert born in the year his father first became Secretary of State. We hear a good deal about the Carteret family-life between 1729 and 1740 in the voluminous correspondence of his cousin Mrs Delany:[2] she was evidently a welcome guest of the Carterets and of his mother the formidable Lady Granville, who all showed her much kindness. But at any rate from 1742 her references to them become scarcer and more acidulous. The reason for this change appears to have been twofold. About the time when Carteret became Secretary of State for the second time she was hoping to obtain some court appointment and expecting the great man to press her claims. But

[1] There is a good account, with illustrations, of the buildings at Hawnes by Mr Christopher Hussey in *Country Life* of 29 Dec. 1934. See also *Victoria County History, Bedford*, II, 339–41. Though there is no documentary evidence that Ripley was Carteret's architect, Mr Hussey's reasons for thinking so seem convincing.

[2] Mary Granville, who married Thomas Pendarves in 1718 and Dr Delany in 1743. To avoid confusion, I call her Mrs Delany throughout.

her friend the Duchess of Portland reported that when she went to see Carteret's mother, 'the Archdragon', as she was nicknamed in polite society, curtly replied that she knew nothing of the matter; that 'her son was never interested in anybody's business, his whole mind being taken up with *doing good to the nation*, and till the French was drove out of Germany and Prague was taken he could not think of *such a bagatelle as that*'.[1] A second grievance was that after she married Carteret's old friend in Ireland, Dr Delany, he did not exert himself sufficiently to procure an Irish bishopric for her husband. But at any rate in her earlier letters she gives a delightful picture of the Carteret family circle. The first daughter to be married was Grace in 1729 to Lord Dysart, on which Mrs Delany comments that Grace 'had a better chance of being happy than most young ladies in her station, because her father and mother are so indulgent to her humour that (altho' they have as much ambition as most people) yet they would not force her inclinations'. In 1733 'the Baron and Baroness were in the highest joy' on the second daughter's engagement to 'Tomasio', Lord Weymouth,[2] related to Lady Carteret, and said by Mrs Delany in a letter to Swift to be 'too inclined to stable and dog-kennel', but hospitable and good to the poor: she, according to Swift, had a jointure of £2500 and £500 p.a. pin money. In the following year Georgina married John Spencer, heir to much of old Sarah Marlborough's great fortune (who was quite out of temper at the marriage), and noted by Egmont as 'fond of frequent bathing, and had a bath in his house'.[3] Carteret's future son-in-law Shelburne relates that at this marriage Carteret, 'more careless than extravagant' in money matters, was hard put to it to pay up this daughter's settlement money, when his father-in-law, Sir Robert Worsley, said to him, 'I have £5000 at my bankers, with which I can accommodate you', to which Carteret replied: 'Can you really? If so, I shall be much obliged to you, for, to say the truth, I have not £100 towards it.'[4] Two years later there was some talk of the youngest daughter Frances marrying the Duke of Bedford, who had recently lost his wife: but this marriage did not come off, and in 1743 she married the Marquess of Tweeddale. Later, when in 1760 his Dysart grandson Lord Huntingtower proposed to marry

[1] *Autobiography and Correspondence of Mrs Delany*, II, 195.
[2] *Ib.* I, 203, 411.
[3] H. MSS. Egmont, *Diary*, I, 279; *Portland*, VI, 42.
[4] Fitzmaurice, *Shelburne*, I, 30. After Spencer's death Georgina married Lord Cowper in 1750.

Sir Edward Walpole's daughter, Granville's (as he then was) characteristic advice to him was 'to choose a gentlewoman and please himself'.[1] These marriages, love-marriages all of them, made Carteret very happy. Writing to Swift after Georgina's, 'I seem to have more friends now', he said, 'than I had when I was in a situation to do them service. This may be a delusion: however it is a pleasing one, and I have more reason to believe a man, now I can do him no good, than I had when I could do him favours, which the greatest philosophers are sometimes tempted to solicit their friends about.' Three years later, in what must have been one of his last letters to Mrs Delany, Swift wrote: 'I think my Lord Carteret is the most happy in all circumstances of life, that I have ever known, as he well deserves it, so I hope he is sensible of it; all my fear is that he will be too rich.'

The marriage of Grace with Lord Dysart, to whom no less than fifteen children were born, brought Carteret into contact with a certain Caspar Wetstein, a Swiss relative of Sir Lukas Schaub, Carteret's ambassador in Paris, and a persistent climber. He had hardly got himself appointed chaplain to the embassy there, when his patron was recalled and was followed by Wetstein on the look out for a post in England. In 1725 he obtained that of bear-leader to Lord Huntingtower on the continent, and two years later, when Huntingtower succeeded his grandfather as Earl of Dysart, remained as his handy-man of business. Dysart seems to have treated him pretty scurvily, expecting him to work without pay and even borrowing money from him: and loud were Wetstein's complaints, not only to Schaub, but also to Carteret himself, who had engaged him to read and talk German with him. In his treatment of Wetstein's shrill complaints Carteret showed the wisdom and courtesy one would expect from the *grand seigneur* he was. 'I think ye best thing you can do', he writes, 'is to write a respectfull letter to ye person himselfe, *Epistola enim non erubescit*;...you will dispose y^r thoughts better y^n in a conversation where you may be interrupted. If there shou'd be any necessity for a mediator, you will then have something regular to lay before him. The complaining to a third person is always to be avoided till this last method has been tried; you will find by this way what reflection can produce, when ye subject is fairly modestly open'd, nothing exaggerated, nothing spared, wch will leave nobody any room to say y^t ye application was improper, since it is made directly to himself, and no one else may ever know

[1] H. Walpole, *Letters*, 2 Oct. 1760.

of it, if he thinks fit. . . . I have now given you my opinion concerning yᵉ first step, and when I know yᵉ effect and when we meet I will be wanting in nothing yᵗ can turn to any use to you.' Carteret did more than give him good advice. For two years running, in 1731 and 1732, he invited him to pass the summer at Hawnes, 'on purpose', as he told Schaub, who duly informed Wetstein, 'to shame his son-in-law into a performance of his engagement to you, . . . and when you come to town he intends to make you a present to help you to jog on'. At last Dysart, on the prompting of his father-in-law, recognized his indebtedness to the extent of procuring for Wetstein the living of Helmingham in Norfolk, where the tithes were said to be worth £140, but he never, apparently, paid him for his past services or for the loans he had occasionally extracted from him.

This scurvy treatment by the son-in-law, however, was more than made up by the father-in-law's courtesy and generosity. For several years Carteret employed him as a tutor in German, in which he probably needed no tuition, and as a reader in Greek, and always thanked him in his grand manner, as if Wetstein and not himself was conferring the favour. 'I hope', for example, he writes in 1733, 'to have yᵉ happiness of seeing you here [at Hawnes] another year, yᵗ we may resume our Greek lectures: yᵉ little I read now is German, I hope you will find me improved when we meet'; three years later he writes in German: 'Lieber von Helmingham, Die schöne übersetzung von Griechischer beredsamkeit so er mir geschict hat, erfordert von mir alle ersinliche erkentlichkeit. . . [I wish you luck in yʳ labours and will end with a Swiss saying wh. I read in some Swiss poems]

Die Tugend wird dir selber geben
Was gutes Ich dir wunschen kan.

Ich verbleibe Ihr Eyfriger Schuler und diener. . . .'[1]

On another occasion, when Wetstein came to pay his respects on his return from a visit to his family in Switzerland, he found the great man suffering from an attack of gout. None the less Carteret came to meet him half-way across the room, embraced him and enquired after his mother, 'come y prenant part véritablement', as Wetstein told Schaub, 'Je trouve quelque chose de bien beau à un

---

[1] 'Dear Lord of Helmingham, For the fine translation of Greek oratory that you sent, I owe you my warmest thanks. . . . "Virtue will confer on thee all the good that I can wish thee." I remain your eager pupil and servant' is a rough translation.

si grand hôme à tous égards d'être si humain. Jugez quel bonheur c'est que la bienveillance d'un tel Seigneur.'

In 1736 Wetstein, probably on Carteret's recommendation, was chosen by the Prince of Wales to teach English to his newly arrived bride, and later as librarian to himself. Even then Carteret's favours did not cease, for in the summer of 1740, after obtaining the Prince's leave, he sent him as tutor to his son Robert for a year's tour of the courts of Europe.

In his early days Robert gave promise of satisfying the great hopes his father placed in him. Like his father he had been sent to Westminster; and in March 1736/7 Carteret had written to Swift: 'Since you mention Greek I must tell you that my son, not sixteen, understands it better than I did at twenty, and I tell him "Study Greek, καὶ οὐδὲν οὐδέποτε ταπεινὸν ἐνθυμηθήσῃ οὔτε ἄγαν ἐπιθυμήσεις τινός".[1] He knows how to construe this and I have the satisfaction to believe he will fall into the sentiment; and then if he makes no figure he will be a happy man.' In planning the forthcoming tour and securing for his son and Wetstein the best of introductions Carteret took endless trouble. He had many friends in Holland, Saxony, Gotha, Vienna and other German states whom he wished them to see, and from the Prince of Wales he obtained a letter to Maria Theresa's husband, the Grand Duke of Tuscany. The Duke of Newcastle, as Secretary of State, was also approached, and he wrote to the English representatives in Copenhagen, St Petersburg, Dresden and Vienna earnestly desiring them, 'out of regard to his Father', to give the boy all the help they could, adding, as a special note to Robinson at Vienna and Finch in St Petersburg, both, like Newcastle and Carteret himself, old Westminsters: 'I am persuaded that, as well on my Lord Carteret's account, as from the consideration that Mr Carteret issues from a place where you, and I, had our Education, you will show him all the Civilities in your power.'[2]

Robert Carteret and Wetstein had a most interesting and even exciting journey, followed with the keenest interest by Robert's father. He was specially interested in the long stay they made in Russia, then a comparatively unknown country, and still more when they began their tour in Germany already alert and seething with excitement on the death of the Emperor Charles VI in October 1740, a death, as Carteret wrote to Wetstein, which will 'unfold a new

---

[1] 'Study Greek, and you will never have a mean thought or desire anything overmuch.'

[2] Add. MSS. 32693, f. 402.

scheme in Vienna'. He writes in January 1741, when Frederic II had already invaded Silesia, enjoining on the travellers not on any account to miss the visit to Vienna: 'Y^e Queen of Hungary is so fine a Lady y^t it will be a shame to have been in Germany without seeing her and ye Duke of Tuscany, who have ye unanimous good wishes of this country and whose interests will be supported powerfully from hence in all events; ye Parliament is unanimous upon this great subject, looking upon it as a national concern.' As time goes on, and all Europe seems to be arming, he becomes anxious for the travellers' speedy return; nevertheless 'if ye coronation of ye Queen should be in a short time...and my son behaves himselfe as he promises me in his last, I wou'd have him see y^t Ceremony'; and it appears from a letter of Wetstein that they were actually present to see the Queen's enthusiastic reception by the Hungarian magnates at her coronation in Pressburg. For the return journey Schaub writes on behalf of Carteret that 'Mylord veut que vous preniez le chemin de la Suisse', chiefly as a kindly thought for Wetstein since 'il est bien aise...de vous procurer le plaisir de revoir la patrie'—but with special injunctions to touch only the Protestant cantons. From Bâle they were to go down the Rhine 'qui est une voiture également promte, commode et agréable'. In a later letter Carteret himself writes that 'the Swiss part of your journey and descending ye Rhine is what pleases me extreamly and wish in y^t respect I was of ye party'. And so, with this agreeable ending for their tour, the travellers were back in England by October 1741.

Unfortunately none of the letters written by Carteret to his son or by Robert to the family at home have been preserved. But even from the letters to and from Wetstein one obtains an inkling of the happy family life at Hawnes or in Arlington Street. Already Carteret was finding great joy and pride in the first two of the fifteen Dysart grandchildren, 'two as fine sons as I ever saw', he writes, and though the elder has had smallpox, 'his beauty is not spoiled'. Robert's letters appear to have given satisfaction, one in French having 'caused great jubilation in Arlington Street', and another to his sister Dysart 'got him great reputation'; and the father rejoices in Wetstein's reports of his 'sense of order and economy'. At the first hint that he had been unwell at Danzig the parents are full of anxiety and send special injunctions as to his health and easier methods of travel: and almost every letter conveys Carteret's and 'the Lady's blessing' to Robert.

Two years after his return from this tour Robert was taken by his father, then Secretary of State once more, to Germany, to introduce him to life in the army, where he is said to have acquitted himself well. But this, unfortunately, is the last good thing heard of him. Less than a year after he had returned from Germany he had taken to drink and began playing strange pranks in the houses he visited. Finally he became so outrageous that his father, after settling a handsome allowance on him, 'but not enough', it was said, 'to maintain his frolics', refused to have anything more to do with him. Elizabeth Montagu, writing in the year after his father's death, gives a sorry picture of him 'with wits enough to ridicule others and folly enough to make himself ridiculous....It is grievous', she adds, 'to see such a creature represent the late Lord Granville, who had all the grace and dignity of manner, added to great talents.'[1] He died in 1776 and with him ended the male line of this branch of the Carterets.[2]

To conclude the story of Wetstein's relations with Carteret, he was appointed, as will appear hereafter, secretary to Carteret when he went to Germany with the King in his second term of office. But Wetstein proved in the end to be a grasping, ungrateful creature. He had been treated most generously by Carteret during the lean days when he could extract no money from Dysart, had been paid unquestioningly and promptly all the expenses, besides his own salary, incurred during the tour with Robert Carteret, and no doubt received full remuneration when he was acting as secretary on the continent. But, not content with these favours, he claimed, on his return from Germany, an English, or at least an Irish, bishopric as his due for this last service, 'some *shabby thing* comme Mylord Granville appeloit les évêchés'. Unsuccessful with Granville himself, as he had now become, he appealed to his former pupil Robert, in a letter of mingled flattery and nauseous humility, to represent his claims to his father: but nothing came of that; and for the rest of his life Wetstein cherished a grudge against his benefactor.[3] Anyhow he was well enough off with his not unremunerative post as librarian and factotum to the Prince of Wales and the proceeds

---

[1] *H. MSS. Bath*, I, 334.

[2] In the *Complete Peerage*, VI, 91–2 are collected records of his outrageous behaviour.

[3] An instance of his mean revenge may be seen in Add. MSS. 32417, f. 335. In the draft of a letter to the Bishop of Norwich about his rectory he wrote that he obtained it 'by the interest of the Earl of Dysart, *or rather the Earl of Granville*', as was the fact. But in the fair copy he carefully expunged the italicized words.

of his rectory, where his duty was performed by a curate for a mere pittance.[1]

During his years of comparative leisure Carteret was always happy with his books and in his relations with authors. For real enjoyment of the classics as literature he was probably unsurpassed in his generation. Homer, Pindar and Demosthenes were perhaps his favourites, but he had read and could quote from most of them. It is said that, when in Denmark, he got to know Sophocles's plays almost by heart, and when he was taken to see one of them acted by Dr Sheridan's pupils in Dublin he amazed his host by his knowledge of the play. This love of the classics brought him into touch with Bentley, the greatest Greek scholar of his age. He seems first to have met him about 1721, when Bentley was engaged on one of his interminable law-suits. 'Should the doctor be sent to prison', Carteret is reported as saying, 'here [brandishing his pen] is Mercury's wand which will soon fetch him out', but later he advised him to apologize, with a quip upon 'University men, who sucked in notions which they called principles, and were resolved strictly to adhere to and die martyrs for them'. It was not till about 1730 that the two men seem to have become intimate. On one occasion, when they were closeted together in Arlington Street, old Lady Granville heard such extraordinary noises coming from the room that she reproached her son for encouraging a clergyman to get drunk; the truth being that Dr Bentley was 'endeavouring to instruct and entertain his noble friend by reciting Terence according to the true cantilena of the ancients'. Carteret more than anybody encouraged Bentley to produce his edition of Homer in order to show the importance of his discovery of the digamma, and took the greatest pains in securing manuscripts of Homer, especially from the great Harleian collection, to assist him in his task. When the last stages of the Bentley lawsuits on his deprivation of the Trinity Mastership by the Bishop of Ely came on in the House of Lords, Carteret opposed Bentley's episcopal antagonists who dwelt on the importance of the chapel disputations on theology and philosophy neglected by the Master. Carteret spoke 'with some respect of the religious exercises' but ridiculed those on the Articles and Aristotle's *Physics* as the distempered frenzies of cloistered zealots. No man, he concluded, 'of tolerable sense or learning could with a grave face expel a Master upon this charge;

[1] The material for Wetstein's relations with Carteret and others is to be found in Add. MSS. 32414–22, especially 32415–7. See my article on Wetstein in *Chambers's Journal* for November 1937.

nor even admonish him, without the censure of dullness and incapacity and the amazement of mankind.' In the end Bentley retained
his Mastership.[1] Another of Carteret's scholar friends was John
[Demosthenes] Taylor, whose editions of the *Leptines* oration and
of Lysias are still useful. For him he obtained from Maria Theresa
the loan of some important Demosthenes MSS. in the Vienna library,
and later a canonry of St Paul's from George II, using as the argument most likely to influence the Hanoverian King that Taylor's
scholarship was famous throughout Germany. According to Taylor,
when Carteret was planning the education of his Weymouth grandchildren, and was asked what he wished them to be taught, his
answer was ταῦτα οἷς καὶ ἄνδρες γενόμενοι χρήσονται—those things
which will be useful to them when grown to manhood.

There were indeed few branches of literature or scholarship, foreign
as well as English, of which Carteret had not a real knowledge and
to which he did not give generous encouragement. Already in 1722
'A Gentleman of Cambridge' had addressed to him the following
verses:

> Carteret will hear, if Phoebus but inspire.
> Carteret in Council, as in Science, prov'd,
> Loving the Muse, and of the Muse belov'd,
> By whom the Chair of Wit is best supply'd
> Since Dorset, rival of Maecenas, dy'd.[2]

In 1726, when he was in Dublin, the philosopher, Francis Hutcheson,
brought out anonymously his *Inquiry into the Original of our Ideas
of Beauty and Virtue*, which pleased Carteret so much that he took
great trouble in discovering the author and made a friend of him.
He helped the Anglo-Saxon scholar Edward Lye to publish his
edition of Francis Junius's *Etymologicum Anglicanum* from the Bodleian
MS., an edition much used by Johnson for his Dictionary. Two
years before he died he was found reading with approbation Gibbon's
first published work, *Essai sur l'Étude de la Littérature*: the scholarship,
the width of view and the sustained magnificence of style of the
Decline and Fall would indeed have found in him a congenial spirit.
In 1735, moved by the scurvy treatment of authors by printers and
publishers—Knapton for example was said to have netted £10,000
out of Rapin's work, for his labour on which Rapin himself was
paid only 10s. a day, while Tonson's profits from Dryden came to

---

[1] For Carteret's relations with Bentley see Monk's *Bentley*, pp. 482, 589, 596, 620.
[2] From a MS. in the Bodleian.

thousands of pounds—he initiated, according to Egmont, a 'generous design' for obtaining 10 guinea subscriptions from noblemen and gentry to rescue 'ingenious authors' from the tyranny of printers and booksellers; the subscriptions going to the printing of their works and all profits remaining to the authors.[1] Nor was his patronage confined to English authors. Overwhelmed with work as he was in Sweden, he found time to establish happy relations with the scholars of Upsala University. Voltaire during his three years in England must have found favour with him; at any rate Voltaire sent him a copy of his *Henriade*, printed in England, possibly even with Carteret's assistance. In 1737–8 he took immense trouble in seeing through the press the magnificent Tonson edition of *Don Quixote, con muy bellas estampas*, published with a life of Cervantes by Don Gregorio Mayens. This edition, now very rare, was highly appreciated in Spain: it was printed in England at a cost to Tonson of £1200, because no other publisher would take the risk.[2] Ten years later there appeared at the Hague Fénélon's *Nouvelle Histoire...sur l'édition procurée à Londres par M.G.* [Milord Granville] and in the same year appeared in London *Récit abrégé de la vie de messire Fr. de S. de la Mothe Fénélon, par les soins de Lord Grandville, ci-devant Lord Carteret*.

Of his own contemporaries among writers one hears much less from Carteret than of the giants of the past. Of his real affection for and admiration of Swift evidence has already been given; and their correspondence continued at any rate up to 1737, soon after which Swift's great mind finally broke down. For Addison, he writes after his death, 'I had a true friendship...and shall always retain great respect for his memory'. Of any close relations with Pope there is no evidence, but that is hardly to be expected, for Carteret's magnanimous nature was not of the kind to accommodate itself with that of the sensitive and waspish poet. Gay, on the other hand, was one after his own heart, and he took to him at once. When he first saw the *Beggar's Opera* in Dublin, he 'laughed his heart out', as Swift told Gay, and meeting him two years later at the Duchess of Queensberry's house at Amesbury, he 'talked with me three hours last night', Gay wrote to Swift, 'he seemed to take to me'; adding modestly, 'which may proceed from your recommendation'. But of other contemporary poets or essayists he is not known to have

[1] H. MSS. *Egmont, Diary*, II, 161.
[2] *Private Correspondence of Sir Benjamin Keene* (ed. Sir R. Lodge), pp. 7, 9, 11: there are two copies of this edition in the British Museum.

taken much account. The fact is that except for Pitt and Carteret himself it was not an age of the μεγαλόψυχος either in literature or in public life, and this may partly account for Carteret's readiness to give up the struggle against intriguing adversaries and return to his beloved studies of the great writers and great deeds of the past, for he never had Pitt's tough certainty of himself and of his own ultimate success against intriguing politicians, whom both of them equally detested.

Not only for his public speeches, never more splendid than during his twelve years out of office, but also for his private talk, Carteret was one of the greatest ornaments of his age. To the charm of that private talk we have two notable testimonies, the first written shortly after his return from Ireland in 1730, when he was at the height of his powers, the second referring to the last years of his life, when he had become the almost legendary elder statesman. In October 1730 the diarist Lord Egmont (Perceval as he then was) records his first impression of him: 'I find him a man of more universal reading than I had imagined, which joined with a happy memory, a great skill in Greek and Latin, a fine elocution, makes him shine beyond any nobleman or gentleman perhaps now living.' The only doubt he then had was about his sincerity, but he soon saw reason to reject such doubt. In this first conversation he was especially delighted to find Carteret 'far from Tory notions in Church matters, though his education when young lay that way': he regarded, for example, 'the confinement of the power of administering absolution to a priest only as a jest' and 'no less a jest to affirm Bishops to be *jure divino* or tithes to be so', and that 'punishing men for their opinions' was 'mere Popery at bottom. He liked the constitution of the Church as settled in England by law...and would have the ecclesiastics acknowledge they hold what they have under Acts of Parliament.... I know not', concluded Egmont, 'any Independent can talk more against the Church.'[1] Egmont's high opinion of Carteret was soon still further confirmed by the ready help he obtained from him in promoting the scheme for colonizing Georgia with the debtors redeemed from prison by his own and Oglethorpe's exertions. Carteret's support was particularly valuable as the owner of a tract of 24,000 square miles in Carolina[2] which it was proposed to incorporate in the new colony: and he not only gave the Georgia promoters leave to take up some of his land but gave useful advice

[1] H. MSS. Egmont, Diary, I, 106.
[2] See above, ch. I, pp. 13, 14.

in securing the Royal Charter and on the best method of starting the colonists.[1]

The second, even more vivid account of Carteret's private talk is that of his son-in-law Shelburne,[2] who in fact saw him only once. As a boy at Oxford he was taken by his father to see Chesterfield and Granville, as he then was, on the same morning. Visiting Chesterfield first, 'I was much struck', Shelburne writes, 'with his wit and brilliancy and good breeding and expected all the same in Lord Granville, but finding him quite plain and simple in his manner and something both commanding and captivating, more in his countenance and general manner than in anything he said, I was much at a loss to account for the difference of impression. I never saw either of them afterwards.' Later he amplified this impression: 'Carteret was a fine person, of commanding beauty, the best Greek scholar of the age, overflowing with wit, not so much a *diseur de bons-mots*, like Lord Chesterfield, as a man of true, comprehensive ready wit, which at once saw to the bottom, and whose imagination never failed him, and was joined to great natural elegance. He had a species of oratory more calculated for the Senate than the people. He was a *bon-vivant* and kept a large, plain, hospitable table. He said that such a man was a stupid man but an admirable hearer.... He said when all other stories failed him Ireland was a constant resource. During his stay there as Lord-Lieutenant, there was no end of the ridicule with which it supplied him. Both he and Sir Robert Walpole were above money, particularly the former. Lord Carteret was more careless than extravagant.... He died at Bath, previous to which he was delirious, and imagined himself in the other world, where meeting an old Clerk of the House of Commons, he gave him an account of all that had happened in the interval between their deaths, with infinite wit, accuracy and humour, insomuch that it was a pity it was not taken down.'[3]

[1] *H. MSS. Egmont, Diary,* I, 278; III, 12, 262.
[2] Shelburne did not marry Carteret's daughter, Sophia, till 1765, two years after Carteret's death.
[3] Fitzmaurice, *Life of William, E. of Shelburne,* 2nd ed., I, 13, 29–31.

Chapter VI

NEWCASTLE, CARTERET & WALPOLE

§ I

In the letters Newcastle addressed to Harrington on his return from Madrid, besides the effusive welcome to his new colleague,[1] he wrote about their association with Walpole in even more enthusiastic language: 'We all owe our happy situation to Sir Robert Walpole's friendship....I hope you will forgive me (who have seen what I daily see), if I assure you greater obligations cannot be to any man than you, my brother [Henry Pelham] and I have to him, tho' it would take up too much of your time to explain them all to you at present. Sir Robert and Horace both write to you by this messenger. Pray write warm and affectionate letters to them both....Sure a better scheme never was made....God bless Sir Robert—'tis all his doing; and lett us in return, resolve to make him as happy as we can, and have but one thought and one way, acting in everything for the King's service; which must make us a happy and, I think, a successful ministry.'[2] What more auspicious beginning could be imagined for the partnership between Walpole, Newcastle and Harrington, destined to continue unbroken for over twelve years? But, though unbroken, it was soon to prove far from harmonious.

At first the change from close alliance with France to an understanding with the Emperor seemed promising. The Emperor, whose chief concern was to secure the succession of his daughter Maria Theresa to the Habsburg possessions by guarantees of his Pragmatic Sanction from as many powers as possible, welcomed England's overtures and agreed to the Treaty of Vienna of 1731. In exchange for the required guarantee given him by England and Holland, he consented to the introduction of Spanish garrisons into Parma and Tuscany to ensure Don Carlos's quiet succession to those duchies as originally stipulated in the Quadruple Alliance of 1718. Thus a difficulty which had kept Europe in a constant state of alarm for thirteen years seemed settled at last. But the calm was short-lived. In 1733 the King of Poland, Augustus the Strong, died; whereupon two claimants appeared to the elective throne, Stanislaus, a former

[1] See ch. IV, i, p. 69.   [2] Coxe, *Walpole*, II, 689–90.

King turned out by Charles XII of Sweden, and now supported by his son-in-law Louis XV, and Augustus of Saxony, son of the last King, backed by Russia and the Emperor. France was unable to give effective aid to Stanislaus, whereas Russia on the eastern frontier of Poland and the Emperor from the south were so menacing to the Poles that they had no option but to elect Augustus. But France found compensation elsewhere. Declaring war on the Emperor, she gained allies against him in his most vulnerable spot, Italy. Sardinia was secured by the promise of gains in Italy at the Emperor's expense; with Spain Fleury made the first of the Family Compacts, whereby France promised to support Spain's claims in northern Italy and her efforts to recover Gibraltar, in return for which Spain agreed, if obstructed by England in Italy, to repudiate the commercial concessions given to England by the Asiento treaty and hand over a share of them to France. As a result of these bargains Spain, unimpeded by any English fleet, landed an army in Italy to act with French and Sardinian contingents against the Emperor's possessions in the Milanese: at the same time French forces laid siege to Kehl and Philipsburg in Upper Germany to prevent any diversions of the Imperialists from the east.

Newcastle obtained full particulars of the treaty with Sardinia and the Family Compact with Spain very shortly after its signature from Keene, his able envoy in Madrid, and even from Essex, the tiresome ambassador in Turin:[1] so at an early stage of the war the question of helping or not helping the Emperor, in accordance, as he claimed, with the terms of the Vienna treaty of 1731, had to be decided. George II as a member of the Empire and anxious for military glory was all for fighting, and at first was strongly supported by his able Queen Caroline. But Walpole was determined not to fight. At the time he was more than taken up by his Excise Bill, but apart from that he dreaded above all things a foreign war as affording his bugbear the Pretender the opportunity of invading the country or at least stirring up another Jacobite rising; nor was he convinced that any important British interest was at issue in this war. Fortunately for him he brought the Queen over to his view, and with her on his side he succeeded in quenching the King's military ardour. Newcastle on the other hand was more bellicose. According to Hervey he 'always talked as his master talked, echoed back all the big words His Majesty uttered and expatiated for ever on regaining Italy for the Emperor, chastising Spain and humbling the impertinent pride

[1] Add. MSS. 32783, ff. 146, 241.

of France. His Grace's predominant sensation was fear; and though the moment the war had been declared all the difficulties pendant to that measure would have kept him in incessant panics, yet, the fear of contradicting the King being the present fear,...he promoted that from timidity, which, had he had foresight sufficient to discern consequences, the same motive would have made him the first to oppose.'[1] Already in 1732, before the death of the King of Poland, Newcastle, flattered by a personal letter from the Duke of Lorraine, Maria Theresa's prospective bridegroom, had committed himself to support the Emperor through thick and thin. Writing to Robinson at Vienna, in Harrington's department, a 'very secret' letter conveying his personal views that 'perhaps may not be those of any other man in the King's service', and were not to be revealed to Harrington or any one else, he declared himself always to have been 'bon Impérialiste', to be ready at all costs to support the Pragmatic Sanction and, if the Emperor wishes it, to support the nomination of the Duke of Lorraine to be King of the Romans [i.e. to be the next Emperor]. As to France, all we now want, he continued, was to keep her quiet, since 'we have nothing to wish from France or to do with them'.[2] Robinson, knowing his Duke, probably paid little attention to this letter, which would certainly have infuriated Walpole, had he known of it; nor, when it came to the issue of war, had Newcastle the courage to insist on a line of his own against his masterful chief.

Walpole, indeed, backed up by the Queen, succeeded in his aim of keeping England out of the war of the Polish Succession. How far he was justified in so doing in view of the engagements undertaken with the Emperor by the Treaty of Vienna is another question. By this treaty we had guaranteed the Emperor's possessions, which were attacked by France in Germany and by France, Spain and Sardinia in Italy. It is true we were not engaged to support the Emperor's candidate to the throne of Poland, but that issue was settled within the first year of the war, which had developed into one of bare aggression by France and her allies on the Imperial heritage. One of the excuses put forward by Walpole for not honouring our engagements was that it was impossible to move the Dutch, our co-guarantors of the Treaty of Vienna, to action; but that was a poor excuse for a major power like England. It is true that in 1734 Walpole did secure the co-operation of the Dutch in proposing terms of peace which might have been satisfactory to

[1] Hervey, *Memoirs*, pp. 344–5.   [2] Add. MSS. 32776, f. 441.

Vienna; but Fleury, after professing to encourage these negotiations, suddenly entered into secret negotiations on his own account with the Emperor, ignoring not only England but even his own allies. By the 'Preliminaries' of 1735, embodied in another Treaty of Vienna in 1738, the Infant Don Carlos was confirmed in his conquest of Naples and Sicily from the Emperor, but only on condition of giving up Tuscany and Parma, secured to him by the Quadruple Alliance of 1718: as the Spanish ambassador in Paris quaintly expressed it: 'The Cardinal as a Prince of the Church, renowned for his piety and learning, ought to know better than others that it is not a crime to favour one's Relations, since Jesus Christ showed constantly particular Marks of Favour to St John his cousin....He ought to have instructed the King of France to have preferred his Cousin the King of Naples' Interests to any others.'[1] Sardinia, France's other ally, was put off with a few insignificant bits of territory instead of the large slice of the Milanese originally promised him. Fleury indeed took care that the lion's share should go to France. By his arrangement with the Emperor, Charles VI, it is true, obtained Parma, but only to lose it in the next war: otherwise the only advantage accruing to him, besides this short-lived possession of Parma, was Fleury's recognition of the Pragmatic Sanction, securing the undivided Habsburg dominions to his heiress, Maria Theresa—an illusory advantage, as Fleury repudiated his promise shortly after the Emperor's death. But Fleury's master-stroke was in his disposal of Tuscany. Something had to be done to compensate Louis XV's father-in-law Stanislaus, for the second time ousted from Poland, so it was arranged that Francis, Duke of Lorraine, affianced to the Emperor's daughter Maria Theresa, should exchange Lorraine for Tuscany; and that Stanislaus should be compensated by Lorraine, but that on Stanislaus's death Lorraine should be incorporated with France. By this provision France rounded off her own eastern frontier and became mistress of a larger self-contained territory than she possessed in the days of Louis XIV's greatest glory. England was entirely ignored in this re-arrangement of Europe; and the Emperor, her one important ally on the continent, was thoroughly estranged by Walpole's refusal to aid him in the war against France and Spain in accordance with the Treaty of Vienna of 1731.

In justice to Newcastle it must be admitted that he had no practical part in these negotiations and results, which reflected little credit on

[1] Add. MSS. 32789, f. 362.

England's diplomacy or fidelity to her engagements. For Walpole, determined to secure peace without venturing anything on behalf of the Emperor, had taken entire control of the abortive negotiations of 1734, employing his brother Horace as his intermediary at the Hague. Newcastle himself was quite right in thinking it would have been better and more honest to begin the negotiation by 'private and confidential' dealings with our ally the Emperor instead of with a secret envoy of Fleury's and characteristically grumbled about 'knowing nothing of what goes on in the other office [Harrington's] where the Austrians are not considered so much as they should be; but this *entre nous*'.[1] However, though he disliked the form which the negotiations were taking behind the Emperor's back, he remained for the time being extraordinarily submissive to Walpole, carrying out the orders sent to him from Houghton as best he could, and lamenting only that Walpole was not on the spot to keep him straight. 'The King and Queen', he wrote, 'are very good to me; but without a compliment, I am always afraid when I have not your assistance and advice'; and again, 'I have done for the best without passion or prejudice of any kind. I have endeavoured through the whole to follow your scheme; and if I have erred I have done it ignorantly. The only way to prevent it for the future is for you to come back; which I once more beg most earnestly.' But, even in this chastened mood, Newcastle plucked up courage to express his qualms, which were soon to be justified, as to the possible failure of this underhand negotiation: 'What a breach this may make for ever between us and the Emperor, and how will it sound in the world when it comes to be known?'[2]

Far more irksome to the sensitive Duke than any difference with Sir Robert must have been the constant sermons and reprimands he had to endure from Sir Robert's tiresome brother. Even Sir Robert himself was bored by Horace's portentously long and often querulous despatches, 'works' as he contemptuously called them; but the Duke himself suffered most and, it must be admitted, suffered with remarkable humility. Many of Horace's reproaches are justified, such as his remark to Sir Robert that 'the Duke looks upon the thoughts of anybody else as reflections upon his own, and, instead of considering the use that may be made of what is suggested by another, looks upon it as a personal thing, and runs out into a long justification of his own performances, which nobody finds fault with'.[3] But his censures might have been more effective had they

[1] Add. MSS. 32785, f. 407.   [2] Coxe, *Walpole*, III, 210, 229.   [3] *Ib*. III, 296.

not been so frequent and couched in such patronising terms. While the secret negotiations were in progress at the Hague, Horace begs him not to go blurting them out 'from want of reflexion in your hurry to go to Claremont'. On other occasions he tells him 'I am glad to find that my lucubrations which doe not immediately relate to your department have mett with your approbation,...[in spite of] your aversion to anybody's thoughts or pen intruding upon your province'; 'the truth being', as he notes to Sir Robert, 'that ye Duke of Newcastle never minds anything that is addressed to him after he has read it'. Then he gives the Duke patronising advice to console himself for the little troubles that had arisen at the end of the session, coupled with the assurance that all his friends 'think well of him notwithstanding some little reprimands [from Sir Robert]; therefore for G–ds sake make yourself easy and fall naturally and merrily into ye old *væilleries* by transacting business in ye morning with the Queen, by walking, talking, joking, and sometimes a little ogling of ye Princess Car—ne in ye evening in ye gallery or gardens; not forgetting a whisper wth Sr R. W. before you goe home, and I fancy all will goe well'. It is astonishing how meekly, as a rule, the Duke took such insufferable preaching: 'I have done my best', he naïvely answers on one occasion, 'and I think I have done well, I am afraid others are of a different mind, but when We differ a little in Things but most widely in persons, This will happen. I am sure I want neither Sincerity or Affection, in that I will equal any the most zealous. If I err from *Capacity* 'tis not my fault.' But sometimes even he turned against his monitor, and gave him a dignified reproof for all these scoldings.[1]

Much of the good Duke's time and energy was taken up in dealing with inefficient or querulous representatives of England abroad. Short work would have been made of such subordinates by a Stanhope, a Carteret or above all a Pitt. But the Duke was too much afraid of hurting his friends' susceptibilities and too undecided in his own policy to take strong action in such matters. The two best representatives of England in his department were Benjamin Keene, our envoy in Spain, and Lord Waldegrave, ambassador to France; but both worked under serious handicaps. Keene was a solid, trustworthy diplomat, never rattled and the writer of admirable despatches, giving clear and accurate accounts of the personalities and policy of the Spanish court. But, unfortunately, in addition to

[1] See, for Horace's tirades and the Duke's generally meek answers, Add. MSS. 32785, f. 325; 32788, f. 383; 32791, ff. 104, 238; 32792, f. 88.

his diplomatic functions he was allowed to combine with them those of agent for the powerful South Sea Company, whose grievances were a main source of trouble with Spain. Thus he was constantly required to put forward those grievances to the Spanish ministers even before he had been instructed to deal with such matters by his own government. Waldegrave at Paris was a sound, painstaking diplomatist, who, in spite of the growing alienation between England and France, maintained, with dignity and some success, good relations with Cardinal Fleury and even the Anglophobe foreign minister Chauvelin. But Waldegrave was also handicapped by the shady dealings he was called upon to have with purveyors of secret intelligence, ranging from high officials in the French foreign office and foreign envoys to Scottish and foreign adventurers. Among the most prominent of these was de Bussy, a *premier commis* under Chauvelin who subsequently was sent to England to negotiate with Pitt in 1761: he was paid a yearly salary by Waldegrave of 1600 louis d'or, with occasional refreshers varying from 1000 to 50,000 livres for specially important information, and was never mentioned by name but only as '101' in the Newcastle-Waldegrave correspondence. Attempts were even made to extract secret information from Chauvelin himself and his successor Amelot by tempting offers ranging up to £100,000, but apparently without success. The Swedish envoy in Paris had 'transactions...relating to his Majesty's goodness to him' for reporting what he was told by the French ministers. But the most useful and the cheapest secret agents were a couple of Sicilian Abbots, as they were always designated in the correspondence. For the modest salary of 300 louis d'or between them they gave English ministers very useful information about the personalities and policy of both the French and Spanish courts. A great deal of Newcastle's correspondence is taken up with this secret service business: Stanhope, Carteret and Pitt were at least as well, if not better, served by their secret intelligence, but they had more important business to transact than to deal personally with the details and remuneration of such agents.

With most of his other representatives abroad Newcastle was singularly unfortunate in his choice. One of the most tiresome was Lord Essex, a connexion of his own, whom he at one time thought of sending to Paris instead of Waldegrave. To console him for losing the Paris post, he was sent in 1732 to Turin to keep an eye on the King of Sardinia and prevent him, if possible, from succumbing to the tempting offers of France and Spain. But instead of attending to business he had been but a few weeks at Turin before he was asking for leave to attend the Carnival at Venice and, on being told by the Under-Secretary that such a premature request might prejudice him with the King, replied that 'if His Grace keeps me this Carnaval he will kill me, and then I shall be pass'd that danger; this is now Hell upon Earth'. Later, during Lady Essex's absence, he found some consolation in entertaining 'a fair lady', remarking that 'the Fair Sex, which tho' to some people might be nothing, to me is everything'; again, just before the signature of the Franco-Sardinian treaty he had been sent out to stop, he was asking for leave to go 'in Cogg' to the fair at Alexandria. His next request was addressed to the King himself, 'the best of Masters and the greatest of Kings.... I am sorry to be forced to own it even to your Majesty y^t I grow old, and I find y^t without the help of a Blue Ribond [the garter] to sett me off my green one will do no longer.' Finally in 1736 he was recalled, leaving the business of the embassy in the hands of the far more diligent secretary of embassy Villettes.

Another unfortunate choice of Newcastle was Lord Kinnoull as ambassador to the Porte, described by his successor as 'the most incompatible character I ever saw'. During the war of the Polish Succession, he was specially instructed to work in close concert with the Dutch ambassador and to prevent Turkey from attacking the Emperor: instead of which he had a violent quarrel with the Dutchman and worked hand in glove with the French ambassador Villeneuve who was inciting Turkey to support the French candidate for the Polish crown. Finally in 1735 he was superseded by Sir Everard Fawkener. The government sent a man-of-war specially to convoy him home, doubtless thinking this use of the navy justified, if he could be got away. But he sent the man-of-war packing and remained for another year at Constantinople, a thorn in the side of his successor.

Then there was the unfortunate affair with that tough old sea-dog Admiral Sir John Norris. It arose from an absurd quarrel between Spain and Portugal in 1735. The cause was trifling, but both parties were getting so hot that the English government was afraid war would break out between them. This they were anxious to stave off, as in that case we were bound by treaty to support Portugal; and Walpole's government wished particularly to avoid a breach with Spain. However, as a precautionary measure, Sir John Norris was sent with a squadron to Lisbon and given credentials as a plenipotentiary to try to settle the dispute amicably, credentials which seemed to Lord Tyrawley, the regular envoy at Lisbon, to trespass on his preserve. The result was a violent quarrel as to their respective rights between the rough old admiral, whom it had taken all Carteret's tact in Sweden to conciliate, and the equally rough old soldier of Marlborough's wars, who was only too disposed to encourage the bellicose attitude of the Portuguese, as he had been promised a command in the Portuguese army if it came to open hostilities. The Hispano-Portuguese dispute was ultimately settled in 1737, mainly by the good offices of France and England, otherwise it might have anticipated the general European war of the next decade, since the Emperor was beginning to hope that if Spain were preoccupied by Portugal, he might have a good opportunity of recovering his losses in Italy.[1] But while Norris and Tyrawley were both at Lisbon they gave an unedifying illustration of the quarrels and insubordination, not uncommon in Newcastle's department, between 'a warm discontented minister and a rough admiral that wants to return home' as Newcastle put it.[2] Neither the admiral nor the minister would listen to the other's suggestions and each sent in separate memorials to the Portuguese court and separate despatches full of mutual abuse to Newcastle and others in England. Tyrawley was not invited to Norris's banquet in honour of Queen Caroline's birthday, so he wrote to the Queen, 'I should have hoped that *Rancune apart* We might have drank the Queen's health together. Nevertheless, Madam, I shall have the honour to drink it at my own home, with my own Friends and in much better Wine than Sir John Norris's Table affords.' Tyrawley took a further revenge in refusing to receive the despatches addressed to Norris by Keene from Madrid, on the ground that he was on board his ship; whereas Norris, as he informed Keene, was 'constantly on shore', and requested him to send any future despatches addressed directly to himself at Lisbon.[3]

Until 1737 there is not much evidence of serious divergence of view between Newcastle and his chief Walpole on foreign policy, even though, as we know from Hervey, Newcastle was inclined to a stronger line in favour of the Emperor during the war of the Polish Succession. He had helped him valiantly in maintaining his majority in Parliament during the election of 1734, after Walpole had suffered his most serious rebuff by the enforced withdrawal of the Excise

[1] Good accounts of this little known dispute are in Michael, IV, 419–25, and Mantoux, pp. 136–7, 178–84, 215–17.

[2] Coxe, *Walpole*, III, 328.

[3] Further details of the peculiarities in the work of Newcastle's office may be found in my article 'The Foreign Office of the Georges' in *Blackwood's Magazine*, no. MCXV (January 1907).

Bill of 1733, and had, as we have seen, followed his chief's directions implicitly in the abortive negotiations for bringing the Polish war to an end in collaboration with the Dutch. But when, about 1737, the dispute with Spain as to the grievances of our traders to the West Indies was becoming acute, he took up a more uncompromising attitude than Walpole, whose ingrained dread of war as a menace, not only to his well thought out economic policy, but even to the security of the dynasty, had become a fixed obsession. But Newcastle was not such an one as Pitt, prepared to play a lone hand against so formidable an adversary as Walpole. Never assured of himself, he always needed a confidant to whom he could pour out his grievances or his hopes, and with whom he could take counsel, before he committed himself to any definite line in politics: and his confidant was chosen generally because he seemed likely to be on the winning side. First it was Stanhope, then Carteret until Townshend and Walpole were in the ascendant. When Townshend was evidently losing ground Newcastle, as we have seen, attached himself with gushing effusion to Walpole and no doubt believed that Harrington, whose claims to the other secretaryship he had pressed upon Walpole, would prove a docile ally. But Harrington in fact proved a broken reed. Hervey describes him as 'infinitely lazy'; and the Queen passed this devastating verdict on him: 'there is a heavy, insipid sloth in that man that puts me out of all patience. He must have six hours to dress, six more to dine, six more for his mistress and six more to sleep;...and if now and then he borrows six of those hours to do anything in relation to his office, it is for something that might be done in six minutes and ought to have been done six hours before.'[1] He was withal an obstinate man and by no means inclined to subordinate his views to Newcastle's, as his Grace had expected. Even so soon as 1735 the Duke actually made overtures to Carteret proposing that he should become his colleague in Harrington's place; and again two years later Hervey records 'one night that the Duke of Newcastle came half-drunk from a Westminster School feast, where he and Lord Carteret (being both Westminster scholars) had dined together, he went directly to Sir Robert Walpole's and made a tender in form of Lord Carteret's service, offering at the same time to be surety for his good behaviour; which Sir Robert Walpole took with a high hand and told his Grace.... "I am glad, my Lord, you have given me this opportunity once for all to let you know my determined sentiments on this matter...and

[1] Hervey, *Memoirs*, p. 346.

that your Grace must take your choice between me and him; and if you are angry at my saying this I care not. I have said it to your betters, and I'll stick to it.'"[1]

But in this year, 1737, Newcastle at last found the confidant he needed for his hopes, and above all his grievances, in the new Lord Chancellor Hardwicke. As early as 1719 Philip Yorke, as he then was, owed his election to the House of Commons for Lewes to the Duke, who, in 1722, transferred him to the still safer seat of Seaford. Appointed Solicitor-General at the age of thirty in 1720 and Attorney-General four years later, he waived his claim to the Chancellorship in 1733, yielding the place to the Solicitor-General, Talbot, and becoming Lord Chief Justice himself. But on Talbot's premature death in 1737 he succeeded him, after stipulating that his eldest son should have the reversion of a Tellership of the Exchequer, a lucrative sinecure which fell vacant in the following year. Until his promotion to the Chancellorship, Hardwicke does not appear to have had any close intercourse with Newcastle, but he still retained, and retained to the end of his life, a deep sense of gratitude to the Duke for having provided him with a seat in Parliament, the first step on the ladder of promotion. But now that Hardwicke as Lord Chancellor had become a minister of cabinet rank, and one who, by his cautious and well-considered expressions of opinion on affairs of state, very soon attained great influence in council, Newcastle discovered in him the friend and counsellor he needed. To him he soon began to pour out all his grievances against colleagues and even relations, to him he imparted his own half-baked schemes of policy, and from him he was always certain of receiving prudent and sympathetic advice. 'Did you know the anxiety I am under, to conduct myself in every respect irreproachably, I am sure you would help me out of it', occurs in one of the Duke's earliest letters to the new Chancellor.[2] Hardwicke's advice was always on the safe side: not for him the daring flights that often mark a really great statesman; but, since Newcastle was to be the executive responsible for the policy, such cautious advice was just fitted for him. Above all Hardwicke seems to have been the only colleague with whom Newcastle never quarrelled. Whereas the Duke was continually pouring out to him grievances about Walpole or Harrington, Carteret and all his other colleagues in turn, including even his own brother, Henry Pelham, Hardwicke alone never incurred his suspicion or his jealousy. The relations between them from 1737 down to the year of Hard-

[1] Torrens, *l.c.* 1, 448; Hervey, *Memoirs*, p. 733.   [2] Yorke, *Hardwicke*, 1, 216.

wicke's death in 1764 may perhaps best be likened to those of a faithful wise old nurse and her fractious and impetuous, but still rather lovable charge.

The first inkling of this new alliance comes, as one might expect, from Hervey, who noted in April 1737 that he and Lord Isla 'were always telling Sir Robert Walpole that Lord Chancellor and the Duke of Newcastle were laying schemes to govern independently of him'; to which Walpole replied: 'they don't govern me, nor they shan't govern me; but you hate the Duke of Newcastle and therefore never will imagine it possible he can do anything right'. Nor would prudent old Walpole hear of parting with them, 'or sour them by letting them know he saw last winter what they were nibbling at'.[1]

§ II

For the first three years after his return from Ireland in 1730 Carteret took no very prominent part in parliamentary debates. In foreign affairs, always his chief concern, he on the whole approved of Walpole's reversal of Townshend's policy in restoring friendly relations with the Emperor by the Treaty of Vienna in 1731; while in domestic affairs there were no acute causes of difference. But at any hint of corruption or of oppression of the poor he was always ready to protest. Thus in February 1732 he warmly supported a Pensions Bill aimed at doing away with the system adopted by Walpole of securing votes in Parliament by the distribution to members of civil list pensions. This was the second year in succession that the bill had been passed by a venal House of Commons in the assured expectation that it would be rejected by the Lords, as indeed it was in spite of Carteret's and his friends' efforts. 'While we are still uncorrupted', he replied sarcastically to the ministers' plea that George II was not likely to bribe members or allow ministers to bribe them, 'we should take precautions and not wait till both Houses of Parliament are corrupted: if this should ever happen to be the unlucky fate of this nation, we may easily judge what would be the success of such bills in such Houses of Parliament.'[2] In the following month he made a strong protest against Walpole's proposed revival of the salt tax, abolished only two years before, in order to make good the deficit he expected from the reduction of the land tax. Carteret's main argument was that the salt tax pressed

---

[1] Hervey, *Memoirs*, pp. 716, 829.   [2] *P.H.* VIII, 990.

with special hardship on the poor: for whereas 'the rich generally live upon fresh provisions, a poor man will live upon salt meat, or he will eat no meat...and we know that there was never a duty laid upon any produce...but what raised the price to the consumer more in proportion than what the duty amounted to'. Moreover the 'prodigious number' of revenue officers required to collect the tax would leave little profit from its imposition, while their dependence on ministers as voters in elections would prove worse than a standing army. It was, he concluded, 'a most insidious bill...a snake in the grass which...would bruise the heel of the constitution', to which Newcastle could only find the school-boyish retort that the only snake was the factious opposition.[1]

In the following year, 1733, when Walpole brought in his abortive excise measure, though its defeat in the Commons precluded any debate on it in the Lords, Carteret began definitely to range himself with the composite opposition of Tories, led by Wyndham, and Whig critics, led by Pulteney, in the Commons, an opposition halloed along by the writers in *The Craftsman* and by Bolingbroke in the background. Their ranks, too, were soon reinforced by former members of Walpole's administration, summarily dismissed for criticism of his policy, notably Chesterfield[2] and Cobham, leader of the Boy Patriots such as Lyttelton and Cornet Pitt. In this temporarily harmonious opposition Carteret and Chesterfield were the most dangerous critics of Walpole in the Lords, where they were very unequally matched by Newcastle and the other government speakers, even when Newcastle's friend Hardwicke was added to their number in 1734. Of the two opposition leaders, Chesterfield, in spite of his mean and ungainly appearance, by his logical mind and the neatness of his arguments no less than by his wit and pungent sarcasm, was at times the more effective in scoring debating points: Carteret, on the other hand, endowed by nature with a noble presence and a melodious voice, in spite of his more discursive speeches, held the House spell-bound by the wealth of illustration he drew from ancient and modern history and literature, from the grandeur of his conception of national policy, and from his devotion to the liberties and privileges not only of his own order, but no less of the humblest of the people. Comparing the two speakers in one notable debate, when both spoke 'with much applause and popu-

[1] *P.H.* VIII, 1040, 1060–1.
[2] Chesterfield, for his opposition to the Excise Bill, was dismissed from his office of Lord Steward.

larity and with as much credit and satisfaction to the audience as they ever did', Hervey specially picks out 'the wit, satire and ingenuity' of Chesterfield's speech and 'the strength, knowledge and eloquence' of Carteret's.[1] If, during the ten most fruitful years of his opposition to Walpole, 1733–42, Carteret did not win many votes, at least he set up a high standard of national policy, which influenced not only Pitt himself, who at this time was put by his patron Cobham to learn statecraft at Carteret's feet, but others of Pitt's and the still younger Shelburne's generations.

It was mainly from a care for the liberties of the people, as well as of the two Houses of Parliament, that in almost every year from 1733 till the outbreak of war with Spain in 1739 he opposed any increase to the standing army. The first and not the least pungent of his speeches on this subject was in 1733, the Excise Bill year, when he advocated the reduction of the standing army from the proposed 17–18,000 to 12,000. Comparing Walpole's fiscal and domestic policy with that of Richelieu, 'the priest who gave French liberties their last stab', he managed to draw an unfavourable contrast between Walpole's and that cardinal's foreign policies, for 'though [like Walpole] Richelieu oppressed the subject at home,...and left it as a maxim that the King ought never to part with any tax he has once got established, even though he has no use for the money, because by giving up the tax he loses the officers that are employed in the collection thereof: [on the other hand, unlike Walpole] he indeed was a great minister...who not only supported but raised the grandeur of the nation abroad; he committed no blunders in his administration, nor did he submit to any foreign power in the treaties or negotiations he had with them.' This contrast between Walpole and Richelieu might have passed in court circles, had not Carteret proceeded to allude to a recent interview between Queen Caroline and the veteran Lord Stair, who, in reference to the recent Excise Bill, had tried to disabuse her of her confidence in Walpole. When France, he continued, was ruled and oppressed by Richelieu's incompetent successor Mazarin, supported by the Queen, Marie de Medici, 'in opposition to the clamour of the people and the inclination of the whole kingdom, the greatest general of his time and a man of the first consideration at the court [Condé] asked an audience of the Queen and at that interview told her, "Madam, you maintain a man at the helm who should be rowing in the galleys"'. Such a

[1] Hervey, *Memoirs*, pp. 435–46. The speeches referred to were in a debate of March 1735 on the army.

comparison was not calculated to endear Carteret to the Queen, who about this time coupled him and Bolingbroke as 'the most worthless men of parts as any in this country, and whom I have not only been often told are two of the greatest liars and knaves in any country, but whom my own observation and experience has found so'.[1] Accordingly when, some months later, the Carterets, with the Sunderlands, took their daughter Georgina and her newly wedded husband John Spencer to court, the King turned his back on them and the Queen merely remarked to Spencer: 'I think, Mr Spencer, I have not seen you since you was a child'; to which Spencer replied: 'No, Madam, I think not.' Egmont's comment on this incident was that it was a pity the King was not more affable, for 'the nobility of England are proud and presently take fire at any slight the Crown casts on them. These Lords Carteret and Sunderland have affection for His Majesty's family, but are no friends to Sir Robert Walpole; but it appears whoever are not friends to him are not to be countenanced at Court.'[2]

It may seem paradoxical that Carteret, an advocate of a strong foreign policy, if ever there was one, for so many years resisted any increase in the army. But during this period there was no question of military action abroad, and even in 1738 when a war against Spain seemed imminent, he still resisted a standing army of more than 12,000 men, while at the same time urging a strengthening of the navy, declaring that it was 'by means of our navy only that we can force Spain to a compliance with our just demands'.[3] It was only in 1740–41, when our treaty obligations called for military help to Maria Theresa, attacked by France and Prussia, that he consented to an increase of the army. Even then he resisted the ministry's extravagant plan of raising new regiments, since two-thirds of the pay voted in such cases went to the officers, instead of the prompter and more economical method he had himself adopted in Ireland of increasing the companies of existing regiments; and pointed out as a model the far less extravagant methods by which Prussia, France and Hanover raised far larger and more effective armies.[4]

One of the main reasons for Carteret's objection to a strong standing army was his fear that it might be used to dragoon the people. True aristocrat as he was, he was greatly before his time in

---

[1] *P.H.* VIII, 1251; see also Hervey, *Memoirs*, pp. 142–4. Later the Queen saw reason to revise this estimate of Carteret.

[2] *H. MSS. Egmont, Diary*, II, 34.   [3] *P.H.* X, 476.

[4] *P.H.* XI, 898 n., 902 n., 911, 923, and *H. MSS. Egmont, Diary*, III, 168.

the exceptionally strong feeling of sympathy he had with the poor and oppressed members of the community. Even on such a proposal as that for taking from the Sinking Fund the £500,000 dowry for the Princess Royal he managed to find expression for this sympathy. His argument was that the Sinking Fund was intended for paying off state-creditors, who otherwise would have to be paid by additional taxes, 'taxes lying heavy on the poor and a clog to trade, as our workmen cannot live so cheaply as those abroad'.[1] In a discursive debate on recent ebullitions of popular feeling against cheap Irish workers, the Gin Act, Turnpikes and the Porteous riots, he went so far as to assert that 'the people seldom or ever assemble in any riotous or tumultuous manner unless they are oppressed, or at least imagine they are oppressed'. The magistrates should reason with them, but when there is real oppression they cannot be expected to listen, 'nor can the severest laws, nor the most rigorous execution of those laws always prevent the people becoming tumultuous; you may shoot them, you may hang them, but till the oppression is removed there will never be quiet, till the greatest part of them are destroyed'. If injustice is found to be done, remove it: 'this is the only human method of preventing riots or tumults...nor should you, if the magistrate cannot execute the law, agree to erecting a barrack at every turnpike'; and he asserted that, with wise dealing, the English and Irish labourers' riots could have been quelled 'without a single soldier'. Then turning to the smuggling trade he asserted that it would never be suppressed merely by severe laws and rigorous execution: 'by such methods we may irritate, we may destroy the subject and at last bring on a temper of a much more dangerous nature. I fear last year's law against smuggling was of this character.'[2] A year later he enunciated the wise doctrine that 'a law which the civil power is unable to execute must either be itself oppressive or it must be such a one as affords a handle to oppression'. For that reason we do not want a 'military government' to support oppressive or dangerous laws.[3]

At a time when Walpole's personal ascendancy in the House of Commons was so great that there he was often able to stifle discussions awkward to the government, it was fortunate that the House of Lords was less accessible to such influence: and on several occasions Carteret and his friends were able to bring up grievances apt to be burked in the Commons. Shortly after the defeat of the Excise Bill

[1] *P.H.* IX, 124, 129.
[2] *P.H.* IX, 1283, 1806.
[3] *P.H.* X, 476.

Walpole had succeeded in stopping an enquiry in the Commons on some highly irregular proceedings of the Directors of the South Sea Company, accused of trading for their own profit and of shady transactions about former directors' estates confiscated after the bursting of the South Sea Bubble. Carteret, however, in the Lords succeeded in the demand for papers on these transactions, in spite of Newcastle's feeble attempt to burke discussion; the first occasion within the last two reigns that the ministry had been defeated in the Lords. Later, however, Newcastle, with the support of 25 of·the 26 tame bishops, managed to negative the proposal to set up a small committee to investigate the charges against the directors; but at any rate Carteret was able to draw public attention to the scandal by the protest he drew up, declaring that 'the impunity of guilt (if any such there be) is the strongest encouragement to the repetition of the same practices in future times, by chalking out a safe method of committing the most flagitious frauds under the protection of some corrupt and all screening minister'. It was as a result of this protest that four of the signatories, Cobham, Stair, Marchmont and Bolton, were turned out of their offices and joined the opposition.[1]

In all his other speeches before 1738, when the imminence of war with Spain caused him to concentrate on his peculiar province of foreign affairs, Carteret is always to be found speaking against acts of injustice and on behalf of the under-dog. He joined Marchmont and other Scottish peers in protesting against the government's barely concealed methods of corruption or even of intimidation in securing that the sixteen elected peers of Scotland should be supporters of Walpole. He found himself unexpectedly on the side of his usual opponents Hardwicke and Newcastle in supporting the Charitable Uses (or Mortmain) Bill to prevent inalienable bequests, mainly for the benefit of the Church, when the whole bench of bishops was ranged against it: his speech is not reported, but one may well believe that, as Egmont observed, he 'spoke tartly and I may say rudely against bishops and clergy in general'.[2] On the other hand he zealously supported the Quakers' Tithe Bill to relieve them of some of the hardships they endured as conscientious objectors to the payment of tithes, finding Hardwicke this time making favour with the bishops, who were united in resisting any concession to the Quakers. He supported, too, against the government, an attempt to amend the iniquitous law in Scotland whereby a man could be

[1] P.H. IX, 100 sqq.; H. MSS. Carlisle, pp. 116–18; Hervey, Memoirs, pp. 184 sqq.
[2] H. MSS. Egmont, Diary, II, 269.

imprisoned on unsworn information. When the great debate came up in the Lords about an allowance of £100,000 to the Prince of Wales[1] to maintain his dignity, especially after his marriage, Carteret took the lead, as Pulteney had in the House of Commons, for the increased allowance. According to Hervey 'he was guarded in most part of his speech and seemed determined to give as little offence as was possible on the King's side of the Palace of St James's, yet in the heat of his oratory...an expression escaped him which the Queen took mortally ill and which...I believe he heartily repented afterwards....Drawing a sort of comparison between the Black Prince and the present Prince of Wales, he said that this Prince was like him in his humanity and virtue...that Edward III was so far from envying him that he retired from the battle on purpose to give him an opportunity of reaping the glory'; and that 'that great and wise king...made so large a settlement on the Black Prince... that his son might not be dependent on his minister, his mistress or his queen'; which, continues Hervey, 'as it seemed to put these three characters on the same foot was a way of arguing that nobody thought very respectful to her present Majesty'. Naturally, so great was the influence of the court in the House of Lords, as in the House of Commons, the motion was rejected: but the dissentient Lords made a dignified and convincing protest, which very possibly was the handiwork of Carteret.[2] There is no doubt that, had it not been for Walpole's docile majority and his refusal to allow a free vote to flout the King's and Queen's hatred of their son, the opposition would have carried their motions in both Houses.

So far Carteret's activities in opposition had travelled over a wide field, but chiefly on domestic grievances. But when relations between England and Spain became strained in 1737, and still more on the outbreak of war in 1739, he was able to concentrate on foreign policy and the conduct of hostilities; his twenty-four speeches during the remaining five years that he was out of office are the most eloquent and constructive of his career.

[1] Carteret, like the rest of the opposition, was welcomed at the Prince of Wales's court, but disapproved of his foolish and wicked removal of the Princess, already in the agonies of child-birth, from Kew to St James's. Thereafter George II and Caroline looked on him with less disfavour.

[2] The *Parliamentary History*'s account is very meagre. I have given this account of the speech by conflating the details recorded in Hervey, *Memoirs*, pp. 696–9 and *H. MSS. Carlisle*, pp. 178–9. They are in practical agreement.

§ III

Even Walpole could not prevent serious differences in his cabinet when, towards the end of 1737, our grievances against Spain were coming to a head. Before that time Newcastle, according to old Horace Walpole, had paid little attention to West Indian affairs, with which the trouble began, though they were a special concern of his department. Writing to him in July 1736, when Spain was attacking the Portuguese in Brazil, Horace reminds him of 'ye W. Indies, a thing y^r Grace has ye least when you ought to have the most concern for, not only on account of ye publick, but by your station; believe me, my Lord, you doe not know what may be ye consequence in all respects of your great indolence and neglect of this Point; if you heard half that I hear from all quarters, friends and foes, on this head, I think it would affect you; when there is danger of a Rupture we are frightened out of our witts; ye Admiralty and ye board of Trade are talked with and councils summoned, but if, while they meet and deliberate, that danger seems to blow over, all thoughts of ye W. Indies are over too, and nothing is done.'[1] Ever since 1713, when by the Assiento treaty the South Sea Company was given the contract for exporting slaves to the Spanish American colonies, and permission to send a ship with a strictly limited cargo of English goods to be sold at one of the two annual fairs in Spanish America, there had been constant bickerings as to the terms of these concessions. Spain was always raising difficulties even in peace time about the sailing of the Company's annual ship from Cadiz, where the cargo had to be measured; the Company in turn was remiss in sending in accounts of their trade on which a percentage claimed by the King of Spain was calculated, and was accused of fraudulently supplementing the cargo of the annual ship from tenders which had accompanied it, so that 'le vaisseau ne désemplit jamais'. But the grievance which loomed largest in the disputes and which ultimately led to war was the interference by irresponsible Spanish *guarda costas* with our traders in the Caribbean Sea. No doubt there was a good deal of illicit trading with Spanish colonies by our ships, but, whether guilty in that respect or merely pursuing a lawful trade with our own colonies, these ships were liable to be seized at sight by the *guarda costas*, the cargoes invariably confiscated by the partial Spanish tribunals, and the crews not infrequently maltreated, the most

[1] Add. MSS. 32791, f. 353.

notorious case being that of Captain Jenkins, who asserted that his ears were cut off by his captors in 1731. Such tales were beginning to infuriate the English people; petitions were brought to the House of Commons to investigate them; Jenkins was heard at the bar of the House in 1738 and solemnly produced one of his ears carefully preserved in cotton wool.

Walpole's withers were unwrung by all this excitement, for he hoped to settle the disputes with Spain by amicable negotiations. But Newcastle, in spite of his previous neglect of West Indian affairs, was all afire for the popular remedy of strong measures, and Walpole expressed to the Chancellor his fear lest 'his Grace should write to Mr Keene, *invita Minerva*, and that should spoil it'.[1] Indeed a few months later Newcastle wrote a stiff despatch to Keene, instructing him to present a strongly worded protest to the Spanish government, though unfortunately, as was pointed out to him by both Horace Walpole and Keene, he was characteristically ill-informed about the treaty rights that he invoked.[2] Nevertheless, even though Spanish and English commissioners were sitting in London to try and reach a compromise, Newcastle continued sending peremptory despatches to Keene almost in the form of ultimatums. In June 1738, however, a compromise was agreed upon by the English and Spanish commissioners and approved of by a full cabinet council, whereby the English merchants' losses were reckoned at £200,000 and the Spanish counter claims at £60,000, leaving £140,000 due on balance to England, but reduced for prompt payment to £95,000. In the course of the debates, however, in Parliament on the convention embodying this arrangement, it leaked out that Philip V refused to pay even this £95,000 until his claim of £68,000 for arrears due to him personally from the South Sea Company was satisfied; so that England would receive no more than £27,000 net. This proved too much even for a docile House of Commons; the country was aroused; and on 19 October 1739 war was solemnly declared by the heralds against Spain, accompanied by the ringing of bells and general rejoicing.

During the months of indecision before this final step was taken, Newcastle and Hardwicke were carrying on a lively correspondence, partly on divisions in the cabinet between Walpole and themselves on the question of conciliation or a bold policy with Spain, but mainly on the Duke's personal grievances. He suspects his colleague

[1] Yorke, *Hardwicke*, I, 217.
[2] Add. MSS. 32796, ff. 77, 94, 168, 212.

Harrington of influencing the King against him; but as Hardwicke points out, and Newcastle himself has to admit, Walpole, 'to do him justice,...has set everything right again'. In another letter he complains 'I was extremely hurt to find myself so universally blamed...by all my best friends' at a cabinet council, but is restored to good humour by a 'most tender and affectionate letter' from the Chancellor. But his main grievance is Sir Robert's decision to raise Lord Hervey to the office of Privy Seal with a seat in the Lords, an office which technically gave him precedence over Newcastle himself. Walpole had much justification for this promotion, since the chief spokesmen for the ministry in the Lords, Newcastle and Hardwicke, were opposed to his policy of conciliation with Spain, while Hervey was his devoted supporter. But it also happened that the good Duke was one of the chief butts of the witty diarist's sarcasms. *Hinc illae lacrymae*, expressed in a letter of portentous length to the Chancellor, only five days before the declaration of war against Spain, when a Secretary of State might have been supposed to have more important matters to consider. The letter is pathetically self-revealing: '...It is so fashionable in all my friends (and when I say this to your Lordship I must except you) to think me in the wrong upon every occasion....My dear Lord, I know myself as well as any of my friends know me. My temper is such that I am often uneasy and peevish and perhaps, what may be called wrong-headed, to my best friends; but that always goes down with the sun and passes off as if nothing had happened....My own party, I think, is taken. I have thoroughly weighed and considered it. I shall not alone, abruptly, at the beginning of the Session, give up because my Lord Hervey is made Privy Seal; but I shall from that moment determine to have nothing more to do with Sir Robert Walpole, and to take my opportunity of withdrawing from the administration, when I can do it with the greatest duty and respect to the King and with the greatest regard to my own honour and reputation....This must be cleared up one way or other, and Sir Robert must take his choice between Lord Hervey and us [for earlier in the letter Newcastle had hoped (and assumed) that Hardwicke would join him in resigning].' A postscript to the letter states that, to spare Hardwicke the trouble of reading his own, almost illegible, script, he had 'made use of the Duchess of Newcastle, upon whose secrecy you may depend'. Replying to this letter a fortnight later, Hardwicke says he has seen Sir Robert's brother Horace, who told him that Godolphin, whom Hervey was to replace, was to remain as Privy Seal for the next session. But Hervey succeeded him in April 1740, without, apparently, any further protest from Newcastle.[1]

But, though this particular cloud blew over for the time being, the Duke was never for long without a grievance. Most of his grumbles were against Walpole and Harrington, but even the Chancellor himself was not immune from his complaints for not attending all the cabinet councils called during the legal vacation, when he was justifiably taking some rest from his arduous duties in the law courts. Walpole was frankly bored with his fussy colleague and took no pains to dissemble his contempt. Hervey describes Newcastle button-holing Walpole after a council meeting and overhearing this colloquy:

'N. If you please I would speak one word to you before you go.
W. I do not please my Lord, but if you will you must.
N. Sir, I shall not trouble you long.
W. Well, my Lord, that's something, but I had rather not be troubled at all. Won't it keep cold till to-morrow?
N. Perhaps not, Sir.
W. Well come let's have it.

The rest of the dialogue was carried on by Newcastle in a whisper, with Walpole ejaculating at intervals "Pooh! Pshaw! O Lord! O Lord! Pray be quiet. My God can't you see it is over?"'[2]

That Hervey's malicious account of this conversation is not far from the truth is apparent from an account given by Newcastle himself to Hardwicke of another such dressing down from Walpole. 'I said then to him [Walpole],' writes the Duke, '"When measures are agreed amongst us, it is very right that everybody should support them, but not to have the liberty of giving one's opinion before they are agreed is very wrong". He said shortly, "What do you mean? The war is yours, you have had the conduct of it, I wish you joy of it."'[3]

It is not surprising that the Spanish war was shockingly mismanaged during the first two years, considering that Walpole himself more or less washed his hands of it, that the two Secretaries, Newcastle and Harrington, had in many respects conflicting views and that Newcastle, to whose province the conduct of operations chiefly pertained, was all of a twitter of anxiety and self-depreciation, or moaning about the shortcomings of his colleagues. On the eve

[1] The letters quoted in this paragraph are to be found in Yorke, *Hardwicke*, I, 221–2, 228–33.
[2] Hervey, *Memoirs*, pp. 935–6.   [3] Yorke, *Hardwicke*, I, 251.

of war, when some of the Spanish treasure-ships had escaped our blockade, he writes to the Chancellor: 'For God's sake, my dear Lord, lett us putt our fleets upon action, somewhere, or all will be called a Farce, and we shall be said to have delayed Vernon, y^t the Azogues might escape', and the best he can hope for is that some good may come 'from the various things flung out the other night at Council'; 'Let us but determine to do Something; we shall soon find out what may be undertaken.'[1] Three months later his friend the Chancellor still had to tell him that in planning a campaign it was essential to have 'an entire Scheme and Plan before us . . . whereas by taking it up as hitherto has been done by piecemeal, at broken hours, with much interception by deviating into other Business, nothing is brought to perfection or consistency and there is great danger that many material things may be forgot or overlook'd'.[2] But Newcastle was incorrigible; and it was not for want of knowing his own failings. 'I perceive', he naïvely tells Hardwicke, 'that it is thought by some that I take too much upon me and spend the time of the Regency in unnecessary discourse.' It may be admitted, however, that, when this was written, ministers were in considerable difficulty, since the King was in Hanover with Harrington, and plans had to be sent backwards and forwards between Hanover and London before any final decision could be made. All the same little light could be obtained from London, with Walpole sulky and irresolute about a war into which he had been driven against his will, and Newcastle—when Norris had been ordered to take a fleet to watch the coast of Spain—bleating to Hardwicke, 'What is he to do, as there are no ships in Ferrol? We must order him to do something against San Sebastian or somewhere', or a little later—'You ask me, Why does not Sir Chaloner Ogle sail [to the West Indies]? I answer, because He is not ready. If you ask another Question, Why is he not ready? To that I cannot answer.'[3]

To add to the confusion, in 1740, on the death of the Emperor, his daughter and heiress Maria Theresa, whose rights the Emperor had fondly hoped to safeguard by his Pragmatic Sanction, which had been accepted by almost every state in Europe, was attacked by Frederic of Prussia, Bavaria, and France.[4] Maria Theresa at once appealed to England and Hanover to honour their treaty obligations;

[1] Add. MSS. 35406, ff. 140, 144, 156.　　[2] Add. MSS. 32692, ff. 510, 523.
[3] Add. MSS. 35406, ff. 274, 221, 253.
[4] France was nominally at peace with Maria Theresa till 1744, but nevertheless was helping Frederic and Bavaria against her.

and this time Walpole could hardly refuse the help demanded, but even so gave it grudgingly and chiefly in the form of a subsidy for Hanover troops to be sent to her aid. The King, as Elector, was at first all for helping her with his electoral troops, paid for by England; but in August 1741, on news of Frederic's alliance with France, he became alarmed for the safety of his electorate, and withdrew his aid, procured a treaty of neutrality for Hanover and actually agreed to vote for the election of the Elector of Bavaria as Emperor. Then, in spite of all this, he expected the English subsidy for his electoral troops to be continued. Once more, as so often occurred in times of difficulty, the King himself, accompanied by Harrington, was in Hanover; and one of Newcastle's complaints was that Walpole had concealed from him the King's letter making this outrageous demand and had actually agreed to it without consulting himself and the other ministers. Newcastle was rightly indignant when he heard of this, and, as usual, complained to Hardwicke of the 'very great dislike at present in the King towards me', adding at the same time, characteristically, 'I am not, my dear Lord, now quitting the King's service...being persuaded that no man alive will seriously think that I have had any hand in any of these measures that I myself am now blaming'.[1]

§ IV

It is refreshing to pass from these dithering proceedings to the vigorous speeches of Carteret in the Lords, whereby he attempted to instil some courage and determination into this feeble and disunited ministry and lay down definite principles for the conduct of the war and of our general foreign policy. In the Lords' first debate, of May 1738, on the Spanish claims, he brushed aside some futile resolutions, proposed by Walpole's son-in-law Cholmondeley and supported by Newcastle, carrying his amendment emphatically repudiating the Spanish claim of search on the high seas: 'I am not for a war,' he declared, 'but if they disturb our navigation, let us disturb theirs.'[2] Next year, in the debate on the King's speech announcing the convention with Spain settling the dispute with the South Sea Company, he recurred to what seemed to him the far more important point of 'no search at sea', which was not dealt with in the convention. Cardinal Fleury, he declared, 'would not have

[1] Yorke, *Hardwicke*, I, 264, 268; Torrens, *l.c.* pp. 531-2.
[2] *P.H.* x, 730 etc.

suffered a minister to come into the tenth antechamber that should talk of searching French ships', and proceeded to give a devastating analysis of the feeble and vacillating foreign policy of Walpole's government since his own resignation in 1724. By our blunders during those years we had been strengthening France; but, he continued proudly, even now, if France joined Spain, we have a fleet to make ourselves respected, if we use it effectively instead of fitting out useless squadrons and wasting money on needless armies. 'Let your fleets and your armies be a terror to your enemies', he cried, 'instead of being a terror to your own people...and when we do strike, I hope care will be taken to give them such a blow as they must remember.'[1] But when after five speeches he had at last dragged from the shuffling Duke of Newcastle the damaging admission that, as an offset to the £95,000 damages agreed upon by the Convention, Spain was still claiming £68,000 due to herself on other counts, leaving only a paltry £27,000 on balance, and that the ministers were also considering Spain's claim to the ownership of Georgia within his own province of South Carolina, his indignation knew no bounds.[2] He strongly supported the merchants' petition to be heard by counsel against the convention, and took occasion to pay his noble tribute to his great patron Stanhope. For now, he said, they had not a Stanhope in the House to speak for the merchants as he did against the commercial clauses of the Treaty of Utrecht.[3] One last speech he made about this unfortunate convention, before the outbreak of war relegated it to the rubbish heap. It was on a motion of gratitude and duty to His Majesty for the convention, which he sarcastically expressed regret at resisting: for the compensation it offered for past injuries was derisory, nor was there in it any settlement of the 'No search' question which put the whole of our South Seas commerce at stake: and 'it is from commerce, my Lords, that I behold your Lordships within these walls, a free and independent assembly.... This nation', he concluded, 'had never so little influence upon the councils of Europe, as since we pretend to give weight to our negotiations by maintaining or increasing peaceable armies or putting out harmless squadrons.'[4] Carteret, had he been living in our days, would no doubt have made the most of the obvious parallel between Walpole's feeble attempt to pacify Spain by his still-born convention and our unfortunate 'peace with honour' policy at Munich.

[1] *P.H.* x, 877, 917.   [2] *P.H.* x, 1013 sqq.
[3] See above, ch. III, p. 45; *P.H.* x, 1041, 1045.   [4] *P.H.* x, 1102.

After the declaration of war against Spain in October 1739 Carteret devoted himself mainly to constructive advice on the conduct of hostilities. He insisted that Parliament, and not least the House of Lords, as the King's 'great and chief council', should have all the facts put before it, to enable it to tender useful counsel to the Crown, otherwise 'our pretences to liberty will, I fear, in a short time become as much the ridicule of foreigners, as our late conduct has already rendered our pretences to the holding the balance of Europe'.[1] On this principle he urged—but vainly—the submission to the House of Vernon's and Haddock's orders for the operations of their fleets in the West Indies and the Mediterranean for examination by a secret Committee.[2] He even went so far as to demand that royal messages asking for supplies should be sent to the Lords as well as the Commons, since the measures on which the money was to be spent ought to be discussed in both Houses: if such things are overlooked, 'this House will come to be an empty room with a great coal fire, a few bishops and two judges and the Lords walking into the Court of Requests to know what Message hath been sent to the Commons separately.... [In that case] our Constitution,...according to its ancient form, the most perfect that ever was established,...will deviate into a democracy, which will...soon come under the absolute rule of one, perhaps one of the lowest rank among them [sc. Walpole]', but he consoles himself by the appearance of 'a spirit of virtue and liberty beginning to prevail among the young Lords of this House [as opposed to] the old men who are perhaps a little too passive: they may sit still under an encroachment, rather than expose themselves to the danger and fatigue of opposing it'.[3] In a later speech he recurs to this topic, declaring that real harmony in the nation can come only when 'Parliament speaks the language of the people': whereas if it speaks only the language of ministers, 'a good harmony between King and Parliament will then have no authority at home, and consequently can have no more effect abroad, than a good harmony between the King and his ministers—I was going to say his footmen....In our capacity as the great council of State we ought to give our advice to our Sovereign upon all important occasions', so, he added in his grandiose way, he had learned from the example of the great Revolution statesmen, Halifax, Somers and Cowper.

Carteret was convinced that, war once declared, Walpole was the last man to conduct it. In this view he was undoubtedly right, for,

[1] *P.H.* x, 1371.   [2] *P.H.* xi, 700, 775; xii, 332.   [3] *P.H.* xi, 450.

as is evident from Hervey and the correspondence between New-castle and Hardwicke,[1] he not only went into the war unwillingly, sneering at a bellicose speech by Hardwicke with the ejaculation, 'Bravo, Colonel Yorke', but in its conduct showed a lamentable want of vigour and decision. Walpole indeed was supreme as a minister for home affairs and for finance. By his fiscal reforms and bold domestic policy he, more than anyone else, planted the Hano-verian dynasty firmly on the throne, and gained for the House of Commons its just pre-eminence in Parliament: but as foreign minister, which he virtually was from 1730 to 1742, he had not the penetrating vision or the power of bold decision possessed by Stanhope and his pupil Carteret. In a series of attacks on Walpole's foreign policy, culminating in a motion of February 1741 for the removal of Walpole from the King's Councils, Carteret traversed the whole field of foreign policy since the Treaty of Utrecht and especially since Walpole had taken control. Contrasting Walpole with the French minister Fleury, of the former he declared that 'for almost twenty years he had been demonstrating that he had neither wisdom nor conduct. He may have a little low cunning such as those have that buy cattle at Smithfield market, or such as a French valet makes use of for managing an indulgent master'; while Fleury 'who so worthily presides over the councils of France and whose great age must make him desire to end his days in peace....He is a minister respected both by the people and the King. This is a great advantage, for it is an infinite loss to a nation to be under the conduct of a minister hated and despised by the people.' Then diverging to one of his favourite topics, the French, he said, 'are more intent upon extending their trade than upon extending their dominions', a policy we might well imitate, since 'our trade is our chief support, and therefore we must sacrifice every other view to its preservation...by covering the sea with our ships of war. The sea, my Lords, when so covered is our defence and our safeguard; when not so covered it is our prison...'. We should also seek allies such as the Emperor and Prussia and 'another power [Russia], which is now as formidable as any in Europe', and also the Dutch, but all this will not be accom-plished by 'our late dealers in negotiation',[2] who, after making a treaty with the Emperor in 1731, had abandoned him in the War of the Austrian Succession.

[1] See *Hardwicke State Papers*, II, 7; Coxe, *Walpole*, I, 637; Yorke, *Hardwicke*, I, 215–77; Hervey, *Memoirs*, pp. 933 sqq.; and cp. my *Whig Supremacy*, pp. 200, 220–1.
[2] *P.H.* XI, 10 sqq., 615 sqq.

But while praising Fleury, in contrast to Walpole, for his conduct of French policy, in his speech against Walpole, said to have been the finest he ever made, he warned the country against French designs, especially after Frederic II's unprovoked invasion of Maria Theresa's Silesia in 1740 with the connivance and eventual support of France. 'France, my Lords,' he declared, 'is the constant and hereditary enemy of Britons, so much divided from her in religion, government and interest, that they cannot both be prosperous together; as the interest of one rises, that of the other must decline. Alliances may form a temporary show of friendship, but it cannot continue; for their situation produces a natural rivalship, which every accidental circumstance has contributed to increase.'[1] Two more speeches, in April and December 1741, his last before Walpole's resignation, sounded the same note of anxiety and warning. In April Walpole had proposed a small vote of credit to Maria Theresa, to honour our obligations under the Pragmatic Sanction, and Carteret, though deserted by two leading opposition peers, Argyll and Chesterfield, spoke warmly in favour of the vote. 'I do not look for popularity,' he said, 'but am now on the popular side of the question.... The Empire may be considered as the bulwark of Great Britain, which, if thrown down leaves us naked.... For if the Austrian dominions are parcelled, France gets enough without getting an acre of land'; and if we do not help the Queen of Hungary, she 'will throw herself into the arms of France.... It shall never be imputed to me that I bury the House of Austria without burying my own country at the same time.' In December, when France had definitely joined in the hunt against the gallant Queen, and Hanover had signed a treaty of neutrality, 'giving a decisive blow to the liberties of Europe', Carteret warned the House that France had attained 'an exalted pinnacle of authority', and Great Britain, when the rest of Europe succumbs, can hardly be long 'exempted from the loss of all our commerce and from the general servitude'. Already, so far from helping the Austrians we had permitted a Spanish invasion of Italy in face of Haddock's superior force in the Mediterranean. But there was still some hope: we could remove the Queen's most dangerous enemy by reconciling Prussia to her; Sardinia was still actively helping the Austrians in Italy; and even the Dutch were beginning to awake from their lethargy; then there was the great power of Russia in the background: she ought above all to be induced to move.[2]

---

[1] *P.H.* XI, 1153 (Feb. 1741).   [2] *P.H.* XII, 152, 226 sqq.

With this final attack on Walpole's policy and a clear forecast of his own, should he come into office, Carteret's work in opposition was completed. In January 1742, Walpole, who had no heart in a war he was hopelessly mismanaging, criticized by an increasingly powerful opposition and intrigued against by Newcastle and others in his ministry, seized the opportunity of an adverse majority in the Commons on a trivial election petition, and resigned from the post he had held continuously for twenty-one years. Newcastle, so far from following his example, had been securing his own position by friendly approaches to certain members of the opposition, and not least to Carteret.

Chapter VII

CARTERET 'THE SOLE MINISTER'

With the fall of Walpole the way at last seemed open for a ministry under Carteret. In spite of occasional attacks of gout he was still at the height of his powers: 'I am still lame,' he wrote at the end of the year, 'but for vigorous measures both as to Mars and Venus.'[1] He had already shown his mettle in two formidable tasks—his embassy to Sweden and his vice-royalty of Ireland. By his great speeches on the Spanish dispute he had been largely instrumental in Walpole's fall and had shown a grasp of foreign politics possessed by no other member of either House. On domestic policy he was less well-equipped, but in that field Walpole had established a fiscal and administrative system on so sound a basis that for the time being this was no handicap; whereas his unique understanding of European politics and systems, coupled with his venturesome spirit and proud confidence in his own and his country's ability to weather any storms, seemed to mark him out, in the confused outlook abroad, as the nation's obvious leader. Unfortunately these merits were counterbalanced by defects in his political equipment. A peer at five years of age, he never had the chance of serving his apprentice-ship in the hurly-burly of the House of Commons, at the very time when Walpole was making that assembly the real centre of power; nor was he ever, like his rival the Duke of Newcastle, interested in the electioneering methods then necessary to secure support for a minister in that House. His personal supporters were a very small group composed of Lord Winchilsea and his relatives the 'black funereal Finches', his cousin Lord Gower and a few others of no great political influence. Nor would he ever condescend to even the most obvious methods of conciliating possible supporters; when, for example, on Walpole's fall, he was asked to attend a tavern dinner to discuss the composition of the new ministry with influential Whigs of both Houses, he refused on the ground that he 'never dined at taverns'.

The new ministry was composed nominally at meetings held either at Carteret's or Pulteney's houses and attended, besides those two opposition leaders, by Newcastle and his brother Henry Pelham

[1] Add. MSS. 32699, f. 603.

with Hardwicke; but behind the scenes Walpole, now Earl of Orford, still had considerable influence. Pulteney was the obvious successor to Walpole at the Treasury; and undoubtedly Pulteney in the Commons and Carteret in the Lords would have formed a strong and coherent ministry. But unfortunately Pulteney had once declared that he did not seek office, and retired to the Lords as Earl of Bath with no executive functions and merely the right to sit in council. In his place Spencer Compton, Lord Wilmington, a nonentity and regarded as 'a tool of Sir Robert Walpole's', went to the Treasury. Carteret indeed became Secretary for the North but with Newcastle as his colleague in the Southern department, bolstered up by his brother Henry Pelham as Paymaster and his crony Hardwicke as Chancellor. Carteret's only real supporters in the ministry were Lord Winchilsea at the Admiralty, an office for which he was quite unfitted, his cousin Lord Gower as Privy Seal after Hervey's dismissal a few months later, Sandys Chancellor of the Exchequer, Tweeddale Secretary for Scotland and a Finch Vice-Chamberlain, none of them carrying much weight. On the day after he received the seals Carteret had a visit from his friend Lord Egmont, a public-spirited Irish peer, who criticized the new ministry as having too many of Walpole's friends and not enough new blood from the opposition or 'country party'. Speaking 'not as a minister but private man', Carteret replied that it would be unwise to have too many changes at first, as long as there were a few like himself to dissipate the King's prejudice against the opponents of Walpole, 'who had poisoned the King against them'; and about the same time his under-secretary Weston wrote to Trevor at the Hague that Carteret 'stakes his whole on keeping the El[ector George II] an Englishman'.[1] In fact Carteret's chief supporter proved to be the King, who appreciated his knowledge of European, and especially German, politics: though even this support in the long run did not prove strong enough to defend him against the Pelhams' intrigues. But, as long as he remained in office, Carteret showed that in foreign policy he meant to be master. Fortunately, as Secretary of State for the North, his business was to conduct the most important negotiations—with Frederic of Prussia, Maria Theresa, the Emperor and all the states of Empire, besides Sweden and Russia: even when Sardinia, in Newcastle's province, was concerned in a treaty with England and Maria Theresa, Carteret managed to keep the negotiations in his own hands. Unfortunately his masterful attitude not

[1] H. MSS. Egmont, Diary, III, 251; Buckinghamshire, p. 82.

only gradually alienated his colleagues but also brought upon him the whole brunt of attacks from such powerful adversaries as Chesterfield and Pitt.

But, though dictatorial, Carteret was never vindictive. He had no cause to love his new colleague Newcastle, who had played a part in jockeying him out of his place as Secretary of State in 1724; but when in 1742 they became co-Secretaries he got on well enough with him until, in the following year, Newcastle began to carp at and obstruct his policy; then Carteret's rejoinder was simply to ignore him. Again, it is notable that Carteret's only recorded speech in his first session as Secretary in 1742 was to prevent what he thought an injustice to his far more formidable adversary Walpole, Lord Orford. A committee had been set up to enquire into the charges of political corruption bandied about against Walpole; but, as it was difficult to obtain definite evidence of these charges, a bill was introduced to indemnify witnesses for any evidence, hearsay or otherwise, they might choose to bring forward in what amounted to a purely fishing enquiry. Carteret strenuously opposed such a proposal, declaring it to be quite contrary to the idea of British justice to allow evidence against a man amounting to no more than common opinion and on no specific charge: he had no wish, he added, to condone breaches of trust, but, if Walpole was guilty, he should be proved so by due legal process, such as impeachment on definite charges, whereas this bill invited a form of testimony unknown to our laws, i.e. 'according to the best of the witnesses' knowledge, remembrance and belief'.[1] Walpole's son, the younger Horace, no friend of Carteret's, was grateful for this speech, declaring that it was chiefly due to him that the proposed irregular procedure was dropped.

When Carteret resumed office in February 1742 the outlook on foreign affairs was bleak. In the war against Spain Vernon's capture of Portobello in 1739 had been followed by the disaster at Cartagena in the following year and the virtual abandonment of attempts to dominate the Spaniards in the West Indies. Maria Theresa, our solitary ally in Europe, had lost Silesia to Frederic of Prussia; France was actively supporting Charles of Bavaria's claims to Bohemia and other parts of her dominions, and Spain was attacking her Italian possessions; and though the Queen had obtained a temporary truce from Frederic in October, in December he had renewed his attacks in co-operation with the French who overran Bohemia. In January 1742 the Elector of Bavaria was chosen Emperor as Charles VII,

[1] *Parl. Hist.* xii, 643-4.

the first non-Habsburg Emperor since 1438. Although Walpole had been constrained by public opinion to honour the Treaty of Vienna of 1731, to the extent of a small subsidy to the Queen and the promise of an auxiliary force of Danes and Hessians, very little material support had been forthcoming; while, as we have seen, George II, alarmed for the safety of his Electorate, had negotiated with the French and Frederic for its neutrality, and had even cast his electoral vote for the Bavarian Emperor.

Such feeble vacillating measures formed no part of Carteret's policy. For conquests in America, as he told Maria Theresa's envoy Wasner,[1] he had no ambition, as long as the balance of power was maintained in the western hemisphere. There he was determined to honour our treaty obligations by giving Maria Theresa effective support, and above all to restore England to the commanding position which he had learned from Stanhope to be her due, and which, as he believed, had been wantonly thrown away by Walpole and Newcastle. Fixed in his intention 'to keep the Elector an Englishman', he told Frederic of Prussia that 'he will much deceive himself if he thinks the King will be frightened from pursuing the system of England and be brought to abandon the liberties of Europe by the danger with which his German dominions may be menaced, since His Majesty can firmly rely on all the weight and power of these kingdoms being exerted in defence of them, whenever they shall be involved with England in the great and general cause'.[2] Accordingly, as one of his first measures, he persuaded George II to abandon the neutrality of Hanover and take his stand, as Elector as well as King, in support of the injured Queen: 'to do my Lord Carteret justice', as Newcastle afterwards admitted, 'the best thing he ever did.' He prevailed on Parliament to increase Maria Theresa's subsidy and to make effective provision for an auxiliary corps of Hessians and Hanoverians in English pay to support her. He also undertook to arouse the lethargic Dutch to their danger from French aggression and if possible to secure their armed assistance.

But he had no desire to plunge into a continental war if it could be honourably avoided and to that end made friendly approaches to Frederic and Cardinal Fleury. As to Frederic he agreed with the view expressed in an opposition pamphlet of 1741 that 'the enmity between England and Prussia, which it was thought the death of

---

[1] F. Wagner, *Kaiser Karl und die Grossen Mächte*, p. 278.
[2] Add. MSS. 22531, f. 7.

the late king would dissolve, still persists and contributes to the peril of the liberties of Germany'.[1] Within a month of assuming office Carteret had a heart to heart talk with Frederic's envoy Andrié, telling him that, though opposed to France's attack on Maria Theresa, and resolved to restore the credit of England destroyed by the last ministry, he was so far from any hostile designs against Prussia that he was most anxious to restore the former good relations between the two countries. Frederic, in his reply to Andrié, admitted that, in what he called 'critiquen und scabreusen conjunctiven', the friendship of England must be secured and told him to assure Carteret that his engagements with France were in no way aimed at England, adding that he recalled with pleasure his meeting with Carteret when he came to Berlin with George I in 1723, and felt certain that such men as he and his colleagues would pursue no policy unworthy of their intelligence. This somewhat cold response was, however, followed by a letter from Frederic to the Emperor urging him to write 'une lettre obligeante à milord Carteret, qui veut que toutes les affaires passent par son canal immédiat...ce que j'appuyerais de tout mon crédit'.[2]

Carteret took a somewhat higher tone when 'opening his heart', as he put it, to the French envoy Bussy. England, he said, attached great value to the friendship of France and had no intention of detaching her from her allies; but, he added, we must know where France stands before deciding on peace or war. Far be it from me, he continued in his grandiloquent style, 'd'employer avec la France ces petits artifices du précédent ministère: entre deux grandes Puissances comme la France et l'Angleterre il fallait faire noblement la Paix ou la Guerre'. War was to nobody's interest, least of all to that of England, 'une nation commerçante'; but, after showing our goodwill by recognizing the Bavarian Emperor, it would not suit our interests or our parliamentary engagements to have Maria Theresa's dominions partitioned and the House of Austria 'absolument renversée'. These advances, however, were coldly received by Fleury and by Frederic, to whom the cardinal sent a copy of Bussy's report. 'V. M. aura jugé assez aisément par tous les discours de my Lord Carteret', wrote Fleury in his covering letter to Frederic, 'qu'il voudrait se rendre Médiateur, et faire reprendre au Roi son Maître l'influence qu'il avait eu ci-devant dans toutes les

[1] *The Groans of Germany*, 1741.
[2] J. C. Droysen, *Geschichte der Preussischen Politik*, v, 246-9; *Politische Korrespondenz Friedrichs des Grossen*, II, 82, 236.

affaires de l'Europe, et je suis bien assuré que rien n'échappera à ses lumières.' Frederic was no less mordant in his criticism: Carteret, he wrote to his minister Podewils, 'se pique de penser et agir en Romain et noblement', his real object being to side-track Prussia 'pour que l'Angleterre et la France partagent l'arbitrage de la paix et de la guerre, et qu'on traite les autres en petits garçons'. Carteret's secret service was good and procured him copies of Bussy's and Fleury's letters, so when, some months later, Bussy accosted him with the question, 'Vous voudriez donc, Milord, nous obliger à une paix honteuse?' Carteret answered him in a very different tone: 'Sans doute, et c'est mon unique occupation depuis que je suis dans les affaires—en ajoutant—et je me flatte d'y réussir.'[1]

No doubt some of the expressions used by Carteret in his early dealings with Frederic II and Fleury grate upon us by their arrogant tone, due no doubt to his anxiety to mark the reaction to Walpole's and Newcastle's timid excursions into foreign politics during the last ten years; and there was certainly some truth in Frederic's complaint that Carteret was inclined to treat other kings 'en petits garçons'. But no such fault can be found with his truly magnificent statement of England's policy addressed to Hyndford, the British envoy in Berlin, in March 1742. The King, he writes, 'is fully determined and resolved, as well in consequence of the engagements he is under, as in compliance with the unanimous voice of his people, and for the maintenance of the liberties of Europe, to stand by and support the House of Austria to the utmost of his power.... As to our trade, which is supposed to be, and is, our favourite object, we don't conceive it to depend on the resolutions of Brandebourg, Saxony and Bavaria, and though France should, by the King of Prussia's assistance, become mistress of the Empire, yet even that melancholy circumstance will not make her mistress of our trade. And with regard to the Electorate, his Prussian Majesty will much deceive himself, if he thinks the King will be frightened from pursuing the system of England, and be brought to abandon the liberties of Europe by the danger with which his German dominions may be menaced, since His Majesty can firmly rely on all the weight and power of these kingdoms being exerted in defence of them, whenever they shall be involved with England in the great and general cause.' As to Frederic himself, the King 'would expect that he should imme-

---

[1] Copies of Bussy's letter to Fleury and of Fleury's to Frederic are in Add. MSS. 22542, ff. 39 and 50; Frederic's letter to Podewils and Andrié's account of Carteret's later meeting with Bussy are in *Politische Correspondenz Friedrich's*, II, 160, 301.

diately settle his affairs with the Queen of Hungary and content himself with what he had already obtained, and depend rather on the Maritime Powers than on France for his security.[1]

Carteret's vigorous policy was in fact even more effective than his vigorous language, language such as Frederic had not hitherto been accustomed to hear. To save Maria Theresa and to protect England from attack by the Bourbon powers, he planned such a combination of allies as even Frederic might find it wiser to join. England's army was small and could not be largely increased owing to the English people's ingrained fear of a standing army as a menace to English liberties. But England had a fleet to guard her shores and trade, and to harass an enemy, and ample means wherewith to support allies and hire auxiliary troops. Besides the subsidies given to Maria Theresa and the money voted for Hanoverian and Hessian troops, Carteret envisaged a coalition comprising Russia, Saxony and several other German states, Holland and Savoy, and he hoped to persuade Sweden and Denmark at least to refrain from actively joining the opposite camp. At the end of 1742 he sent Villiers, our envoy at Dresden, on a roving commission to Vienna and thence to some dozen German principalities to secure their adhesion; and thereby succeeded in detaching Saxony-Poland from the camp hostile to Maria Theresa.[2]

With Russia Carteret achieved a striking success. In his instructions of April 1742 to the new envoy to St Petersburg, Sir Cyril Wyche, he warned him about the intrigues of the French envoy La Chétardie, since 'to be mistress of the North is as much the scheme and system of France as the destruction of the House of Austria, for the sake of enslaving the rest of Europe'; and he had the satisfaction, two years later, of seeing La Chétardie expelled from Russia for his palace intrigues. In his Russian policy he had a strong supporter in the Tsaritza Elizabeth's chief minister Bestuzhef, through whose influence the first treaty of alliance with Russia was signed in December 1742, whereby the imperial title claimed by the Tsars was admitted, and Russia and England by a secret clause agreed to provide 12,000 men and 12 men-of-war respectively to the common cause if either power were attacked by a new enemy. There were indeed difficulties to be overcome thereafter. Russia and England supported rival candidates for the succession to the throne of Sweden, but Carteret avoided a quarrel by finally agreeing to the Russian candidate. Again in 1743 Russia took offence at the marriage of George II's daughter

[1] Add. MSS. 22531, f. 7.　　　　[2] Add. MSS. 22530, ff. 9, 17, 31, 70.

Louise with the Prince Royal of Denmark, a country with which Russia had serious differences: but Carteret turned away Muscovite wrath by his Olympian remark that it was 'an affair purely of a domestic nature, and we accepted it as such without any view to politics; for God knows these alliances sometimes produce effects different from what is imagined'.[1] Another obstacle to Carteret's Russian policy was the attitude of Frederic of Prussia. Throughout his reign Frederic dreaded an attack from his northern neighbour more than that of any other power—for, as the English envoy to Prussia remarked, 'Frederic fears Russia more than God'[2]; and he was always ready to fish in the troubled waters of Russian palace intrigues. Thus in 1744 he scored a success by getting Maria Theresa's envoy Botta expelled from Russia on an unproven charge of an anti-dynastic plot. But, in spite of all these difficulties, Russia, partly owing to her favourable trade relations with England, remained a fairly reliable ally during the War of the Austrian Succession. There were still diplomatic difficulties to be overcome after Carteret's resignation in 1744; nevertheless, in accordance with his policy, Russia actually sent a contingent to the Rhine in 1748 to support England's allies.

But Carteret's main efforts in support of Maria Theresa were first to persuade Frederic to content himself with his gain of Silesia and make a definite peace with the Queen, and secondly to form a composite army, destined to relieve the pressure on her from the Bavarians and the French. His first object was attained without great difficulty. By his second campaign, after repudiating the Convention of Klein-Schnellendorf, Frederic had consolidated his hold on Silesia, and was then only too willing to obtain a guarantee of his gains from England. Moreover, having used the French for his own purposes against Maria Theresa, he had no wish to see them established in too strong a position in Germany. Maria Theresa was harder to move. Finally to part with Silesia to a prince who had already broken two engagements was hard to bear, all the more as the tide of success in favour of her French and Bavarian enemies was beginning to turn. Her chancery, as pedantic as any in Europe, supported her in her obstinacy; but Carteret's appeals at length prevailed. If she refused terms now, he wrote, 'it might prove fatal to the Queen and her posterity, as

---

[1] Add. MSS. 22528, ff. 5, 132. In this instance Carteret proved a true prophet: the marriage was subsequently dissolved on a charge of infidelity against the English princess.

[2] Droysen, l.c. v, 149.

well as to the whole present system and the common liberties of Europe';[1] so, though with no good grace, she at last gave way. By the Treaty of Breslau of June 1742[2] Silesia was finally yielded to Frederic under England's guarantee, as the price of his secession from the war against Maria Theresa, a treaty chiefly due, as Frederic willingly testified, to Carteret's 'grandes lumières', and Hyndford's 'sage conduite et zèle infatigable'.[3] And no sooner was this treaty concluded than Frederic pressed for a further treaty with England alone to guarantee his own dominions from attack. Carteret was not unwilling and negotiated with the Prussian envoy the Treaty of Westminster of 14 September 1742. But this treaty proved of doubtful benefit to England, who got no useful guarantee in return; while Frederic, who had asked for it, said in the end, 'Je fais cette alliance à contre-cœur, et s'ils ne me satisfont sur mes intérêts, et qu'ils n'entrent pas dans mes idées, ils en seront les dupés'.[4]

There still remained Maria Theresa's other antagonists, the Bavarian Emperor and his French allies, the latter, however, acting without an official declaration of war against the Queen. In his turn Carteret proposed to form a composite force to maintain the Queen's rights under the Pragmatic Sanction, likewise without any formal declaration of war. This force, known as the Pragmatic Army, was to be composed of 14,000 English troops, all that could be spared from our small army, 22,000 Hessians and Hanoverians in English pay, 14,000 contributed by Maria Theresa, and, it was hoped, a contingent from the Dutch. But there came the rub. Exhausted by the Marlborough war, in debt and torn by intestine quarrels between the ruling republican party and supporters of the Prince of Orange's claim to be Stadtholder, the Dutch had no stomach for more military adventures. However in July 1742 an English contingent had been landed at Ostend and the rest of the Pragmatic Army was being gradually assembled in Flanders under the command of Lord Stair, a crusty old fire-eater of Marlborough's wars, who was also named ambassador to the republic to secure their contingent. His choice for this purpose was not happy, for he set everybody by the ears, 'talking big', as Frederic said, 'in Louis XIV terms like a *fou furieux*' to the Dutch, and making shrill complaints to Carteret for 'over-

[1] Add. MSS. 22529, f. 29.
[2] Later incorporated in the definitive Treaty of Berlin of 28 July 1742.
[3] Add. MSS. 22531, f. 35; and see Frederic's *Mémoires*, I, 168.
[4] See Lodge, *Great Britain and Prussia in the 18th Century*, pp. 40-2; Wiese, *Die Engl. Parlsche. Opposition*, p. 26; *Marchmont Papers*, I, 24-5.

turning the fair fabric of your own building', by not taking a stronger line when everything was 'on the point of succeeding even beyond our wishes to the great glory of the King our Master and to the greater honour of Lord Carteret'.[1] Finally Trevor, our regular minister at the Hague, in despair suggested that Carteret himself should come to smooth matters over. The King approved; Carteret remarked: 'I did not enter into discussions, but said I was *toujours botté*', and, though warned of the difficulties he would encounter in Holland, replied that he had adopted the principle that nothing in the world was impossible; and had found it his experience in life that one had to keep that principle before one and stick to it if one wanted to arrive at a successful issue'[2]; and he set forth accordingly. But even to his 'smiling and open countenance, winning dexterity and light touch in business transactions' the Dutch were impervious; and it was not till the following Christmas that they at last decided to grant an additional subsidy to Maria Theresa and contribute 20,000 troops to the Pragmatic Army.[3]

Thus in less than a year from his resuming office Carteret had brought about a marvellous change in the foreign outlook and a no less remarkable return of self-confidence in England. As early as June 1742 a London friend of Robinson at Vienna told him that 'all has taken an amazing turn and the spirit of disquiet seems greatly to subside; Lord C. gains great esteem and ground by his resolution and unshaken *fermeté* and will carry matters, I doubt not, in such a channel that the people will be, as they daily are, more and more pleased'.[4] The French envoy in London wrote to his colleague at the Hague in July that Carteret's prompt announcement in the *Gazette* of Frederic II having, by the Treaty of Breslau, taken over payments on a Silesian loan originally made by England to Vienna, had stopped wild speculation in the shares and made the best impression on the public, 'Walpole', he added, 'used to seize such opportunities for letting in his friends, as well as himself, to profitable speculations. The contrast', he adds, between Carteret's and Walpole's practice in such matters, 'has won him the hearts of the merchants; while the gratification afforded by that treaty to the public hatred of France has silenced all domestic hatred against Carteret, who, from

---

[1] Friedrich, *Politische Correspondenz*, II, 261 sqq.; Add. MSS. 22537, f. 30.

[2] Add. MSS. 32699, f. 404. Pitt uttered much the same sentiments about 'impossibilities', see my *Chatham*, I, 330–1.

[3] Droysen, *Geschichte der Preuss. Politik*, v, 283 sqq.; Adelung, *Pragmatische Staatsgeschichte Europens*, III, i. 294.

[4] Add. MSS. 9180, f. 113.

having been the least popular man in England and openly despising methods employed by other politicians to curry popular favour, has suddenly, between night and morning, become the most popular man in the nation and will be able to raise all the money needed by the government.'[1] Carteret himself, at the opening of the session in November, was fully justified in taking credit for the improved outlook abroad. 'The French', he declared, 'were no longer lords of Germany'; the Dutch were delivered from their terrors and ready to support the Pragmatic Sanction; Frederic of Prussia had been gained, and 30,000 men turned from the scale of France; adding in a characteristic aside that 'Princes, like other men, are inclined to follow that scheme which shall promise them most gain'.

Even with these widespread activities in foreign politics Carteret found time in his first year of office to turn for a moment to interests nearer home. The excessive consumption of raw spirits, entailing the horrors illustrated in Hogarth's *Gin Lane*, had for many years been the concern of the legislature, where various measures with the object of mitigating the abuse had been successively passed without any obvious results. One more such bill was introduced in February 1743 and in the course of the Lords' debates on it, lasting three days, Carteret made no less than six speeches. In describing the previous, abortive, attempts to lessen the evil he was in his most rollicking mood. The first Act had forbidden the manufacture of 'compound spirits', since uncompounded spirits were 'not agreeable to the palate', but only resulted, said Carteret, either in the clandestine retail of 'compound spirits' on a large scale, or in forcing the lieges to drink 'a nauseous or at least unpleasant sort of spirit, which in derision of the authority of the Legislature they called Parliament brandy'. Next an attempt had been made to reduce consumption by imposing taxes on distillers and licence-holders, taxes so enormous that they resulted in a great increase of smuggling, and could not be enforced without calling in military aid, and 'I hope', he said, 'the law will always be able to execute itself without the assistance of the military power', otherwise the military would become 'the dictators, not the directors, which would put an end to the constitution'. To illustrate the contempt of the law and the savagery of the mob caused by this Act, he gave 'an instance of their fury I very particularly remember; on a shout being raised, "an informer passing", the populace united in pursuit, as of a beast of prey...the populace rolled on after him with a torrent not to be resisted... [till]

[1] Add. MSS. (Secret Intelligence), 22539, f. 10.

one of the greatest persons of the nation...opened his doors to the distressed fugitive, and sheltered him from a cruel death.' By the new bill he was advocating, the duties on licence-holders and on still-heads for spirits would be considerably lowered, whereby he hoped the licence-holders would have an interest in suppressing illicit gin houses: 'it is not', he said, 'a tax on vice but may help to prevent it'; though he admitted that some hardened offenders might still follow their inclinations at the risk of death, like 'the gentleman who being dangerously ill of a dropsy sent for a physician. When the physician came he found the gentleman with a pot of fine ale with toast and nutmeg upon his table. The physician immediately said, Sir, you must not touch it: it is certain death for a man in your condition: Not touch it doctor! replies the gentleman, why, if my grave were on this hand and that pot of ale on the other, I would drink it, were I sure of being thrown into my grave next minute.' Carteret then in confessional mood admitted that he allowed himself 'some indulgence which I cannot prevail upon myself to forbear'; his hearers were no doubt prepared for a frank admission of his notorious taste for good burgundy; but, if so, they were disappointed, if not amused, by his ingenuous παρὰ προσδοκίαν that 'the indulgence is too much snuff, to which it is well known that many persons of rank are not less addicted;...therefore I do not wonder that the law is ineffectual, which is to encounter with the habits and appetites of the whole mass of the common people.... If it were possible at once to extinguish the thirst of spirits, no man who had any regard for virtue or for happiness would propose to augment the revenue by a tax upon them.'[1]

Though Chesterfield and all the bishops were against the bill, it was passed into law: it was an improvement on the law it replaced, but was not really effective till it had been amended in 1751, as a result of Hogarth's *Gin Lane* and Fielding's agitation against the drink evil.

But this discussion was only a passing interlude in the parliamentary opposition to Carteret's policy in foreign affairs. Already in the first debates of the new session, begun in November 1742, came mutterings of the storm which was to prove one of the chief causes of Carteret's downfall. The obvious preference of the first two Hanoverian kings for the interests of their electorate over those of their kingdom had been a chronic cause of complaint, and these complaints were brought to a head when the services of Hanoverian

[1] *Parl. Hist.* XII, 1223 sqq.

troops in a cause as vital to Hanover as to England were to be paid for by the English taxpayer, whereby, as Pitt, 'speaking like ten thousand angels', declared in the Commons, 'this great, this powerful, this formidable kingdom is considered only as a province to a despicable electorate'. It is a misfortune that Carteret and Pitt were never able to cross swords in the same house, for in the Lords Carteret never met an adversary so worthy of his steel, but only brilliant debaters such as Chesterfield, in answer to whose philippic against the Hanoverians he argued that without them the Pragmatic Army would be too weak to hamper French designs, whereas with that accession of strength against them the French had been forced to defend their own frontiers instead of overwhelming Italy. In a second debate of February 1743 Lord Sandwich preluded his attack on the Hanover troops by a long disquisition on the constitution of the Empire, thus laying himself open to Carteret's tart retort about his own 'long acquaintance with that constitution, which I understood before the noble lord, who has entertained you with a discourse upon it, was in being', and a refusal to take up the time of the House by a 'superfluous disquisition' on that intricate subject. Then, speaking, says Horace Walpole, 'with great concern', he argued that we were as fully entitled to defend Maria Theresa as the French were to attack her without a formal declaration of war, and, since the King was the first to oppose her spoliation with his electoral troops, the least we could do in recognition of his courage as Elector was to take them into our pay. Both in the Commons and in the Lords the ministry obtained comfortable majorities, so that now Carteret felt himself free to carry out his ambitious schemes on the continent. Accordingly, early in May 1743, accompanied by his wife, he set sail for Holland as sole minister in attendance on the King.

Rarely has an English minister appeared to have such unrestricted power as Carteret had during the seven months of this year that he spent on the continent. He had won the confidence of the King, still a power to be reckoned with, by his knowledge of German and of the intricate constitution and problems of the Empire, by his support of the Hanoverian policy, and not least by his ambitious schemes for the dominating role to be played by England in European politics. It is true he had to reckon with his colleagues in the ministry left at home, but, by keeping the threads of all negotiations in his own hands, he was often able to present them with decisions already taken, so that only minor details could be altered by them. To us, accus-

tomed to see ministers, especially those concerned with intricate
foreign negotiations, accompanied by hosts of secretaries and interpreters and other officials, it appears marvellous that Carteret could
have conducted all his business abroad almost unaided. He needed
no interpreters, of course, since he was familiar with almost every
European language; but, as far as appears in the records, he took
with him as his only secretary the Reverend Caspar Wetstein, his
son's bear-leader on the continental tour and reader in German to
Carteret himself in his days of greater leisure, but hardly qualified
to be a busy minister's sole secretary. It might have been wiser to
take more and better clerkly assistance, for he was so much engrossed
with the details of his manifold negotiations that he had not always
enough leisure to keep his colleagues at home fully and promptly
enough informed of the agreements to which he was committing
them.[1] Indeed a certain ὕβρις took possession of him when occupied
in the congenial task, as he once described it to Fox, of 'knocking
the heads of the kings of Europe together and jumbling something
out of it that may be of service to this country'. Above all it was
a game at which he enjoyed himself hugely, so much so that he never
felt rancour even against the backbiters and plotters like Newcastle
who succeeded finally in cutting it short.

When the royal party landed in Holland in May 1743, the King,
accompanied by his second son the Duke of Cumberland, his mistress
the Countess of Yarmouth and by Lady Carteret, hurried off forthwith to his beloved Hanover, leaving Carteret himself to complete
negotiations with the Dutch at the Hague. There he found a much
better disposition to accept his proposals than during his last visit in
October 1742. The Emperor's defeat, the French retreat from Bohemia
and parliamentary support for Carteret's policy had removed the
Dutch doubts about contributing their quota to the Pragmatic Army,
now already preparing under Stair to march into the Empire. By
the end of May he had rejoined the King in Hanover, where he found
his wife very ill, and his time was much taken up not only by her
illness, but by the reviews, boar-hunts and dinners at which he was
obliged to attend the King, whom he saw killing several boars and
Cumberland spearing four more at one hunt. 'It is inconceivable
in what good humour and spirits the King is', he reports to Newcastle, 'how much he eats at dinner, how affable and obliging and

---

[1] Carteret's correspondence with Newcastle, reporting more or less fully on
his continental activities in 1743, with Newcastle's answers, is to be found in
Add. MSS. 22527, 22536 and 32700.

what attention he has to the most nice civility; if my Lady Carteret
had been in London, He had not enquired after her, but here He
has shew'd the attention of a friendly and private gentleman—
Arcana Arcanorum.' With Cumberland he is equally pleased 'and I,
who am not easily caught with young men, tho' Princes, begin upon
acquaintance to have a very good opinion of him'. But such jun-
ketings were soon interrupted by more serious business.

During the years 1742 and 1743 one of Carteret's most persistent
correspondents was Prince William of Hesse, brother of Carteret's
old friend Frederick, King of Sweden;[1] who was also Landgrave
of Hesse Cassel. As king, Frederick was now closely allied with the
French, who had supported him in his differences with Russia; as
Landgrave, he had hired 6000 of his Hessians to England—a characteristic example of the international topsy-turvydom of the period—
leaving the details for the march of these Hessians to be arranged with
the English ministers by his brother William. But Prince William
was by no means content with this subordinate role, and assumed
to himself the task of pacifying Europe. Coming to London in 1740
to arrange details of the Hessian treaty and to attend the marriage
of his own son William with George II's daughter Mary, he thereafter felt himself entitled to be constantly giving advice to the English
ministers.[2] Unfortunately he had from the first conceived the idea
that Maria Theresa's prospects were hopeless and that the only means
of restoring peace was for her to yield all along the line. Before
Carteret assumed office he had been writing to Harrington begging
that George II should make her see the need of a dictated peace,
and, even when, at the end of January 1742, her troops were marching
into Bavaria, he insisted that England should persuade her to give
way, and, as a sop to England, suggested that the puppet Emperor
would obligingly mediate between England and Spain. When
Carteret assumed office he politely expressed the King's obligations
to the Prince for his kind suggestions, but assured him that we were
not prepared to let France give the law to Europe. In answer to
further absurd proposals from Prince William he told him roundly
that England and Holland looked on 'la Maison d'Autriche comme
la cause de l'Empire et de l'Europe, comme celle de la Foy et de
la sureté publique'; and that in view of our treaty obligations to

[1] See above, ch. II.
[2] The correspondence between Prince William and the English ministers is to
be found in Add. MSS. 22527. Hervey has details about the Princess Mary's
marriage.

the Queen it would not beseem us to act as neutral mediators, still less at a time when she was regaining ground and when the troops promised to the Bavarian Emperor by princes of the Diet were very unlikely to be forthcoming. But Prince William, impervious to rebuffs, for the rest of the year kept bombarding Carteret with fresh proposals on behalf of the Emperor, while Carteret, ignoring these, kept urging the Prince to hasten the march of the Hessian contingent to join the Pragmatic Army.

Within a week, however, of Carteret's arrival at Hanover, this self-appointed negotiator appeared there, fresh from a tour to various German courts, including Frederic II's, with further proposals from the Emperor for his own rehabilitation. 'Touché des maux que la guerre fait souffrir à mon Peuple et ceux dont l'Empire est menacé' wrote the Emperor in a letter entrusted to Prince William for George II; he declared himself willing to sacrifice his own interests and leave the terms of his peace with Queen Maria Theresa to the King, provided they were honourable and suitable to his Imperial dignity. But it appeared that among these 'honourable' terms were still the cession of parts of the Queen's dominions, and a new proposal, apparently approved of by Frederic II, to secularize some of the ecclesiastical states of the Empire and hand them over to the Emperor to provide him with a revenue of some six million crowns. Carteret, with the King's full assent and with Newcastle's subsequent approval, made short shrift of such outrageous demands: 'not a village' of Maria Theresa's would be given to the Emperor, nor would the King as Elector do anything to prejudice any state of the Empire, whether Protestant or Catholic, by its secularization for such a purpose: if the Emperor really wanted peace, he should show it by abandoning such claims and detach himself publicly from France. Carteret's only concession was that if Charles VII, now a fugitive from Bavaria, chose to take refuge in his Imperial city of Frankfort, he would be unmolested there, but if he were intercepted before he reached that city, the King could not be blamed. Prince William's report, as Carteret drily observed, would not be 'fort consolant' to the Emperor. By the beginning of June his French allies had been driven out of Bavaria and the Austrians were in possession of it, and also of the Palatinate: Stair had brought the Pragmatic Army to Aschaffenburg on the Main, whence he hoped either to cut up de Broglie's army retreating from Bohemia or to oppose another French army under de Noailles sent across the Rhine to give a helping hand to de Broglie.

So at the end of June George II, a still martial veteran of Marlborough's wars, decided to join his Pragmatic Army and take part in the hoped-for victory. Carteret of course accompanied him and was quartered with the King in the castle of Aschaffenburg, whence he had a full view of Noailles' army only three miles away across the river. 'The whole Pragmatic Army', he writes, 'is under arms, and we are all booted: this is something different from Hounslow, but as my good fortune began there, I don't think it will end here.'[1] The French and English, not being officially at war, were for the time being on the best of terms with one another, mutually exchanging deserters or stragglers from each others' armies 'with much civility' says Carteret; while even after Dettingen, where they had met in battle, though only as auxiliaries to the Emperor and Maria Theresa respectively, the same courtesies continued. Carteret, sending over to Noailles the Marquis de Fénélon's son, a wounded prisoner in the battle, reminds him that many years ago they met in Paris and that he is still 'exempt de tous préjugés nationnaires [et] au dessus de la moindre démarche contraire à la bonne foi et à la candeur dont j'ay toujours usé envers ami et ennemi'; on another occasion he sends back a thieving and horse-robbing French valet 'wanted' in the French camp.

But such courtesies did not interfere with more serious business. In view of the numerical inferiority of the Pragmatic Army, the King had specially ordered Stair to keep all his forces together during his advance. But Stair, as cantankerous in the field as in diplomacy, had disobeyed these orders and marched on without waiting for Hessian and Hanoverian regiments still at Hanau, farther down the river Main. Moreover, the position he had chosen for the King's headquarters at Aschaffenburg was not at all secure. So George decided to risk a flank march in face of Noailles's superior army back to Hanau. Setting out on this flank march the King found a strong French detachment facing him at Dettingen about half-way, with Noailles's main army within easy cannon-shot of him across the river on his left. Nevertheless, by bad generalship on the French side and spirited resistance by the Pragmatic Army, the King routed the French and had his way clear to Hanau. During the battle Carteret's coach was drawn up on a road by a wood with a 'great guard' to protect him; next to him was an invalided officer who said 'he never saw so much anxiety in anybody's countenance in his

[1] Carteret's good fortune at Hounslow does not appear to have been recorded.

whole life' as to the safety of the King.[1] Later Carteret's meditations were interrupted by the Archbishop Elector of Mainz's envoy, who thrust his head in at the coach window, shouting, 'Milord, je proteste contre toute violence', a sentiment with which Carteret, always more inclined to gain his ends by diplomacy than on the battlefield, no doubt heartily agreed.

However, his first duty on reaching Hanau was to send an account of the battle to Newcastle. He himself was not satisfied with this composition, which he afterwards described as 'a letter expressed in terms not fit for a tallow-chandler to have used', but it gives a clear account of the engagement, dwelling especially on George's courage 'on foot and sword in hand', when he led the English infantry on the right wing. Any shortcomings in the despatch may well be excused by the circumstances in which Carteret composed it, 'in a poor cottage' by the roadside, where he had taken shelter with the Austrian general Neipperg on the night of the battle,[2] and still more since he had just received news from Hanover of his beloved wife's sudden death as she was playing the harp. At any rate he turned over to his secretary Wetstein the official account for publication in the *Gazette*.[3]

Had Pitt been with the victorious army at Hanau instead of Carteret, he would certainly have supported Stair's proposal to undertake 'something very useful to the Common Cause...against the French army,' defeated as it then was and dispersed in scattered posts, and so perhaps have saved five more years of dreary and aimless warfare.[4] But Carteret had never been a cornet of horse: his training had been at Stockholm, where, maybe, he had come to believe that wars could always be avoided by vigorous diplomacy. At any rate when, only a week after Dettingen, his pertinacious correspondent, William of Hesse, came with fresh proposals, he at once cast aside all thought of decisive military operations and threw himself optimistically into what proved a morass of negotiations. As a military correspondent with the army at Hanau wrote to

[1] *H. MSS. Frankland-Russell-Astley*, p. 266.
[2] Add. MSS. 22537, f. 291. This volume contains Stair's correspondence with Carteret.
[3] Add. MSS. 32417, f. 17.
[4] Stair's proposal is to be found in Add. MSS. 22537, f. 338. In September, after other much less promising proposals of his had been turned down, Stair sent the King a memorial recounting his grievances and asking for permission to 'retire to his plough': a permission readily granted him. See *Stair Annals*, II, 454–6.

England: 'Our able and mighty minister, as we hear, is no less than sixteen hours out of the twenty-four busy with pen, ink and paper. Schemes of pacification must doubtless be the result of his present labours.'[1]

His negotiations with Prince William were the subject of considerable controversy at the time, and subsequently were one of the causes of Carteret's fall from power, so must be dealt with in some detail. At their first conference on 6 July (N.S.) 1743 the Prince proposed as a basis for discussion:

1. That the Emperor should dismiss the French troops supporting him in his pretensions to the Habsburg dominions.

2. That when the French troops had left Germany, Bavaria should be restored to him, and the Austrian troops should leave the Empire.

3. That the Emperor should receive a sufficient revenue to maintain his troops and support his Imperial dignity.

4. That the Empire and other mediating powers, including England, should arrange a solid peace.

5 and 6. Provisions for a general amnesty and exchange of prisoners of war.

To these proposals Carteret replied that he could not act without Maria Theresa, who was not likely to agree to give up Bavaria at present. He then sent copies of Prince William's proposals to Newcastle and to Vienna. Nine days later Prince William returned with amended proposals for an agreement between the Emperor and Maria Theresa whereby Charles VII, as an inducement to the Queen to give up her conquest of Bavaria, agreed to renounce all his claims on the Habsburg dominions and promised to restore the Queen's vote in the Diet in respect of Bohemia; he also proposed a secret agreement between George II and the Emperor whereby George was to negotiate an accommodation between the Emperor and Maria Theresa and, as a sign of friendship and to relieve his immediate necessities, pay him 300,000 crowns, pending some arrangement, such as the secularization of ecclesiastical estates in the Empire, to provide him with a revenue of 6,000,000 florins for the upkeep of his Imperial dignity. Carteret in reply demanded as a *sine qua non* that the Emperor should insist on his French allies leaving Imperial territory and also that he should agree to a satisfactory peace. But he thought it very unlikely that Maria Theresa would abandon Bavaria unless she obtained some other compensation for her loss of Silesia, adding that nothing could be done about this scheme

[1] H. MSS. *Frankland-Russell-Astley*, p. 258.

without consulting Maria Theresa, and that he 'did not think matters were yet ripe enough in the great crisis of affairs, to make these propositions to the Queen of Hungary'. As to the secret agreement proposed with George II he declared that it must be referred to the Regency in England (practically Newcastle, Pelham and Hardwicke), but that meanwhile he was prepared to advance the first 100,000 crowns to the Emperor[1] on the understanding that he would break with France and clear Germany of French troops. In his despatch to Newcastle giving an account of these negotiations he waxes lyrical on the hoped-for results: 'all Europe', he exclaims, 'sees what a scene this is, and what a glorious figure H.M. makes', and predicts that if the Emperor, the Empire, Maria Theresa, George II, the Dutch and the King of Sardinia could, as he hoped, by his diplomacy be brought to co-operate against France, 'there is the probability and, I will venture to say, as much certainty as human affairs will admit of, to trust that, by the blessing of God, a safe, lasting and general Peace may be procured, not impossible in this campaign...'; and in a 'most secret and particular' postscript, adds, 'if so the King will make a great figure and yr Grace, and I, and Harry [Pelham], and Stone [Newcastle's secretary], may *quidnunc* with impunity and with pleasure, unless we quarrel amongst ourselves, which I don't believe we shall...most faithfully and affectionately yours, Carteret.'[2]

In this negotiation and in his optimistic view of its results Carteret made two cardinal mistakes, first in believing that this puppet and landless Emperor would ever gain the authority to unite Germany, and secondly that Frederic II, already restive at the motley Pragmatic Army's intrusion into Germany, would ever admit the strengthening of Maria Theresa, or that anybody but himself should take the lead in Germany. At any rate Newcastle and his colleagues took the sounder view that the Emperor was not worth gaining, and that if the French were forced to leave Germany we could no longer depend on any help from German princes and would have to bear alone the whole brunt of the war against the two Bourbon powers; accordingly they sent a decided negative to Carteret's proposals. Even before this decision reached Carteret the Emperor had retracted his offer to break with France and his acceptance of Carteret's advance to

---

[1] To avoid the need for a formal grant from Parliament Carteret proposed to take this 100,000 crowns from the Secret Service Fund.

[2] Add. MSS. 22536, f. 119. This volume contains all Carteret's correspondence with Newcastle and Add. MSS. 22527 his correspondence with Prince William on the Hanau negotiations.

him of 100,000 crowns. Carteret himself in a letter to Newcastle attributed the final breakdown of the negotiation, first to Maria Theresa's refusal to give up Bavaria till she was assured of some other equivalent for her loss of Silesia, and secondly to the Emperor's demand for territory worth an income of 6,000,000 florins and involving the secularization of ecclesiastical states of the Empire. But this was not the last Carteret heard of this Hanau negotiation, which, in 1744, proved a fruitful source of controversy against him both with Frederic II and with the English Parliament. But at least one charge brought against him was unfounded, that he concealed the negotiation from Vienna: on the contrary he kept Robinson at Vienna fully informed of the negotiations and gave copies of the proposals and his replies to the Austrian generals at Hanau for transmission to Maria Theresa.[1]

Meanwhile Carteret was already busy with a far more important negotiation between England, Maria Theresa and the King of Sardinia, Charles Emmanuel of Savoy. Queen Elizabeth of Spain, flushed with her success in securing the kingdom of the Two Sicilies for her elder son Don Carlos, was now aiming at a principality to be carved out of the Habsburg possessions in northern Italy for her second son Don Philip. In the early days of the war Maria Theresa, facing the combined attacks of Frederic of Prussia, Charles of Bavaria and their French allies in Silesia and Bohemia, could not spare enough troops to hold her Italian territory. To supplement her resources she had to depend partly on an English fleet in the Mediterranean, to prevent the landing of Spanish troops in north Italy, partly on the help Charles Emmanuel could give her. Unfortunately the English fleet had not prevented two Spanish contingents from reaching Italy, and, though Charles Emmanuel's support had enabled her to hold her ground, its continuance could not be counted upon. For that Prince, faithful only to the traditional opportunism of his race, had stipulated in his convention with the Queen that he should be at liberty to repudiate it at any moment convenient to himself: and already in 1742 he had been receiving tempting offers from Spain. Carteret, fully alive to the danger of a Bourbon power in control of north as well as south Italy, and of the Mediterranean thereby becoming a close preserve of the Bourbon powers, was determined to prevent Maria Theresa losing her only ally in Italy. The negotiations for a definite treaty, to include England, as well as Maria Theresa and Charles Emmanuel, had begun as far back

[1] See Add. MSS. 32701, f. 174 and 23815, f. 33, and articles by Sir R. Lodge in *E.H.R.* xxxviii, 384, and 509 and by me in xlix, 196.

as the spring of 1742, but had been dragging on for over a year owing to the high price demanded by Charles Emmanuel, and still more to the obstinate refusal of the Queen to part with any territory or rights she ever possessed in order to save the rest. By the summer of 1743 Carteret saw that an immediate decision was essential. France was now joining Spain with tempting offers to Charles Emmanuel of a large increase of territory if he sided with the Bourbons, while the Austrians were still raising captious objections to any proposal for accommodation with that King.

One of Carteret's chief difficulties in negotiating with Vienna was the arrogant language of the Austrian ministers, inherited from the Imperial court in its palmiest days. They could not realize that the old tune would no longer do. On one occasion, after a succession of impertinent and dilatory rescripts from the Austrian chancery, Carteret fairly lost patience and instructed Robinson to state roundly that 'Written memorials may sooner or later come to be published, and the author of those that come from Vienna makes so little difference between friend and foe, and is so˙ entirely devoid of management, either in magnifying the merits of his own court or in vilifying others, that it would be impossible to answer his productions without a suitable asperity of style'. Then, with a significant reminder of the more popular form of government in England, he adds: 'It would not be to the interest of your court that this Parliament and Nation, in the generous efforts which they enable the King to make for the support of the House of Austria, should see His Majesty perpetually put upon justifying that very conduct to which the Court of Vienna owes its preservation.' The King, he adds, will persevere in helping Vienna, but will not allow his servants to be always refuting the chicanes of their ministers. The gist of this despatch he orders to be reported to Maria Theresa herself.[1]

On this occasion, however, Carteret was able to keep the negotiations entirely in his own hands by their transference to Worms near Hanau, where he could deal directly with the Austrian envoy Wasner and the Sardinian Osorio. Fortunately, too, in spite of the Bourbons' alluring offers, he found Charles Emmanuel more disposed to an Austrian than to a Franco-Spanish alliance; for that Prince had no mind to have another Bourbon principality established in Parma on his borders. So he had immediately informed Carteret of his adversaries' offers, with an intimation that he would have to accept them unless Maria Theresa would agree to his terms forthwith. Carteret thereupon summoned Wasner, showed him Charles Emmanuel's

[1] Add. MSS. 22529, f. 320.

letter and insisted that, without further cavilling as to terms, he should accept the proposed treaty between England, Maria Theresa and Sardinia. Wasner, faced with this ultimatum, agreed to the treaty. But this was not quite the end of the business. When the treaty was sent to Vienna for ratification, Maria Theresa was highly indignant at the concessions required of her: she had to give up considerable tracts of territory to round off Charles Emmanuel's dominions, besides Finale as a port on the Mediterranean; in addition, out of the £500,000 subsidy voted to her by Parliament, she had to pay £200,000 to Charles Emmanuel for the upkeep of his contribution of 40,000 troops (to Maria Theresa's 30,000) for operations against the Bourbons in Italy; and, whereas his £200,000 was guaranteed to him for as long as the war or the need for it lasted, her £300,000 was not so safeguarded. A further grievance was that she was given no guarantee either that she should remain in possession of Bavaria or that some other 'dédommagement' should be secured to her as compensation for her loss of Silesia. Before ratifying the treaty she demanded that at any rate her £300,000 share of the subsidy from England should be assured to her on the same terms as Charles Emmanuel's £200,000 share, and that she should be compensated for her territorial losses. Carteret met her to the extent of promising, by a separate convention attached to the treaty, to procure her 'le meilleur dédommagement qu'il serait possible suivant les conjonctures et le succés de la guerre' for her loss of Silesia, and that her subsidy of £300,000 should be continued for the duration of the war. But these concessions proved unavailing. When, on his return to England, the cabinet met to consider ratification of this supplementary convention, Carteret was defeated by nine votes to four,[1] and had the unpleasant task of informing Vienna of this decision. Making the best he could of a bad case, he remarks that when the concession was made 'the King was at a Distance and had not the same opportunity, as now, of observing the Dispositions of Those who must be Ultimately consulted [i.e. the ministers in Council] in the Performance of all onerous Engagements... [and that] in regard to the Temper and Disposition of the People here [it was regarded] as a reproach to the British Nation... and a Provocation on the part of your Court to the Parliament and Nation in a Country so jealous of its Principles and Honour', to require promises of a subsidy for the future after their punctual payment in the past: as to the 'Indemnification to the Queen for the loss of Silesia', the people here most devoted to the Queen's interests were convinced

---

[1] Yorke, *Hardwicke*, I, 322-5, has an account of this cabinet council.

that Vienna's insisting 'that we should do a thing, which according to the Events of War might prove impracticable, and that the Charges upon the Nation should however continue till that Thing was done, would extremely alienate People's Minds, and raise a general outcry against your Court, instead of that general Prevention in Her Favour, which has hitherto supported the Austrian cause in this Parliament and Nation'.[1]

Another objection, of which Carteret was to hear more in the following year, came from Frederic II, who, in addition to his grievances about the terms proposed to the Emperor at Hanau, found another in the absence from the Treaty of Worms of any explicit guarantee of the clause in the Treaty of Breslau which confirmed his possession of Silesia and made him suspect that Carteret was abetting Maria Theresa's intention to repudiate it at her convenience.

Successful as Carteret had been in his negotiations at Stockholm in the heyday of his youth, when he was working under the direction and with the full approval of one of England's ablest foreign ministers, these two negotiations conducted entirely by himself at Hanau and Worms resulted in no such success. He had in both antagonized Frederic II, whose power for mischief he appears to have underrated, and who made Carteret's two negotiations an excuse for repudiating the Treaty of Breslau and once more throwing himself into the arms of France, in order to assert himself as the real master of Germany. He had also antagonized his own ·English colleagues in the ministry, who resented what Newcastle called his 'insufferable silences' about his negotiations, due no doubt chiefly to his attempting to do too· much himself, without a sufficient staff to draft the despatches needed to keep the cabinet fully informed of his plans and activities. Still more had he antagonized the House of Commons, where he came to be regarded mainly as the inveterate supporter of the hated 'Hanover connexion', and became odious under the designation of 'Hanover troop minister'. No doubt his general policy was wise, in his attempt to isolate France, which he rightly regarded as England's inveterate enemy; and still more in his proud assertion of England's rights and importance, which had been allowed in the last ten years of Walpole's regime to sink to a low ebb. It was in this respect that he was a worthy pupil of his master Stanhope, and himself a teacher whom Pitt himself acknowledged as his master in statecraft.

[1] Add. MSS. 23815, f. 483, which also contains the specific alterations made in the ratification of the treaty.

Chapter VIII

NEWCASTLE HAS HIS REVENGE

When Carteret went to Germany with the King in the spring of 1743 he and Newcastle seemed to be on the best of terms, just as at the beginning of Carteret's first ministry in 1721; and these friendly relations lasted throughout the month that Carteret spent at the Hague and in Hanover. Carteret, jovially optimistic as ever, describes everything *couleur de rose* both in Holland and in Germany and looks forward to an early peace 'with the King acclaimed as the "Libérateur" of Europe'. He signs his letters, with messages from Lady Carteret and himself to the Duke and Duchess, 'most faithfully and affectionately yours', and, besides full accounts of his negotiations, retails all the gossip of the court. In his turn Newcastle was no less forthcoming: 'I write to you as freely', he declares, 'as I could talk at Stone's; but it is to you and you only'.[1]

These halcyon days of affectionate intercourse soon passed. As Carteret became more and more absorbed in continental politics and had his time fully taken up in attending on the King and negotiating at Hanau and Worms, he found less and less time to keep Newcastle and his other colleagues in London fully informed of his proceedings. On the eve of Dettingen he could not be spared to go to Hanover even on the death of his wife. 'You may easily judge', he wrote to her companion Mrs Favre, 'how much I suffer for my irreparable loss, and I should be distracted if I did not know that you had been with her and that she was affectionately taken care of by you'; he even had to entrust to Mrs Favre all the arrangements for embalming her 'dear remains', which were to be kept in the vault of a church until he could personally convey them to England.[2] After Dettingen, as he explained to Newcastle in excuse for his silence, he himself was so ill for a fortnight that he thought he 'should not be able to hold out'; then an illness of the King gave him renewed anxiety.[3] Apart, too, from these interruptions, his absorbing negotiations with Prince William at Hanau and then with

[1] Add. MSS. 32700, ff. 138, 173.
[2] Add. MSS. 32416, f. 410. Lady Carteret's remains, when finally brought over to England by Carteret in November 1743, were buried in Westminster Abbey.
[3] Coxe, *Pelham*, I, 86.

Wasner and Osorio, the Austrian and Sardinian ministers, at Worms, and his difficulties in smoothing over the differences among the commanders of the various contingents in the Pragmatic Army were more than enough to take up his whole time, without writing at length to his colleagues. Nor had he, as we have seen, an adequate staff of secretaries to prepare his despatches or even take copies of his confidential letters to London. When, for example, Newcastle complained that he could not understand passages in one of his letters, Carteret was fain to confess that, 'as I never keep any copy of my private letters, I cannot remember what your Grace alludes to: whatever my expressions may be I know my heart is clear, and therefore I thank y^r Grace for putting the best interpretation, which you may depend on is the truest'.[1] It was indeed not only to his colleagues that he was remiss in writing. Horace Walpole, answering his friend Horace Mann, who had written to Carteret about his uneasy position as envoy at Florence, told him to have no fear 'from Lord Carteret's silence to you; he never writes: if that were a symptom of disgrace, the Duke of Newcastle would have been out long ere this: and when the Regency were not thought worthy of his notice, you could not expect it'.[2] Such silence as to the details of his various negotiations was clearly not due to any reticence about his ultimate objects, on which to both Parliament and the cabinet he was perfectly open. Even Bolingbroke, one of his bitterest opponents, admitted that 'to his frankness this justice is due, that he never disguised his opinions nor his intentions'.[3] But, though perfectly open about the main lines of his policy, when it came to details and the give and take inevitable in delicate negotiations, he was doubtless not sorry to have an excuse for being somewhat sparing of his information to such muddlers as Newcastle. Moreover, during his absence from England, a change had been brought about in the ministry, which, for all his optimism and self-confidence, may well have given him an inkling that, in order to secure the line of policy he had adopted, he must rely entirely on his own judgment.

Had Newcastle alone been Carteret's most serious adversary in the ministry, he might well have surmounted the obstacle, especially as the King had the greatest contempt for the Duke. But behind Newcastle and his brother Pelham loomed the figure of Lord Orford, still regarded by George II as his safest adviser and consulted by him on two critical occasions during Carteret's ministry. Orford had

[1] Add. MSS. 32701, f. 96. [2] H. Walpole, *Letters*, 24 Jan. 1744.
[3] *Marchmont Papers*, II, 283.

no cause to love Newcastle, who had already betrayed him, but he had the highest opinion of his brother Pelham, his true disciple in financial and administrative government. On the other hand he had never forgiven Carteret for the injury he had himself done him in 1724 or for his powerful diatribes against his foreign policy in the last years of his own ministry. Writing to Pelham about him in October 1743: 'I cannot conceive', he says, 'what measures this bold adventurer forms to himself to secure success in the King's business. To stick at nothing to gain the King, to indulge him in all his unhappy foibles, and not to see his way through a labyrinth of expectations, which he must have raised, deserves no better title than infatuation; wherein, if he miscarries, his labour is all lost, and his credit must sink, with the disappointments he shall meet.' Then, alluding to Carteret's supposed affiliations with the Tories, he continues: 'Upon this ground you will be able to contend with Carteret. He gains the King, by giving in to all his foreign views; and you shew the King, that what is reasonable and practicable, can only be obtained by the Whigs, and can never be hoped for by any assistance from the Tories. He promises, and you must perform.'[1]

The first occasion for a rebuff to Carteret came on the death of Lord Wilmington on 2 July 1743. Unimportant as Wilmington himself was, he held the post of First Lord of the Treasury, which, as Walpole had shown, could be made the most important in the state. To succeed him Carteret urged the claims of his old associate Pulteney, now Lord Bath, but Hardwicke and Newcastle put forward a rival candidate, Newcastle's brother, Henry Pelham; and the King, prompted by Lord Orford behind the scenes, decided on Pelham. Carteret was naturally disappointed, but characteristically bore no malice for the rebuff. On the contrary he sent Pelham a generous letter of congratulation, admitted by Newcastle himself to be 'a manly one'.[2]

If I had not stood by Lord Bath [he wrote], who can ever value my Friendship? and you must have despised me. However, as the Affair is decided, in your Favour, by His Majesty, I wish you joy of it; and I will endeavour to support you as much as I can, having really a most cordial affection for your Brother and you, which nothing can dissolve but yourselves, which I don't apprehend will be the case. I have no jealousies of either of you; and I believe that you love me: But if you will have

_____

[1] Coxe, *Pelham*, I, 103–4. It is somewhat ironical that when the Pelhams had got rid of Carteret, they opened their ranks to several of the Tory opposition.
[2] Yorke, *Hardwicke*, I, 337.

jealousie of me, without Foundation, It will disgust me to such a degree that I shall not be able to bear it. And as I mean to cement an Union with you, 'I speak thus plainly. His Majesty certainly makes a very great Figure; and the reputation of our country is at the highest Pitch; and it would be a deplorable Fatality if Disputes at home should spoil all the great work.

I am, Sir, with all affection and Respect,

Your most humble and obedient Servant,

CARTERET[1]

But already, while he was still in Germany, Carteret had begun to realize that the opposition to him in England was becoming formidable. On the same day that he wrote to congratulate Pelham he also wrote to Newcastle: 'As I have courage, God be thanked, to risque, in a good cause, my natural life, I am much less solicitous about my political life, which is all my enemies can take from me; though I must own that my friends have been near ruining me at various times, of which I shall take care in the future, being past fifty-three.'[2] He evidently had not yet realized how industriously Newcastle had been trying to undermine him, and had been collecting from correspondents in Germany material for a regular vendetta against him. These correspondents' original grievances were the undue favour shown by the King to his Hanoverian troops and his neglect of the English regiments and their aristocratic officers. Lord Harcourt complained, for example, that, when he with Lord Delawar and the Duke of Richmond went to pay their court to his Majesty, he did not 'show the regard for us that men of quality might have expected'. But the most persistent and venomous of these tale-bearers was the Duke of Richmond, colonel of the Blues, a regiment whose conduct at Dettingen had, he said, been maliciously aspersed. He retailed diligently to Newcastle all the camp gossip about 'our dear Master's venal partiality to those damned Hanoverians', and about his wearing the hated 'yellow sash' of Hanover instead of the British red at Dettingen. Turning from the King to the minister, Richmond 'trembles at the thought of what will certainly happen if we are to be solely governed by my Lord Carteret', and tells Newcastle it is 'your duty to turn him out if you can...but then the *quomodo*?' concluding that the grievance about the Hanover troops would be the best stick wherewith to beat him, especially as the King himself could not well be attacked in Parliament. But even Richmond's animus was not entirely proof against Carteret's great

[1] Add. MSS. 32701, f. 29.   [2] Coxe, *Pelham*, I, 88.

qualities. After relating a discussion with him about the ministerial changes, when 'Carteret fell into a violent passion and swore that he had a better personal interest than anybody in the House of Commons and whilst in a passion talk'd in my poor opinion as weak as any Putt[1] did', he nevertheless continues, 'but that did not last a minute, and then he was the man of sense again'; and when Newcastle reproves him for showing some partiality to Carteret, Richmond is fain to admit that with all his annoying ebullitions he undoubtedly had great qualities; his final conclusion being that 'my Lord Carteret is to be sure a man of great parts, but surely sometimes his talk is so incoherent that (if one did not know him to be the man he is) I should not take him to be what he is; but I take it for granted *il se moque de moi*, which God knows he need not muster half his parts to do'. Newcastle treasured the criticisms without minding the qualifications, and told Richmond that 'Lord Carteret has no other view than his own, absolute sole power'; that he himself, Pelham and Hardwicke were willing to act with him 'in confidence and friendship... but it must be on the foot of Equality and not Superiority; of mutual Confidence and Communication of all things as well Foreign and Domestick', whereas his conduct to his colleagues was 'the most contemptuous Usage that ever was towards men of some consideration, and perhaps one time or another his Lordship may find them so in this Country....I believe such a Treatment was never before heard of from one gentleman to another.'[2] Carteret indeed, apart from difficulties of communication, was never inclined to wait before taking prompt action till his colleagues, 'timid warblers of the grove', to use the phrase of his even more masterful pupil Pitt, had talked about and around any measure that he thought essential.

Carteret's seven months on the continent had, it is true, finally established him in the King's confidence, but it had given his enemies in the opposition and in the ministry an opportunity for combining their forces against him. Quite apart from his 'obstinate silences' which infuriated his colleagues, especially Newcastle, a most effective battle-cry was found by his enemies in the employment of the hated Hanoverian troops, and the King's supposed favouritism to them. As early as February 1743 Chesterfield, in the first number of the journal *Old England*, had begun stirring up popular feeling against Carteret's alleged partiality to Hanoverian interests: 'I think', he wrote, 'that there can be no treason equal to that of a minister who

---

[1] I.e. country lout.
[2] The Richmond-Newcastle correspondence is in Add. MSS. 32701.

would advise his Majesty to sacrifice his great concerns to his little ones; because, as I think his Majesty's virtues have firmly riveted him in the hearts of his subjects, he is as sure of the Crown of England as of the Electorate of Hanover; and therefore every measure in favour of the latter, in prejudice of the former, is the blackest treason against the King and the people.'[1] Even before Carteret's return from abroad Newcastle had been suggesting to Hardwicke that the King should be advised not to propose a vote for the pay of Hanoverian troops in the next session, one of the five reasons he gives being that 'it will be an entire victory over Lord Carteret...on a point that will give us the greatest advantage, both in the nation and with our own friends;...whereas; if we go on supporting Lord Carteret...we shall give him great advantage over us, [and] dirty ourselves in his dirty work, of which he will have all the merit.... The only objection', he naïvely adds, 'is the visible difficulty there may be in carrying on the war afterwards', an objection fatal in the eyes of his prudent brother Pelham and of Hardwicke.[2] But they entirely agreed with him in seeking an alliance with some of Carteret's bitterest opponents in the opposition, such as Chesterfield, Marchmont, an intriguing Scottish peer, Cobham's cubs Pitt, Lyttelton and the Grenvilles, and even that fly-blown politician Bolingbroke. Then they could always reckon, as a last resort, on the support of Lord Orford, the bitterest of his foes, who in August 1743 had warned Pelham about 'your dear friend [Carteret] crossing you; for it is certain what advantage presence has against absence with *somebody* [i.e. the King]'.[3]

Thus when Parliament met on 1 December 1743 Carteret was left almost alone to defend his policy, especially against the repeated attacks made on the hiring of Hanoverian troops. Within the first two months of the session no less than three debates were held in each House on this grievance: and in both Houses Carteret was under fire as the minister mainly responsible for it. In the Commons he was personally attacked by Pitt as 'an execrable, sole minister, who had renounced the British nation and seemed to have drunk of the potion described in poetic fictions, which made men neglect their country'. In the Lords, with hardly any support from his colleagues against bitter attacks, especially from Chesterfield,[4] Carteret defended himself with a zest and vigour which many younger men might

---

[1] Dobree, *Chesterfield*, I, 101.   [2] Coxe, *Pelham*, I, 107.
[3] Torrens, *History of Cabinets*, II, 25–7.
[4] 'Chesterfield,' it was said, 'who never loses his jest, said [in private] that Carteret had at last voided his Worms.' Add. MSS. 9198, f. 66.

have envied. In the third of these debates (January 1744) Sandwich proposed a motion for dismissing the Hanoverian troops in practically the same terms as those of a motion already rejected seven weeks before: but, when Hardwicke pointed out that it was contrary to the standing orders of the House to bring up a question which had already been debated and voted on in the same session, Carteret refused to ride off on such a technicality. 'I am so confident', he said, 'of the invariable force of the arguments which may be produced against the dismission of these forces, that I cannot but wish for a proper occasion to produce them'; then, when some of their lordships urged that the debate should at least be adjourned, owing to the late hour, he was equally ready to continue or adjourn the proceedings. 'I am, indeed, enabled by the happiness of a very vigorous constitution', he boasted, 'to support the fatigue of unseasonable hours; nor shall I feel any inconvenience from attending this debate beyond midnight....As I am convinced, my Lords, of the rectitude of the measures which have been pursued, I am at all hours prepared for their defence; nor do I need any time for premeditating arguments which crowd upon me faster than I can utter them; but this conviction...assures me likewise that it is superfluous to take any advantage, and that since I do not fear that length of time can give those whom I am to oppose any real advantages, I am under no necessity to push them to a sudden contest.'

In these three debates Carteret did not waste much time in dealing with the factious opposition to the employment of Hanoverian troops. He reduced to its proper proportions the camp gossip retailed by English dukes and other aristocratic officers who thought their services not sufficiently recognized by the King. One such, for example, had come to tell him that the whole camp was in an uproar because an English soldier had been killed by Hanoverians, but when he came to investigate the matter he found that the whole story was a mare's nest. He entirely agreed with those who said that 'if England was to be steered by the electorate, it was necessary for the rudder to be separated from the ship'; but, so far was this from being the case, he declared, our hiring of the Hanoverian contingent had alone made it possible for the Pragmatic Army to divert the French from overrunning Germany and crushing our ally Maria Theresa. Hanover in fact was now subservient to England instead of taking an independent line of her own, as in Walpole's time, for, quoting the great Duke of Marlborough: 'the English may for a time be misled, but will come back into the right way sooner than any people on earth'.

Then, turning to the charge that the Pragmatic Army had won no decisive battle after Dettingen, he replied: 'If we have not slaughtered our enemies, we have obliged them to destroy themselves; if we have not stormed towns and citadels, we have compelled those who had taken possession to evacuate them; [we have restored our ally Maria Theresa]; and, if this has been done without a battle, the reasons for congratulation are not less but greater than if we had bought our triumphs with the blood of thousands and had weakened ourselves together with our enemies.' Turning to considerations of general policy he pointed out that Spain had 'forgotten that the lords of the sea were their enemies', enemies who had successfully shut up their army in Italy and had prevented supplies and reinforcements from reaching them: and after all, he concluded with accurate precision, their present enmity was due to the 'particular interest of a single prince or the private opinions of the present minister', on whose death or removal we shall have the friendship of Spain. Far different was the case of our persistent enemy France, the enemy always aiming at our destruction, whose 'ambition is hereditary and whose pride is universal'. But now by the peace of Breslau with Prussia, by the recovery of Maria Theresa, helped by the Pragmatic Army, the French had been forced to retire behind the Rhine: they will no doubt try to recover, but will only succeed 'by our indolence or folly, or become formidable...by our cowardice'. But though we must act vigorously we need not 'irritate our enemies by unnecessary provocations. It will surely be proper to imitate the French in mixing politeness with hostilities, and, though we oppose all their schemes, and disappoint their ambition, to treat them with all the outward form of civility. But the decency with which we shall mention the King of France will afford no protection to his fleets or his armies'; and he continues with the typical remark that 'In common life...injuries are more patiently borne, and more easily forgiven than contempt;[1] and it cannot but be imagined that the delicacy of princes is greater than that of other men'. Other gems from these speeches are his *obiter dicta* as to the reports spread of discussions in the Cabinet. 'There may be disagreement without discussion', as must always be the case among men differing in capacity, education, etc., 'who have all equal right to declare their opinion'; and his appeal to his hearers to 'disentangle ourselves by industry and

[1] A *dictum* he might well have remembered more often in his dealings with Newcastle.

fortitude'. It was ominous, however, that in the first two of these debates Newcastle pointedly abstained from defending his fellow-Secretary, and that, when he did speak in the last debate, he seemed to admit all the charges bandied about of undue favouritism to the Hanover troops.

The attacks on Carteret and his policy, especially in the employment of Hanoverian troops, were not confined to Parliament. A far wider public was appealed to by a spate of pamphlets issued during the years 1743 and 1744 and even later. The hunt seems to have been started by Chesterfield's *The Case of the Hanover Forces*, which not only attacked the hiring of these troops in this war, but also suggested that ever since 1714 British policy had been constantly deflected from its proper aims by Hanoverian interests. This was promptly answered, probably by old Horace Walpole, in *The Interest of Great Britain steadily pursued*, and as promptly followed by Chesterfield's *Vindication* and *A Further Vindication of a late Pamphlet* and *The Interest of Hanover steadily pursued*. This battle of pamphlets went on without respite throughout 1744, the majority of them being anti-Hanoverian and anti-Carteret and undoubtedly contributing to the unpopularity of Carteret's policy and to his fall at the end of 1744.[1]

Meanwhile Newcastle was once more at his old game, which he had played before against Walpole, of secret understandings with the opposition, and even of back-stairs intrigues with subordinates in Carteret's own department. There is, for example, an illuminating letter from old Horace Walpole to Trevor, the English minister at the Hague, telling him that Newcastle was not pleased with his despatches as too full of flattery to his immediate chief Carteret: 'for you must know', he writes, 'that notwithstanding the common danger, they are, if possible greater enemies than ever, and that appears in all the deliberations in Council at this great and critical juncture. The truth is that his Grace is generally not much esteemed; and his Lordship is generally, I am afraid, hated, not to say worse'; and in a later letter he writes of 'the perpetual and irreconcilable discord among our Ministers here'. Pelham himself, who was generally above such intrigues as his brother Newcastle delighted in, sends his own 'private thoughts' to the envoy, adding, 'Nobody knows of my writing to you on this subject but Lord Harrington and the Duke of Newcastle'.[2]

[1] E. v. Wiese, *Die Englische Parliamentarische Opposition*...1740–44, 1883, gives a list and epitome of over thirty of these pamphlets.

[2] H. MSS. *Buckinghamshire*, pp. 93, 95, 97.

Carteret's opponents even found support from abroad. That inde-fatigable intriguer, Prince William of Hesse, never forgave Carteret for the breakdown of the Hanau negotiations and was untiring in pursuit of his revenge. In the first place he drew up a highly coloured version of the Hanau affair, in which he attributed all the blame for the breakdown to Carteret; next he persuaded his brother, who, besides being the ruler of Hesse was also King of Sweden, to repudiate the treaty hiring 6000 Hessians to England and transfer their services to the Emperor.[1] More serious was a new *volte-face* by Frederic of Prussia. He had many causes of grievance against Carteret, who had never taken Frederic and his mushroom kingdom at his own valua-tion. Carteret, for example, had once remarked in his lofty way that 'as Prussia is a new erected kingdom, we do not reciprocate with them in signing treaties, as with the ancient crowns', and for-bade the English plenipotentiary 'to yield the pas' on such an occasion.[2] Then he was offended at the secrecy of the Hanau negotia-tions, to watch and to take part in which he had sent a certain Count Finkenstein; but George II and Carteret had been careful to keep this emissary at arm's length, so that he had to return from Hanau no wiser than he came, describing Carteret as 'un homme qui se cache, qui se déguise, jusque dans les éclaircissements que je lui arrache'.[3] But a far more deep-seated grievance with Frederic was the mere existence of the Pragmatic Army. This grievance was partly, of course, due to self-interest, as that army might interfere with any further designs he had against Maria Theresa; but it also had a more patriotic side since he really resented all foreign intervention in the affairs of the Empire and may be called one of the earliest exponents of the 'Germany for the Germans' idea. Indeed he had definitely complained to the English envoy Hyndford of the entrance into Germany of this army, 'dont la plus grande partie est étrangère', adding that 'si votre Maître fait la guerre à l'Empereur, je le prie de se souvenir que le Hanovre est à une petite distance de chez moi et que j'y peux entrer quand il me plaira'. Above all, Frederic was seriously alarmed at Maria Theresa's recent successes and suspected that Carteret's Treaty of Worms contained a clause promising her

[1] In Add. MSS. 22541 (Intelligence) there are many intercepted letters of Prince William about these Hessian troops. It was finally arranged that France should pay for their service with the Emperor (f. 238).
[2] In the case of 'ancient crowns', such as England and France, the two copies of any treaty were signed first by the English and second by the French pleni-potentiary in one copy and *vice versa* in the other copy.
[3] Droysen, *Geschichte der Preussischen Politik*, v, 99.

either the restitution of Silesia or some equally valuable equivalent in Germany.

Accordingly, when Prince William came to visit him in 1744, Frederic, already planning to ally himself once more with France and form an anti-Pragmatic League of German states to support the Emperor, was delighted to obtain the Prince's *ex-parte* account of the Hanau negotiations to use as one of the pretexts for a new *volte-face*. Prince William's version was that Carteret had never reported the proceedings to his colleagues in London and without their knowledge had withdrawn his offer of 300,000 crowns to the Emperor, who had been quite willing to come to terms; the facts being that Carteret had sent full details of the negotiation to the cabinet, that it was the cabinet council that had refused payment, and that the Emperor himself, even before the answer had come from London, had broken off the negotiation. Frederic, of course not in his own name, published an account based on Prince William's version, had copies distributed in Holland, Sweden and Germany, and instructed his minister in London, Andrié, to invite the chief members of the opposition to hear a reading of it: Carteret, he added, would no doubt find 'subterfuges pour se disculper de ne pas avoir profité des bonnes dispositions de S.M.I.', but such subterfuges would not deceive the English nation, for whom Frederic had 'une véritable affection et une estime distinguée'. Accordingly Chesterfield, Marchmont and other leaders of the opposition sallied forth, at night and disguised, to hear and discuss Andrié's revelations. These intrigues did not indeed escape the attention of Carteret himself;[1] who, when he met Prince William's envoy told him, in his lordly way, that he was well aware of the substance of this account, and showed no particular desire to have it read out to him from beginning to end, merely stating that there had been no question, as Frederic stated, of the Hanau negotiation during the proceedings at Worms. But Frederic's purpose of undermining Carteret's position was well served by the dissemination of this *ex parte* pamphlet, of which the opposition and ministerial opponents made full use in their campaign of vilification.[2]

But these measures of Frederic and of political opponents at home

---

[1] Among other sources of information was one of Andrié's lacqueys.

[2] The whole plot is exposed in Add. MSS. 22541 (Intelligence) in Carteret's papers. Full accounts are in Frederic II, *Pol. Corr.* III, 288 sqq. and R. Koser, *Preuss. Staatsbriefs*, I, 374–82, 432–55; see also F. Wagner, *Kaiser Karl VII*...1704–5, pp. 577–8.

did far less harm to Carteret than his own self-sufficiency and arrogance. Convinced that with the King's support he could hold his own against jealous colleagues, he hardly troubled to conceal his contempt for their judgment and ability. He once told Hardwicke that if he did not obey the King's command in two hours, he had another person ready to supply his place; and of Pelham he remarked in a moment of pique, that he had been 'only chief clerk to Sir Robert Walpole, and why he should expect to be more under me, I can't imagine: he did his drudgery, and he shall do mine'. It was at this time, too, that the need for stimulating his restless energy by ever deeper potations of his favourite burgundy wines became most evident, a habit which no doubt tended to impair his judgment and gained for his ministry the nickname of 'the drunken administration'.

Nor was his self-confidence abated when, in April 1744, at the age of fifty-four, less than a year after his first wife's death, he won as his second bride Lady Sophia Fermor, a girl of twenty-four and the reigning beauty, who had been expected to marry Newcastle's nephew and heir Lord Lincoln. It was on this occasion that the following verses were handed round polite society:

> The beauty like the Scripture feast
>   To which the invited never came,
> Deprived of its intended guest,
>   Was given to the old and lame.

Horace Walpole, as one might expect, made very merry about this marriage, all the more as Lady Pomfret, Sophia's mother, was a noted blue-stocking and bore, 'who will think to govern her son-in-law out of Froissart', which she had translated. 'The chief entertainment', he writes to Horace Mann, 'has been the nuptials of our great Quixote and the fair Sophia. On the point of matrimony she fell ill of a Scarlet fever, and was given over, while he had the gout, but heroically sent her word, that if she was well, he *would* be so. They corresponded every day, and he used to plague the Cabinet Council with reading her letters to them. Last night they were married; and as all he does must have a particular air in it, they supped at Lord Pomfret's: at twelve, Lady Granville [his mother 'the Dragon'] and all his family went to bed, but the porter: then my Lord went home and waited for her in the lodge: she came alone in a hackney chair, met him in the hall, and was led up the back-stairs to bed.'[1] Carteret himself, elated by his successful wooing,

---

[1] H. Walpole, *Letters*: to Mann, 15 April 1744.

wrote round to his friends and acquaintances in high spirits: to Buys, the acting Pensionary of Holland's congratulations, he replies: 'je ne suis pas encore marié, quoique dans l'espérance de l'être dans quelques jours, ayant toujours été accoutumé à une vie réglée. La dame est de la première qualité. C'est Lady Sophie Fermor, fille du comte de Pomfret'; and finishes the letter with a plea for closer union with Holland against France. Later to Lord Tyrawley, an old friend then envoy in Russia, he is more expansive in the postscript to a business letter: 'Now for a joke. Was it not a bold thing in me to marry so young and so fine a woman as Lady Sophia Fermor? But it turns out well, with all the *Laudades* imaginable. Adios, lo muy atente y seguro servitor hasta lu muerte, Carteret.' Tyrawley replies: 'In answer to your joke, I always took you for a bold man. My Lady Carteret is certainly what your lordship says. I used to see her sometimes at the Duchess of Richmond's, and I thought her in person, understanding, behaviour, and by all reports the finest young lady in England.'[1]

Apart from this domestic success Carteret's schemes went very much awry in 1744. His public achievements had so far been solely in the field of diplomacy; but as a war minister he showed none of the qualities of his master Stanhope, who had actual experience of campaigns in the Low Countries and the Peninsula, or of his critic, Pitt, who had studied methods of warfare to such purpose that he could plan and direct his own campaigns, and above all possessed that fiery enthusiasm which enabled him to call forth their utmost from his chosen admirals and generals and to arouse the whole people in support of the national endeavour. Carteret's choice of military leaders for his own special Pragmatic Army was deplorable, nor does he appear to have taken any interest in the morale and efficiency of the navy, which at that time were at a low ebb. As for his colleagues in the ministry he antagonized them by his independence, without reducing them to submission when it came to open conflict. On the other hand his rival Newcastle, without any of Carteret's great qualities as an orator and debater in Parliament, with no real understanding of foreign, or indeed of domestic, politics, had one great purpose in life, to maintain himself as an indispensable member of the government, partly by his mastery of electioneering technique, which made him essential for the maintenance of a

[1] Add. MSS. 22526, f. 185, and 22631, ff. 33 and 81. The marriage lasted little more than a year, for this second wife died in October 1745, and was also buried in Westminster Abbey.

government majority in Parliament, partly by his mole-like success in underground intrigues against any colleague who had taken the measure of his incapacity and seemed likely to threaten his monopoly of influence.

In October 1743, barely more than a month after Carteret had disappointed the Bourbons' hopes of an alliance with Charles Emmanuel, France and Spain renewed the Family Compact, binding them to closer co-operation in the continental war. In February 1744, though France had not yet declared war on England, her intentions were made clear enough. In that month she sent a fleet of her own to escort a Spanish fleet, that had taken refuge in Toulon harbour, past Admiral Mathews's fleet, which had been keeping watch outside Toulon. In the engagement that followed, owing to the insubordination of Mathews's second in command, Lestock, who ignored his chief's signal to join forces in the pursuit, the Franco-Spanish fleet got away with little damage and landed troops in Italy; whereupon Don Carlos of Naples, abandoning his enforced neutrality, joined the forces against Maria Theresa. In the same month London itself was alarmed by the threat of an invasion. A French fleet was known to have put off from Brest on its way to the Channel, and early in February news arrived that a flotilla of transports and a concentration of troops were being assembled at Dunkirk under Marshal Saxe, and that the Young Pretender had arrived to take part in the projected invasion of England, at a time when there were less than 3000 guards, horse and foot, quartered in London, and barely 6000 more within call to defend the capital. It was unfortunate that only a few weeks before Carteret, in one of his jovial moods, had said that Spain could do nothing and would be only too glad to cease hostilities, and that he had 'France in his pocket and could make peace with her when he chose'.[1] But happily Carteret's old friend Norris, the rough admiral, had been sent to watch the Brest fleet and was ready to pounce on it as it came up Channel: and once more in our island story the winds came to our aid. The French fleet was dispersed by a storm, which also played havoc with the transports assembled at Dunkirk. But it was a near shave; and during the anxious days of waiting there was something approaching a panic in London.[2] Then by the middle of March France had declared war on England and a month later on Maria Theresa, thus regularizing

[1] Droysen, *l.c.* v, ii, 24.
[2] Egmont in his *Diary* 26 Jan. to 31 March 1744 gives a graphic account of the alarm in London.

the absurd position of English and French, nominally at peace but in fact fighting one another as auxiliaries of Maria Theresa and the Emperor respectively. Thereafter Carteret seemed free to make full use of his Pragmatic Army and of his alliances with Saxony, Russia and Savoy in the struggle against the ancestral foe that he had anticipated with gusto.

At first prospects seemed hopeful. Maria Theresa, secure in the possession of Bavaria, was able to spare her brother-in-law Prince Charles of Lorraine to make an incursion into France, and Louis XV had been obliged to withdraw his troops under Marshal Saxe from the Dutch border to meet Prince Charles in the neighbourhood of Metz. That indeed would have been the moment for the Pragmatic Arn.iy to co-operate with Prince Charles by at once marching into the north-east of France and even circumventing Louis XV's main army at Metz. In May 1744 that hardy veteran Stair, from the 'plough' to which he professed to have retired, sent Carteret two projects for the invasion of France and the capture of Paris. These were duly forwarded to the allied commanders of the Pragmatic Army, but it was not till September, far too late for any such advance, that they were returned to London as 'téméraires, impraticables, contraires à toutes Règles sensées de guerre'.[1] Anyhow it was perhaps as well that no such bold adventure was attempted. In the previous year the presence of the King and Carteret had alone been able to impart some unity of purpose and warlike spirit into the motley crew of which the Pragmatic Army was composed: unfortunately this year, owing to the threat of another attempt of invasion by France and the Young Pretender, neither the King nor Carteret were able to leave England to inspire it with some spirit of adventure. The Dutch, as usual, were behindhand in providing their quota of troops, and even when Marshal Saxe was threatening their own borders would not commit themselves to a declaration of war against France; still less were they prepared to move beyond their own line of Barrier fortresses. Wade, the English commander, though exactly the same age as his predecessor Stair, both being septuagenarians, had none of that fiery marshal's vigour, unregulated though it may have been; indeed he found it difficult to ride his horse without undue fatigue, and was quite incompetent to hold his own against his Austrian and Dutch colleagues, Aremberg and Nassau; it was also hinted that being 'fort protégé par MM. Walpole...qui ont tout crédit sur M. Wade...[il] a quelques vues contraires à My Lord

[1] Add. MSS. 22538, ff. 102, 285.

Carteret lui-même'.[1] Finally, in July Carteret had to write to him in two successive letters that it was 'His Majesty's pleasure that the army in Flanders should no longer remain inactive...and his positive command...forthwith [to] enter upon Action...and march up to the Enemy and attack him with a Spirit suitable to the glory of the British Nation'.[2] But nothing would do to galvanize the Pragmatic Army into life: so Marshal Saxe, free to return to the Low Countries by the recall of Prince Charles of Lorraine to defend Maria Theresa's possessions nearer home, was able to resume his successful campaign against the Barrier fortresses; and Wade, an impotent observer of these victories, in October requested and obtained leave to return to England.

To add to England's difficulties Frederic II chose this moment to re-enter the war against Maria Theresa, in co-operation with France. He had, as we have seen, many grievances against England, and especially Carteret, whom he directly attacked in the manifesto he published to justify his action, accusing him of having caused the breakdown of the Hanau negotiations and the Emperor's desperate plight, and of having encouraged Maria Theresa, if not to recover Silesia, at least to find some compensation in Germany; above all he renewed his complaints of the Pragmatic Army's activities on German soil, of which he regarded himself as the chief protector. He had delayed taking action for almost a year since Hanau, because he wanted French money to assist him and was anxious to give an entirely German façade to his new offensive by forming a general confederation of German states in a Union of Frankfort. His preparations were also somewhat delayed by France's support of the Pretender, since he did not wish to appear as assisting a Roman Catholic to recover the throne of the chief Protestant power; and by his failure to bring about a palace revolution in Russia, thanks to the action of the pro-English chancellor Bestuzhef. Moreover, he had received only a moderate response from the German states for his Union of Frankfort, Saxony, the most important state after his own and Hanover, pointedly standing out and adhering to Maria Theresa.[3]

However, by August 1744, he felt ready to throw off the mask and once more invaded Bohemia. Maria Theresa, hard pressed at home, had to recall Prince Charles from the Rhine and some of her troops

[1] Add. MSS. 22538, f. 268.   [2] Ib. ff. 197, 214.
[3] The best account of Frederic's manœuvres before renewing hostilities against Maria Theresa is to be found in F. Wagner, l.c. pp. 466–563.

from Italy, and even then had to evacuate Bavaria and could not prevent Frederic from capturing Prague, while Saxe was pursuing his victorious course in the Low Countries. In Italy she was no better off: her troops under Prince Lobkovitz after advancing to the borders of Don Carlos's kingdom of Naples were driven back into their own territory in the Milanese, while Charles Emmanuel in September sustained a crushing defeat outside his own capital Turin, and was only saved by the retreat of the 'Gallispan army', as it was called, into their own borders on the approach of winter.

Thus all Carteret's great schemes for the reinstatement of Maria Theresa in her rights by an ingenious system of continental alliances and the establishment of a Pragmatic Army to support her and overawe France seemed to have crumbled away. He had still, it is true, two strings to his bow, Russia and Saxony-Poland, both of which powers had entered into the orbit of his alliances. But neither of them seemed ready yet to take an active part. In Russia, though Frederic's intrigues had failed to achieve the palace revolution, the chancellor Bestuzhef, friendly to England, still had to reckon with the vice-chancellor Vorontzov, who preferred an alliance with France and Prussia, with the result that a waiting policy was kept up till 1747, when Russia obtained a more favourable treaty and actually sent her troops into Germany in 1748. The Elector of Saxony, too, though he had raised a considerable army, professed to be too poor to set it in motion without a substantial subsidy from England. Carteret was quite prepared to pay this, but Pelham refused to grant another subsidy, though in the following year, when Carteret had resigned, he made no difficulty in providing it. However, Carteret did succeed in persuading him to increase Maria Theresa's grant from £300,000 to £450,000, on condition that she handed over £50,000 to the Elector for the movement of Saxon troops against Frederic.[1]

As long as Carteret could show solid achievements, as he did in 1742 and 1743, he could afford to ignore the criticisms of his colleagues in the ministry and of Parliament. But his open contempt for most of his fellow-ministers, his monopoly of the King's favour and the suspicion that he was truckling to George's undue partiality for his detested Electorate had been gradually inflaming anger against him till at last it burst out in the autumn of 1744, when his schemes seemed all to have been brought to naught.

On his return to office in 1742 a pamphlet entitled *The New Comers*,

[1] The terms of the treaty are given in Pribram, Österreich. Staatsverträge, I, 686–94.

or the Characters of John the Carter... was published, which, though unjust in the attack on his honesty and his public spirit, had a grain of truth in it. 'John Carter', it begins, 'is a man of parts and vivacity capable of any understanding but faithful in none....When he was formerly postilion [1721–4], before Bob Monopoly [Walpole] took the reins in his hands, it appeared he was for driving on through thick and thin over hedge and ditch, without fear or shame, purely to show his own skill....At present [as Clerk of the Vestry]...it must be allowed he makes a much better figure than his predecessor. If he picks the pockets of his parishioners he does their business at the same time and carries on their law suits with more spirit and success than they have been lately used to....I do not find anything yet prevails over his love of country. But other thoughts, other pursuits are crowding for room and bid fair to jostle out by degrees his public spirit. John may do well for a twelve month, while his honesty is only on the wear, but by that time it will be pretty well whetted down and he must be laid by to recover his edge. This he soon does out of the verge of the court and gives deeper cuts to those in it than any other man of his age. Bob Monopoly hath often felt him and smarted for it severely.'

When he came back to office Carteret quite rightly saw that the country was disgusted with Walpole's and Newcastle's handling of foreign policy, and was determined to restore to England that pre-eminent voice in the councils of Europe which he felt to be her due. As far as he could attain this end by vigorous diplomacy he succeeded for the time being, and at any rate made England's voice, as it had not been in Walpole's later years, one to be reckoned with in the chanceries of Europe. But, unlike the elder Pitt, he was no war-minister: his choice of generals in the field was deplorable; nor did he realize the importance of America and India in our struggle with France, or of the rising power of Prussia, which he treated with barely veiled contempt. But perhaps his worst mistake was his 'contemptuous usage' of Newcastle, of which the Duke complained so bitterly: for, as we have seen, Newcastle's electoral and sub-terraneous activities could not prudently be left out of account. As a statesman indeed Newcastle was almost beneath contempt, but his nuisance value was immense until a greater than Carteret, the Great Commoner, had called his bluff.

Newcastle, ever since Carteret's long sojourn on the continent, had made up his mind to get rid of him, his fellow-conspirators being his brother Henry Pelham and his crony Hardwicke, with the powerful aid of Orford, the chief he had himself betrayed, in the background; and, as we have seen, had begun with his old game of interfering in his colleague's department. It is true that Newcastle's attempt in February 1744 to start a private intrigue with Trevor, Carteret's envoy at the Hague,[1] had failed, for Trevor had had the courage to tell his correspondent, old Horace Walpole, that 'my new master [Carteret] has rather coincided with me than I with him.... He set out like a minister who proposed to *serve* rather than *please* his master [the King].' In May 1744, however, the conspirators scored a first success in obtaining the King's consent to the despatch of a formal letter to the Dutch requiring them to make a declaration of war against France, a consent obtained without Carteret's knowledge, though Holland was within his province. When told of this action, Carteret, says Newcastle, 'took it patiently and seemed to acquiesce'. But a few weeks later, when other such incidents had occurred, Carteret, driving down with the Duke to see the King at Kensington, told him plainly, so Newcastle reported to Hardwicke, 'that things could not remain as they were [and]...must be brought to some precision; that he could not be brought down to be over-ruled and outvoted upon every point by four to one; that if we would take the government upon us, we might; but if we could not, or would not, undertake it, there must be some direction and he would do it. Everything passed coolly and civilly, but pretty resolutely on both sides....My brother and I...both look upon it that either my Lord Carteret will go out (which I hardly think is his scheme or at least his inclination) or that he will be uncontrollable master.' Newcastle's conclusion on the matter was that 'we must either take upon us the government, or go out': Carteret's 'that there was anarchy in Holland and anarchy at home; that the former might be removed by a Stadtholder; that in order to remove the latter things must be brought to a precision'.[2]

So the two parties in the ministry seemed agreed only on the conclusion that the existing condition of tension was intolerable, but for months allowed matters to drift in the same hopeless confusion. In June Newcastle writes one of his characteristic letters to Pelham: 'I have, you know, long thought that it was not possible to go on with my Lord Carteret with any satisfaction to ourselves....This opinion chiefly arose from the nature of the man; who never will

[1] See above, p. 154.
[2] See Coxe, *Pelham*, I, ch. v; and Coxe, *Memoirs of Horatio, Lord Walpole*, II, ch. xxvi.

have any fixed scheme of action; lives upon events, and has such a contempt for everybody else that he will not so much as vouchsafe to communicate his thoughts to those with whom he acts....His chief view in all that he does or proposes to do, is the making court to the King by preferring Hanoverian considerations to all others. By this method he secures the Closet.....There is the sore, there the grievance,...I shall not upon this immediately resign my employment, which...would turn the criticism of the world upon my immediate conduct, rather than upon that of Lord Carteret. My intention, therefore, is to remain until my friends think they can go on no longer...and whilst I do remain to confine myself to the business of the Southern province;...to go into the King's Closet as seldom as possible, to avoid being there with Lord Carteret whenever I can, and...to explain to the King my reasons for my particular conduct.'[1]

This contest between the two parties in the cabinet was rather one-sided, for Carteret's only ally of any account was the King, whereas the Pelhams and their friends in the ministry knew that they could rely upon the support of Parliament, which Carteret had never thought it worth his while to conciliate. It was by the bogy of parliamentary objection that the Pelhams were able to exercise pressure on the King, as in the cases of the Saxon subsidy and the pay of Hanoverian troops, though in both cases, when Carteret had been got rid of, they showed themselves quite able by subterfuges to obtain the consent of Parliament to these measures. But it soon became obvious that in order to get rid of Carteret more direct attacks on their colleague would be required. Newcastle complains, after one of his audiences in the Closet, that the King shows 'all the resentment that can be shewed by manner, by looks, by sharp expressions to those (and to me in particular) who he thinks have obstructed his views', which coincided with Carteret's, and concludes: 'Upon the whole I am of opinion that he thinks at present that he has nothing more to hope from us, and nothing to fear; that we will go on with his favourite Lord Carteret, and he will use us accordingly.'[2] Finally, on 14 September he writes to Hardwicke that 'the only means to act effectually for the public, and honourably for ourselves, is to remove the cause and the author of all these misfortunes, or to continue no longer ourselves'; and accordingly asks the Chancellor to draw up a Remonstrance detailing their grievances for submission to the King. The Chancellor soon produced the

[1] Quoted from Torrens, *l.c.* II, 37–8.   [2] Yorke, *Hardwicke*, I, 357.

required paper, which, after due discussion and amendment by Newcastle, Pelham, Harrington and the Chancellor himself, was on 1 November presented by Newcastle to the King. The Remonstrance made no direct attack on Granville—as Carteret had become in October by the death of his mother Countess Granville—but by implication suggested various measures in which he had been supposed to be remiss. These were principally: to insist that the Dutch should be brought to more vigorous action by sending an ambassador 'of rank and consequence' [Chesterfield was contemplated]; to enforce on them a declaration of war against France and a more vigorous participation in the war; to detach Frederic once more from the enemies of Maria Theresa; to obtain support from Russia and Saxony; to secure definite treaties with our allies stipulating the strength of their armies and their objectives, 'so as to prevent such mischances as the ill-conceived and unsuccessful operations in Italy'. Within a few hours the King returned the paper and when on the following day Pelham reinforced its arguments in the Closet 'the effect produced was sullenness, ill humour, fear, a disposition to acquiesce, if it could be done with Lord Granville's approbation, for that is the whole'. In fact there was nothing in the suggestions with which Granville himself could not have agreed, for he himself, by his personal visits to the Hague and by his instructions to Trevor, had done his utmost to induce the Dutch to take a more active part; but, presented as it was to the King by a clique in the cabinet, it had the obvious air of an attack on his previous diplomacy and on his continuance in office: and so it was taken to be by the King and Granville himself. At first Granville made an attempt to form a new ministry by inviting members of the opposition into the government; but most of them had received more alluring offers from the Pelhams and professed that 'his schemes were so wild, so impracticable and so inconsistent with the interest of England that they could not concur with him'.[1] So the King, faced with the loss of either Granville himself or of most of the ministry, as before in a similar dilemma, consulted Orford, who, too ill to come to London, sent a message advising him to follow the wishes of the majority. So, on 24 November 1744, only three days before the meeting of Parliament, Granville resigned the seals.[2]

[1] *Marchmont Papers*, I, 88.
[2] The Pelhams' intrigues, which culminated in Granville's fall, can best be followed in Coxe, *Pelham Administration*, I, 154–90, and Yorke, *Hardwicke*, I, 318–72, which give the most important correspondence of Newcastle and his friends on the subject.

'Who would not laugh', was Horace Walpole's comment, 'at a world where so ridiculous a creature as the Duke of Newcastle can overturn ministries?' But after all it is not so surprising. Newcastle, with all his ridiculous ways, his petty jealousies of men abler than himself, and his limited intelligence, had at any rate a quality somewhat lacking in Granville, obstinate persistence, in spite of humiliating rebuffs, in making himself indispensable. With this object the Duke was willing to put up with such rebuffs from men greatly his superiors in attainments, and to work hard at what he had the wit to recognize as his main asset, a power of concentrating on the petty details of elections and of patronage which brought him influence which could not be neglected. And if he came across difficulties from colleagues—from his own brother downwards—colleagues even so eminent as Walpole or Granville—he worked with the industry of an ant until he had removed them from his path. Granville, on the other hand, was too conscious of his supreme abilities, too solely occupied with the higher elements of government—emperors, kings and nations—to trouble himself with the waspish attacks of jealous inferiors, who resented his arrogant self-confidence. His great speeches in the House of Lords no doubt entranced that noble assembly, but they rarely penetrated to a wider audience, and he never took the pains to consolidate a party in the House of Commons, already the governing element of the legislature. To repeat Winnington's pithy phrase: 'Had he studied Parliament more and Demosthenes less, he would have been a more successful minister;' with the result that, as Egmont records in his Diary for November 1744, 'the clamour of the populace was great against Lord Granville, and he had so haughtily and negligently used his power, slighting all friendships and doing no favours to anybody and being confirmed in a character of insincerity that he had no party in the House of Commons'. Even on the rare occasions when he did stoop to intrigue, he was too inexperienced in the by-paths of politics to choose the right methods. In his first ministry he chose the wrong King's mistress as the object of his attention, in his second he did not realize that even the King was no longer powerful enough to shield him against a horde of 'disobliged' rivals such as Newcastle and Hardwicke. Great too as were his accomplishments and some of his successes in foreign politics, even there his arrogant language made him formidable enemies. Frederic II, for example, whose means of obtaining secret intelligence were almost unrivalled, no doubt came to hear of his contemptuous remark about his 'new-erected kingdom',[1] and was needlessly antagonized by being persistently ignored by Carteret in the Hanau and Worms negotiations. Thereafter Frederic carried on a persistent vendetta against him. Not content, when Carteret was still in office, with secretly forwarding to the Secretary's political opponents his own *ex parte* account of the Hanau negotiations, on Carteret's fall the Prussian King openly expressed his pleasure to the remaining members of the cabinet through his envoy Andrié, who was instructed to convey to Harrington his congratulations at the change in the ministry: 'Vous lui direz...qu'il n'y a que les principes outrés de son prédécesseur, le lord Carteret, son traité de Worms, le mépris qu'il a témoigné pour ma concurrence au rétablissement de la paix...m'a forcé de prendre malgré moi le parti que j'ai pris en dernier lieu, puisque, depuis le traité de Worms et le système violent que le lord Carteret avait embrassé, je ne voyais plus de sûreté pour moi....J'ai oublié d'ajouter à ceci...qu'il a ouvertement intrigué en Russie pour empêcher l'Impératrice de me garantir la Silésie [this was false].' Newcastle and Pelham were also to be specially congratulated, since 'le système violent de Lord Carteret...ne me laissait entrevoir d'autre perspective que ma ruine, avec celle de l'Empereur et du système de l'Empire'.[2] Frederic, of course, was then specially concerned in defending his own sudden repudiation of treaties in August 1744 by making Carteret the scapegoat.

One of the few in England who at the time deeply regretted Carteret's departure from the ministry was the poor, somewhat forlorn old King, bereft for the last seven years of his wise and loving counsellor, Queen Caroline, but who had found in Carteret a man who could talk German to him, who knew the intricacies of German politics almost better than himself and who so far from joining in the hue and cry against his own 'despicable' Electorate, was quite at home there and recognized frankly that in the interests of the dynasty, and no less of England itself, it had a full claim to our protection. In the end too it was left, as will appear, to Carteret's ablest antagonists at home, Chesterfield and Pitt, to recognize that in him was embodied the highest statesmanship of their time. Even at the moment of his downfall three of his opponents testified that he showed no rancour and quitted his high office with imperturbable good humour. Murray said of him: 'Lord Granville had behaved

---

[1] See above, p. 155.
[2] *Pol. Corr.* III, 368–70. The letters were to be read out verbatim by Andrié to Harrington, Pelham and the Duke of Newcastle.

extremely well, never having lost his temper in the whole affair';
and Chesterfield told Marchmont 'that Lord Granville had wrote
yesterday a very civil letter to Lord Harrington, acquainting him
that this day he would give up the seals, and that he heard his Lordship was to have 'em; on which he gave him joy'.[1] Even old Horace
Walpole, who had no love for him and had generally criticized his
policy, was fain to admit that though 'no doubt Lord Granville was
an overbearing presumptuous minister, and made his great court
to the King upon his German points; and in the Dettingen campaign,
either through his own or his master's fault, he managed but awk-
wardly: but truth obliges me to say, that the war was not better
conducted on the continent after he was turned out, nor did lord
Chesterfield bring the Dutch up to our propositions; and the duke
of Newcastle himself, under the wing of a military prince of the
blood grew as fond of the war abroad as lord Granville himself.
His brother and he almost came to a rupture about it in 1747 and
1748.'[2]

[1] *Marchmont Papers*, I, 86, 88.
[2] Coxe, *Memoirs of Horatio, Lord Walpole*, II, 103.

Chapter IX

NEWCASTLE, GRANVILLE AND THE PELHAM MINISTRY 1744-54

Newcastle had now got rid of the one statesman likely to overshadow him, and seemed to have the ball at his feet. On Granville's fall the ministry was reinforced by the admission of several of its former critics and established as the 'Broadbottom' administration. George Grenville and Lyttelton, two of Cobham's 'Young Cubs', and even a Tory, Hynde Cotton, were admitted into its ranks; but Pitt, the most effective of Granville's critics and Newcastle's only possible rival, was left out in deference to the King, who could not forgive his anti-Hanoverian diatribes. With his brother Henry Pelham, first Lord of the Treasury, Chancellor of the Exchequer, and virtually Prime Minister, Newcastle should have had no quarrel, since, except on the question of paying subsidies to foreign powers from the English Exchequer, Pelham was not particularly interested in Newcastle's province of foreign affairs. The Duke's former colleague, Harrington, now restored to the Northern province, though occasionally exhibiting a streak of obstinacy, was constitutionally too indolent to take a strong line of his own; while, except for the Chancellor Hardwicke, his unwearying adviser and comforter, the other ministers were of little account. The only weak spot in his armour was that George II, another obstinate man, though he had been obliged to give up his favourite minister Granville, had no love for those who had forced this decision upon him, and took little pains to conceal his distrust of his present advisers and his contempt for the Duke himself.

One of the main ostensible reasons for Granville's fall was his supposed predilection for the 'Hanover connexion' as opposed to a purely English interest. Accordingly, one of the first acts of the reconstituted ministry had perforce to be at least an appearance of cutting themselves adrift from this hated connexion. The subsidy previously voted for the services of the Hanoverian contingent in the Pragmatic Army, financed and organized by England, was ostentatiously dropped; but it soon appeared that this renunciation was a mere parade, since the subsidy granted to Maria Theresa was increased by the same amount as was paid for the Hanoverians, on the understanding that the Queen should nominally take them into her own service. Another grievance against Granville had been that he had failed to persuade the Dutch to take efficient measures for the protection of their own country against the French, or to join England in a declaration of war against Louis XV, though in fact in his first year of office and also in 1743 he had personally visited the Hague and made attempts, as Carlyle expressed it, 'to boost the Dutch'. Newcastle and his friends had nevertheless been demanding that an ambassador of high rank should be sent to the Hague to press a more energetic policy upon the Dutch republic, and, when Granville had been cleared away, they proposed to the King that Chesterfield should be sent on this mission, with a promise that he should thereafter obtain the vice-royalty of Ireland. At that time George II had a particular aversion to Chesterfield as one of the most pertinacious critics of the Hanover connexion, but finally yielded on the consideration that in neither post would Chesterfield be brought into personal contact with himself. In fact Chesterfield had no more effect on the Dutch than Granville or the regular envoy Trevor, and very soon gave up his mission to take up his post in Ireland. Indeed to the end of the war, even when their own territory was actually invaded, the Dutch persisted in keeping up diplomatic relations with the French. Nor was the war in the Low Countries conducted with more success than in 1744, in spite of the super-session of 'disobliged' or superannuated veterans, such as Stair and Wade, by the youthful Duke of Cumberland—at that time a close ally of Newcastle's—who to some extent made up for inexperience by youthful ardour.

Apart from any shortcomings in the government, all continental plans were entirely upset by the sudden and unforeseen invasion of Britain in 1745 by the Young Pretender. In February 1744, it will be remembered,[1] there had been a scare of such an invasion, when a bill had been passed, with Carteret's support, for attainting the Pretender's sons and the forfeiture of the estates of any who had correspondence with them. But that danger had passed away, and the ministers had since acted as if no such scare were again possible. So unprepared indeed were they for such a stroke, that the King, with Newcastle's co-Secretary, Harrington, in attendance, was actually in Hanover at the time, and the Duke of Newcastle, writing to Argyll, had to confess as a 'melancholy consideration that the government has at present no friends and no force to defend it',

[1] See above, ch. VIII, p. 159.

whereas, if a proposal of Argyll's to increase the forces in Scotland had been accepted, 'we might now have had a much more considerable number in arms for the government than can in all probability be brought against it'.[1] To make matters worse, just at this time Ostend, the most convenient port for embarking reinforcements from our army in the Low Countries, was captured by the French; while Tweeddale, the Secretary for Scotland, was pooh-poohing the danger and refusing to allow arms to be given out to the loyal clans.

With the return of the King from Hanover at the end of August a little more energy was put into the ministry: the militia was called out, loyal associations were formed throughout England, the merchants of London alone raised two new regiments, and Dutch troops were brought over. Even so the ministers could find little else to do but complain, as Hardwicke expressed it, that the King would not allow 'the old servants of his family to do his business' while 'his principal midwife' Granville, who was accused of pooh-poohing the danger, 'does not undertake to deliver him'. Indeed, after the shameful rout at Prestonpans in September, Newcastle wrote that 'the confusion in London would not have been to be described and the King's crown in the utmost danger'. He himself had ocular demonstration of the panic in the capital, for the rumour was spread about that 'his Grace had fled; nay, the mob gathered in crowds about his house and saw some of the shutters unopened, from whence they concluded he had gone, and when he went out they surrounded his chariot and look'd him in the face, and said "It is he, he is not gone"'.[2]

It was during the black winter that followed, two months before the Jacobite forces were finally disposed of by Cumberland's victory at Culloden, and while the country still seemed in the utmost peril, that the whole ministry, including Pelham, Hardwicke and the two Secretaries, Newcastle and Harrington, decided to throw up their employments and leave the country in the lurch. Their pretexts were that since Granville's enforced resignation the King had treated them with curt displeasure in the Closet, talking of Pelham's 'incapacity' and of the rest of them as 'pitiful fellows';[3] and also that he had refused to accept their recommendation of Pitt as Secretary at War. They were indeed fully justified in this recommendation; for Pitt, by his practical insight, his confidence in his countrymen and by his stirring speeches, already stood out as the leader he was to become

[1] Coxe, *Pelham*, I, 251–2.   [2] Yorke, *Hardwicke*, I, 461.
[3] *H. MSS.* I (Duke of Richmond), 115.

in the next war. But the King not unnaturally resented Pitt's criticisms of his beloved Hanoverians and oblique references even to himself; so, for want of courageous guidance from his incompetent ministers, he took counsel with Granville's friend Pulteney, Lord Bath. He, though without office, was still a member of the cabinet and encouraged the King in resisting Pitt's entry into office. So on 11 February 1746 the procession of ministers into the Closet to resign their offices began. The first to bear the brunt of the King's anger was Harrington, followed by Newcastle, each of whom gave up his seals; next day they were followed by Pelham, Bedford, Gower and Pembroke; the cautious Chancellor postponed the surrender of the Great Seal till later, on the plea that he was busy in the law-courts. But by that time the game was up, and the King had been obliged to throw up his hand. On 11 February he had ordered Granville to come and receive both Secretaries' seals and they were at once accepted: on the following day he proposed to give the Treasury to Bath. But Bath, who had at first assured the King that, if need be, he and Granville could easily form a new ministry, was a timid soul, and when he saw the long procession of resigning ministers and found that the City would not advance a farthing to him for next year's supplies—'no Pelham, no money' was the reported answer[1]—he shied off and threw up the job. So the King was compelled to call Pelham, Newcastle and their friends back on their own terms, which included office for Pitt.

'Lord Granville is as jolly as ever', writes Horace Walpole in his entertaining account of this palace revolution,[2] 'laughs and drinks and owns it was quite mad, and owns he would do it again tomorrow.' Granville's own account, as reported by Charles Yorke, is much to the same effect: 'Upon my soul I knew nothing of it. I was sitting quietly by my fireside, reading in my study [some say Demosthenes]; the King sends to me to take the seals. I saw 'twould not do and was amazed at it. But like a dutiful subject of the crown I obeyed. I waited on the King. I took the Seals, went directly to my office, wrote a few letters of form,[3] and signed a pass. That's all the business I have done. But give me leave to tell you, my Lord, you and your

---

[1] H. MSS. Lothian, p. 158; Egmont, Diary, III, 315.
[2] H. Walpole, Letters, 14 Feb. 1746; see also Id. Memoirs of George II, I, 171-5.
[3] Copies of letters from Granville to envoys abroad announcing his appointment are still in the Carteret MSS. Horace Mann at Florence complained that he did not get one: the reason given by Granville being 'To Italy? No, before the courier can get there I shall be out again'.

friends have done a thing not known before in any country, deserting the King by troops in a dangerous crisis....I could raise a flame about it, but I won't. Family circumstances, which have lately detained me at home, shall now engross me. I will go home, into the country, to my books, to my fireside. For I love my fireside.'[1]

It would be doing Newcastle no great injustice to suspect that when, though himself the senior Secretary, he allowed Harrington to be the first to resign in February, he must have foreseen that the King's resentment would be especially concentrated on the man who appeared to be the leader in the ministerial strike. At any rate it was so, for when, after Bath's failure, the King was forced to accept the Pelhams' terms, while courteous enough to the other ministers, he never forgave Harrington, so that when, as inevitably happened, Newcastle began to undermine Harrington's position, he had a strong supporter in the King. Suddenly, in the course of Maurice de Saxe's campaign of 1746, so disastrous to the allies, d'Argenson, the French foreign minister, proposed terms of peace—very onerous terms, which included the return of Cape Breton Island captured by the English, permission to fortify Dunkirk contrary to the Treaty of Utrecht, and the cession of Tuscany to a second Infant, don Philip, at the expense of Sardinia and the Austrians. Pelham and Harrington were inclined to peace at any price, since no help could be obtained from the Dutch even in defence of their own territory; but Newcastle, though willing to negotiate, was not prepared to accept such humiliating conditions. As a compromise it was decided to send Lord Sandwich, a young man under thirty and an adherent of the Bedford clique in the cabinet, to hold a watching brief on the course of the Franco-Dutch negotiations. Now, though Sandwich was ostensibly under Harrington's direction, the Low Countries being in his Northern province, Newcastle began playing his well-established game for getting rid of a rival, as his brother Pelham complained, by keeping up 'a correspondence with Sandwich ever since the latter went to the Hague without ever communicating or owning anything of it to Lord Harrington'.[2] As Newcastle had intended, Harrington was driven thereby to resign his seals as Secretary: but some sort of provision had to be made for him. Offered the post of Lord President, he refused that, as bringing him into close contact with the King, and demanded the post of Lord-Lieutenant of Ireland vacated by Chesterfield, who was to succeed him as Secretary. Unfortunately Ireland had been promised to the Duke of Dorset,

[1] Yorke, *Hardwicke*, I, 507.   [2] Coxe, *Pelham*, I, 339.

who at first refused to give up his claim, but ultimately was induced by Hardwicke and the Pelham brothers to give way to Harrington. To such shifts were the Pelhams driven by Newcastle's insatiable jealousy of colleagues whose co-operation he had at one time been foremost in welcoming.

It seems at first sight surprising that Newcastle should have chosen as his next colleague Chesterfield, who in fact was even more of a pacifist than Harrington. But Newcastle's sudden and, as it proved, short-lived enthusiasm for Chesterfield was no doubt due to their common antipathy to Granville, to whose fall nobody perhaps had more contributed than Chesterfield by his speeches in the Lords and still more by his pamphlets against his policy; and after Granville's fall Chesterfield had been the chief agent with Newcastle in putting the administration on its so-called 'Broadbottom' basis. From that time forward Newcastle had been carrying on a confidential correspondence with Chesterfield, not only about his negotiations in Holland, which were really in Harrington's province, but also about his grievances against the King. In fact the *coup d'état* of a mass resignation in February 1746 had been suggested to Newcastle by Chesterfield almost a year before it actually took place, when he wrote to him in April 1745: 'Your strength is irresistible if you exert it and must be submitted to. But then you must exert it effectually, and not let little notions of frivolous decency or compliment enervate either the reality of your strength or weaken the appearance of it in the Publick. You must mark out Lord Granville by exterminating without quarter all who belong to him.'[1] Such a sympathetic adviser was just after Newcastle's heart and the little difficulty about his pacific views happened for the time being to be in abeyance, since the French had broken off the peace negotiations at Breda, while both Newcastle and Chesterfield agreed in deploring our conquest of Cape Breton, the importance of which was appreciated by few except Pitt. Newcastle's ingenuous account to Hardwicke of how the whole affair was managed throws an interesting light on that arch-intriguer's methods. He first saw Chesterfield and found him willing to agree to a subsidy of £900,000 to Russia for sending 30,000 troops to help the allies, and also to accept the Secretaryship on Harrington's resignation. The narrative then continues: 'When I came to Court I saw Lord Harrington, who had just come out from the King. He told me he had quitted. I seemed surprised....He

[1] *Private Correspondence of Chesterfield and Newcastle*, ed. Sir R. Lodge (R. Hist. Soc.), p. 45.

said...that he told the King things could not go on, that the King agreed with him, that he spoke of my private correspondence, and the King owned he had seen all my letters. I went in immediately. The King said, "He has quitted, I am glad of it". I answered, "Who does your Majesty think of for successor?" "I have nobody; whoever you will"—and then of himself, "Chesterfield is the man that naturally occurs, but he differs so far from you as to peace and war, that can't do". I then told him Lord Chesterfield's discourse, but that I would not recommend him or any body His Majesty did not like. He seemed pleased, but said "I know him better than you.... You shall help to get rid of him, if I don't like him." I answered, "That is already done. The moment the King dislikes him, he told me he would make his bow."...Chesterfield accepts. I should have spoke to you and my Brother. I had no notice. I thought you must like this, and sure it is right." [1]

The Newcastle-Chesterfield honeymoon was of brief duration, for Newcastle was soon at his old game of communicating behind his fellow-minister's back with an agent of his own in his colleague's department. This time the agent was Sandwich, whom he kept egging on to a stiffer attitude in the negotiations for peace than had been enjoined on him by Chesterfield. As Chesterfield himself complained to his friend Dayrolles: 'I can no longer continue in a post in which it is well known that I am but a *commis*, and in which I have not been able to do any service to any one man, though ever so meritorious, lest I should be supposed to have any power, and my colleague not the whole'; accordingly, while intimating that he meant 'no sullen retirement from the world, but would indulge his ease and preserve his character', he resigned office in February 1748. Newcastle's next choice as a colleague was Sandwich, a man still young enough to take orders from himself without repining. Here Pelham took a firm stand: Sandwich was obviously too young and of too light metal for so responsible a post; and he gave a decided negative to the suggestion. But Newcastle, not to be beaten, sought to attain his end by a subterfuge. He proposed as an alternative successor to Chesterfield the chief of Sandwich's special group in politics, the high and mighty Duke of Bedford, not that he thought Bedford likely to be an accommodating colleague or without a will of his own, but suspecting that he would soon get tired of the drudgery of office and be only too willing to make room for his adherent Sandwich. And so it was settled: the King, not over-fond

[1] Yorke, *Hardwicke*, I, 637–8.

of Bedford, being placated by Newcastle's suggestion that he and Bedford should exchange provinces, so that Newcastle should take the Northern department, including Germany in which the King was specially interested. The result was not exactly as Newcastle had calculated; for, though Bedford took his duties as Secretary very lightly, devoting for many months of the year little more than a day a week to office work, he proved very obstinate in his opposition to many of Newcastle's views and much more difficult to get rid of than had been hoped.

One duty that fell on Newcastle when he changed to the Northern department was to accompany George II on his visits to Hanover in 1748, 1750 and 1752. These journeys, quite apart from the Duke's dislike of sea-voyages, were no light undertaking. On the first occasion he was accompanied by the Duchess, who brought with her a doctor in theology, another in medicine, a surgeon and an apothecary, 'suite très convenable', as that vivacious Frenchwoman Lady Bolingbroke remarked, 'pour faire les honneurs d'une table magnifique', while, as to the Duke's silver and gold plate brought over to furnish his table, she adds, 'on vient de tous costées voir sa vaisselle, comme chez nous le trésor de St Denis':[1] 'To convey all the tables and chairs and conveniences that he trails along with him', says Walpole, 'he has hired a transport, for the yacht is not big enough.' Moreover, both on board the yacht and for the land voyage to and from Hanover precautions had to be taken for airing the beds to be slept in by the ducal pair. On the return from the Duke's last voyage to Hanover Sir Joseph Yorke, then ambassador in Holland, records the following precautions taken for that purpose. 'On the day before they were to pass the sea a messenger came at 5 o'clock in the morning and drew Sir Joseph's bed-curtains. Sir Joseph, starting, asked what was the matter…."Is the King ill?" "No." After several fruitless questions the messenger at length said, "The Duke sent me to see you in bed, for in this bed he means to sleep."' For the sea voyage the Duke 'despatched the messenger, Cleaverley, to Rotterdam to lie in his bed on board the yacht that was to convey him to Mœrdyk, and ordered that the Duchess's bed should be lay'n in likewise. On his arrival at Rotterdam he enquired very earnestly whether the messenger was sure he had lay'n therein, which after he had swore to, "Well," says he, "but who lay in the Duchess's bed?" "One of the sailors, my Lord." "Very well, you are sure of it?" "Yes." "Well, that's well."'[2] We also get an entertaining glimpse of the

[1] H. MSS. Denbigh, v, 164.   [2] Yorke, Hardwicke, II, 175-6.

Duke's naïve curiosity at a review of the troops provided for him by the Duke of Cumberland after his landing in the Low Countries in 1748. 'As he passed through the army he hurried about with his glass to his eye crying, "Finest troops, greatest general." Then broke through the ranks when he spied a Sussex man, kissed him in all his accoutrements—"my dear Tom such an one"—chattered of Lewes races; then back to the Duke with "finest troops, greatest general"; and in short was a much better show than any review.'[1] On landing from his second journey in 1750 peace with France was already made, and he must needs get the French officials to show him their fortresses of Lille and Dunkirk. The account is full of 'His Grace's curiosity and the infinity of questions he asked....He tired...l'Intendant de Flandres...by walking him all over and under the works both of the Town and Citadel. He was in high spirits, of which nobody has a greater fund.'[2]

When Newcastle went over to the continent in 1748 he had taken the precaution of holding a general election in the previous year, whereby he had been assured of a perfectly docile Parliament. It was then unusual, except in the case of a demise of the Crown, to have a general election before the termination of the seven years provided for in the Septennial Act: but in a letter to the Duke of Cumberland in March 1746/7 he had given an ingenious reason for forestalling the normal date by a year. 'The memory of their late deliverance [from the Pretender], owing, under God, entirely to your Royal Highness, and their obligation to the King, for his...royal protection and support, under the dangers this nation was so lately in, is, at present, too fresh, not to give us a certainty of chusing a good Whig parliament. The uncertainty as to the success of the [continental] war, and the terms of a future peace, will keep all people in suspense, and hopes. Whereas, any reverse of fortune, though not to be prevented, and any final conclusion of the war, by almost any peace that can be obtained, would undoubtedly give strength to opposition, raise some flame in the nation, and render the choice of a parliament more difficult....What the course of a year may produce, nobody can tell. Unfortunate public events, or private disappointments, and personal views may render that opposition formidable, which, at present, is far from being so.'[3] So the elections had been held, not in 1748 but, as Newcastle suggested, in the summer of 1747. The only serious attempt to interfere with New-

---

[1] H. Walpole, *Letters* 14/25 July 1748.   [2] Yorke, *Hardwicke*, II, 24.
[3] Coxe, *Pelham*, I, 491.

castle's efficient electioneering methods came from the Prince of
Wales, who confided to an adherent that 'my duty towards my
father [is]...to redeem him out of those hands that have sullied the
Crown and are very near to ruin all....I hope...to rescue a second
time this kingdom out of wicked hands.'[1] But Newcastle's masterly
electoral strategy had proved more than a match for the Prince of
Wales's feeble opposition; and with a docile House of Commons
and a ministry adjusted for the time being to his liking, he was able
to start for the continent in 1748 in a far less trammelled condition
than had been the lot of his predecessor Carteret in 1743.

When Newcastle arrived at Hanover he found that Sandwich had
practically reached an agreement with France, but that our Austrian
allies were characteristically raising all manner of objections, all the
more futile since Marshal Saxe had practically overrun the Austrian
Low Countries and no help could be expected from the Dutch in
that quarter. Sandwich was now urging that, in view of the Austrians'
impotent obstinacy, we should come to terms with France and leave
the Austrians to come in later, as they would have to perforce. The
Duke would not hear of any peace without the Austrians and
stigmatized Sandwich, hitherto praised to the skies, as 'abominable'
and his proposals as 'wild, ignorant, indecent', thus justifying his
brother Pelham's comments that 'he first drives all men of business
out of office, and then, if those he substituted do not happen to act
according to his mind in everything, he quarrels with them also....
I have long seen no reasoning signifies a farthing with his Grace;
it must be an implicit resignation of your opinion to his, and a fulsome flattery of his own works that will ever bring him to be satisfied
with any correspondence....We all know he quarrelled with every
minister at home he was ever joined with; if it should be his fate
to do the same with everyone he himself has sent abroad I leave your
Lordship [Hardwicke] to judge of the consequence.'[2] Hardwicke's
comment to his sons on the differences between Newcastle and his
brother was that they were 'disagreeable to their friends and everybody else; [he himself] had carried the bucket between them for
many years, almost at the end of his line'.[3]

However, after shrill complaints from the Duke as to his own
treatment, the peace, such as it was, of Aix-la-Chapelle was patched
up by October 1748. It was an inconclusive peace, merely providing
an uneasy pause between the War of the Austrian Succession and

[1] Coxe, *Pelham*, I, 492–3. [2] Yorke, *Hardwicke*, I, 665, 668, 675–6.
[3] *Ib.* I, 629.

the far more important Seven Years' War, but none the less hailed by Newcastle as a great achievement, 'under the delusion I am thinking', he observes sarcastically to Hardwicke, 'that I have, almost singly, brought this Treaty to the perfection it is now in'. He is very sore that his services in attaining this perfection were not appreciated at home as much as they were by himself. 'Nothing I can say or do is approved by your lordship', he whines; 'I will not pass at home for a fool or a knave when I know I am not.... I am horribly hurt....I've done in three months what Lord Townshend and Lord Harrington could not do in three years....It may be vanity but', he adds with a glimpse of the obvious, 'vain I am.' Again, 'though I have been in the office [of Secretary] above four and twenty years, I have never till now been allowed to be myself.... I do not talk of quitting, and have no thoughts of it...but, if I am to continue, nobody shall be employed...in my department who shall think himself...wiser than I am', a dig at his brother Pelham, who had ventured the opinion that Sandwich had 'great merit in the peace'; and he magnanimously concludes one of these letters to Hardwicke: 'You shall always find me your affectionate and sincere friend, tho' at present your angry humble servant.'[1] There is something engagingly childlike in these self-satisfying outpourings: but he must have been an impossible colleague.

Pelham for the remaining six years of his life had indeed much to bear from his fussy self-opinionated brother. For, while Pelham, foreseeing that this inconclusive peace was only a breathing-space before another and more serious war, was doing his utmost by economic and careful management to husband the country's resources for the coming struggle, Newcastle was spending all his energy in securing, by subsidies, mainly at England's expense, allies, nearly all of whom proved broken reeds when the occasion arose. He had conceived the absurd scheme of procuring the election of Maria Theresa's son Joseph as King of the Romans to ensure his succession to the Imperial throne on the death of his father Francis, in the mistaken idea that the 'Old System' of close alliance with the Habsburgs would hold good in the next war. It was a costly scheme for it involved bribing a majority of the Electors. Cologne was at first obtained cheaply enough by an annual subsidy of £40,000, to which Holland and Hanover also contributed; but that Elector soon began to demand more and finally, being offered better terms by France, repudiated his engagement to England. Bavaria had to be

---

[1] Yorke, *Hardwicke*, I, 678–81; II, 13.

given a subsidy of £30,000 and Saxony £48,000, Pelham protesting against every fresh commitment, but feebly yielding to his brother's pertinacity. The best criticism of the Duke's plan was made by Hardwicke who doubted 'how far the giving small subsidies to the German princes in time of peace will secure them to your side, when a war shall break out. It will be doubted whether your money will really be applied to keep up troops, or rather to supply a vanity or profusion unequal to their own revenues. It will be apprehended that, when a new war breaks out, they will raise the market upon you, and having received small subsidies for doing nothing, will demand the larger when they enter upon service.'[1] Frederic of Prussia, the only Elector capable of delivering the goods, was ignored in this distribution of largess. Pelham and Hardwicke, as well as Granville, believed, quite rightly, that he was the only German prince worth securing as an ally, but the King's prejudice against his nephew, shared at that time by Newcastle, was such as to prevent any approach to him. On the other hand Newcastle at first found a strong supporter in the King for his subsidy policy to the other Electors, flattering him by the suggestion that, having made one Emperor in the late war, he would also have his successor to his credit: but soon even the King began to lose faith in 'the great system', which, according to Newcastle was 'to bring him the greatest honour in the world'. As for Maria Theresa, who was to be the chief beneficiary by Newcastle's plan, she took not the slightest interest in it. She was in fact already throwing out feelers to France for an Austro-French alliance, which was consummated in 1756 and removed all danger of another non-Habsburg emperor: indeed in 1765 Joseph's election as King of the Romans was obtained from an unbribed and unanimous College of Electors.

By 1751 the ministry at home had been once more re-constituted, chiefly to suit Newcastle's passing prejudices. It will be remembered that on Chesterfield's resignation in 1748 Newcastle had seriously proposed as his successor the youthful and inexperienced Earl of Sandwich, but, yielding to Pelham's protest, had agreed to the seals being given to Sandwich's patron the Duke of Bedford, in the belief that Bedford would soon get bored by the office routine and yield his place to Sandwich. But this ingenious scheme had gone awry: Sandwich, by taking a line of his own at Aix-la-Chapelle, had seriously 'disobliged' Newcastle; while Bedford had not only clung to his post but had contrived to secure the Admiralty for Sandwich.

[1] Yorke, *Hardwicke*, II, 19.

By 1751 Bedford, who constantly opposed his fellow-Secretary's schemes, had become so obnoxious to Newcastle that he was determined to get rid of him. This was not so easy as usual, for Bedford was too important, as a great magnate and the chief of an indispensable Whig group, lightly to be dismissed. So Newcastle, never at a loss for ingenious devices for getting rid of a rival, had the happy idea of persuading the King and Pelham to dismiss Sandwich, calculating that the proud Duke, taking offence at this slur on one of his dependents, would of his own accord resign in a huff. The device succeeded. On 13 June 1751 Newcastle sent Sandwich a curt note dismissing him from the Admiralty: on the following day Bedford's secretary wrote to Newcastle informing him that, though it was not usual for a Secretary of State to inform his colleagues of his own resignation, he wished Newcastle to know that he had resigned that morning.[1] By this masterstroke Newcastle had got rid of the two members of the administration he had come most to dislike. He then persuaded Pelham to rearrange the ministry to his liking. Anson, his special confidant Hardwicke's son-in-law, came to the Admiralty, a really good appointment, as it turned out. But Pelham jibbed a good deal at the appointment of Holderness, proposed by Newcastle as his colleague in the Southern department, believing him, quite rightly, fit at best to take orders from a Secretary of State in a foreign mission. But again Newcastle had his way, being convinced that 'though a d'Arcy, he is not proud, you can tell him his faults and he will mend them'; and after a few months' trial reported that he and Holderness 'go on purely well, and I have not the least apprehension that we shall not continue to do so. It is very agreeable to have such a companion, which never happened to me before';[2] so that at last the Duke had a colleague ready to follow implicitly his own ideas in foreign policy. Dorset, the Lord President, who had made so many difficulties at yielding his promised post as Lord-Lieutenant, now got his wish, while Harrington, dismissed from Ireland, finally disappeared from the political scene. There still remained to be filled the post of Lord President vacated by Dorset. For this office, *mirabile dictu*, Newcastle pitched upon his old antagonist Granville.

By this choice Newcastle showed considerable political acumen. For the Granville of 1751 was a much altered man from the vehement and masterful Carteret of the years up to 1744. After his rebuffs

---

[1] Add. MSS. 32724, ff. 358, 360.
[2] H. MSS. *Mrs Stopford Sackville*, I, 180.

in 1723 and 1744 he seems finally to have given up his ambition to dominate the country's foreign policy, and to have been content with reading by his fireside and entertaining his friends with good talk, good fare and plenty of good wine at his hospitable table. His appearances in the House of Lords were rare and then only on subjects that happened to have a special interest for him. Such, for instance, were the trials of Lovat and the other rebel lords, when he had two skirmishes with Hardwicke, his *bête noir*, insisting on the right of the accused to brief counsel and pay them out of their estates, which, he successfully urged against the Chancellor, could not be impounded until their owners had been duly convicted of treason and sentenced to the pains of forfeiture.[1] On the other hand he spoke warmly in favour of Hardwicke's bill to abolish the Scottish Heritable Jurisdictions and to supersede the lairds' authority over their clansmen by the King's courts of justice throughout Scotland.[2] In the debate on the Regency Bill of 1751 he took occasion to applaud the government's precautions against a possible attack from the ever-watchful foe France during a minority by a clause forbidding a general election for three years after the establishment of a Regency, since 'rebellions were best carried out during elections; it had been the policy of Louis XIV to foment them here at that season; and...among the secrets that had not come to light had been an advice given in the Council of France during the very last Rebellion, to wait for a general election'.[3] But the only subject on which he really let himself go was, of all things, a British Fishery Bill to encourage the herring fishery by a bounty from the Crown to be distributed by a 'Free British Fishery Company' presided over by the Prince of Wales. In recommending the measure he contrasted our own ineffectual attempts to compete with the successful methods of the Dutch fishing industry, expatiated on the excellence of the herrings he had eaten at Stockholm, and became almost lyrical on a present of Scottish herrings he had received from Lord Eglinton: 'upon trial every gentleman agreed that they were most exquisite both for taste and flavour, and far exceeding any Dutch herring they had ever tasted: yet they were despised by the country people; even my own servants could hardly be induced to taste them...but if herrings should once come to be frequently served up at the tables of the great, they would soon come to be coveted by the poor and would be as cheap and as wholesome a food as any they now use. I may be sanguine,' he

---

[1] H. Walpole, *Letters*, 1 Aug. 1746.   [2] Yorke, *Hardwicke*, 1, 614.
[3] H. Walpole, *Memoirs of George II*, 1, 121-2.

concluded, 'but I hope that soon our fisheries will bring us more than the mines of Mexico and Peru ever did to Spain, hopes founded on the excellence of our home-cured herrings.'[1]

For some time Newcastle had been casting a favourable eye on Granville as a colleague in the ministry. He had realized not only that his old rival had finally abandoned any hope of being 'the sole minister', but might even prove a useful ally against his brother Pelham in his schemes for continental alliances in peace-time. When the King gave Granville the Garter in 1750 he had made no protest, and in the same year was already urging Pelham to substitute him for Bedford as his co-Secretary. But at that time Pelham would not listen to such a suggestion: he would agree, he said, to anything his brother proposed, 'providing indeed that Lord Granville was not to be introduced into the Council', whereupon Newcastle desisted for the time being from the proposal. In fact he wrote to Hardwicke: 'I believe your Lordship and I agree more as to Lord Chester[field] than as to Lord Gran[ville]. I fear neither; I esteem the last the most, for the great superiority of his talents, and his right way of thinking in foreign affairs. But I opinionâtre nothing. Lord Gran[ville] is dropped. I will never mention him more'.[2] All the same he had formed a juster estimate of Granville's actual disposition than either Pelham or Hardwicke when he remarked to Pelham that 'My Lord Granville is no longer the terrible man; *Non eadem est aetas, non mens*',[3] and he was keen enough to observe that his intimate knowledge of continental politics would be of immense value in council. Moreover, though changeable in his affections and animosities, Newcastle was apt to be very persistent in pressing his momentary predilections on his colleagues, so, in spite of his promise to Hardwicke, he always kept Granville in view. Only five months later, on 10 March 1751, his secretary Stone told him that Pelham seemed floating between Granville and Pitt as successor to Bedford.

Ten days later the sudden death of Frederick, Prince of Wales had helped to precipitate matters. Owing to his death it had become necessary to provide for a Regency council in case the old King died before the next heir George (III) had attained his majority; and it was feared by the Pelhams and Hardwicke that Cumberland, with whom Newcastle had now quarrelled, and who was suspected of wishing to introduce a military regime, might obtain too commanding a position on the council. Newcastle was confirmed in his desire to

[1] *P.H.* xiv, 770.   [2] Add. MSS. 9224, f. 78.
[3] Coxe, *Pelham*, ii, 388.

secure Granville's co-operation by a despatch he had intercepted from Wall, the Spanish ambassador, to his court. In this despatch Wall reported that he had found Newcastle 'out of humour at the Prince's death' and very apprehensive of Cumberland obtaining too much power on the Regency, whereas Bedford seemed disposed to favour Cumberland obtaining the chief authority during a minority: Granville, on the other hand, had told him that ministers had asked him for his opinion, 'in order', as he said, 'to gain courage to move the matter themselves'; whereupon with a flash of his old spirit he had told them bluntly that 'it was proper to take such a resolution (without attending to private [i.e. the King's] affections) as might make the nation easy and the consistency of the government known abroad...if they did not do so, it were better to trust to Providence; but he gave them warning that, if they made a false step, they would give him occasion to declare himself the most popular man in England, though he had never courted the approbation of the people.'[1]

Accordingly, in these critical circumstances, Newcastle was all the more anxious to secure Granville's support, and succeeded in overcoming his brother's objections to his re-entering the ministry as President of the Council. Granville himself had no wish to be in too close relations with Newcastle as his co-Secretary; but in a conversation with Stone, duly reported to the Duke, 'expressed great friendship and affection for your Grace and an entire satisfaction in the situation [of Lord President] he was now entering upon, which', he often said, 'was more agreeable to him than any other could have been. He is', concluded Stone, 'I really think determined to give your Grace all the support, and ease, and satisfaction in his Power.' Accordingly, on 16 June 1751, Newcastle wrote an effusive letter to Granville on the 'agreeable command he had received from the King' that he should be formally declared President of the Council and on his own delight to be 'once more a Fellow Servant with you...founded upon a thorough persuasion that nothing will ever happen that can lessen or alter that Friendship which is now so happily and so cordially restored between us'. Granville in response dwelt on the 'absolute necessity of a strict union between your Grace and Mr Pelham...which is all I can desire, dreading nothing so much as disputes, which I will never occasion or promote'.[2] And, as will appear, Granville remained true in essentials to his word. He had ceased to have any ambition to domineer over the cabinet,

---

[1] *H. MSS.* VIII, App. Part i, 284.
[2] Add. MSS. 32724, ff. 175, 362, 372-4.

being content with the role of conciliator and prudent adviser in what, as he saw them, were the country's best interests.

As Lord President he became third in precedence of the King's servants, after the Chancellor and the Lord Treasurer, an office now in abeyance. Almost his only official function was to preside over the Committee of the Privy Council dealing with appeals or other business from the islands of Jersey, Guernsey and Man, and from the Plantations in America. To quote Blackstone,[1] 'whenever a question arises between the provinces in America or elsewhere, as concerning the extent of their charters or the like, the King in Council exercises original jurisdiction. And so likewise, when any person claims an island or a province in the nature of a feodal principality by grant from the King or his ancestors, the determination of that right belongs to His Majesty in Council.' Granville, as one of the former proprietors of a large territory in Carolina, was naturally interested in such questions and entered with zest upon these new duties. When he came into office he found long-standing arrears of such cases left by previous Presidents; so he set to work to such good purpose 'that within two years he had cleared off more business than was formerly done in ten, and more than the ordinary law-courts do in thirty years'.[2]

Apart from this official duty, he was always prepared to advise his colleagues and Parliament on general policy. An excellent example of his now mellow wisdom is a speech he made on the proposed repeal of the Jews' Naturalization Act passed in May 1753. All that the Act permitted was what was already law in the American Plantations, that Jews could be naturalized by private acts on taking the oaths of supremacy and allegiance without the words 'upon the true faith of a Christian'. But this Act of 1753 had raised such a quasi-religious fervour of antagonism in the country that in the new session beginning in November of the same year the Duke of Newcastle, in a panic about possible results at the general election due in the following year, introduced and passed a bill to repeal it. Granville, though not dividing against the repeal, showed up its illiberality and absurdity.[3] If, he said, the original Act had been called an Act to prevent the profanation of the Lord's Supper, since by it Jews could be naturalized without partaking of the Communion, instead of the

---

[1] *Commentaries* (4th ed.), I, 231.
[2] *Archives de la Maison d'Orange-Nassau*, 4e Série, II, 284.
[3] For the absurd agitation against this harmless Act see Hertz, *British Imperialism in 18th Century*, pp. 60–109.

Jews' Naturalization Act, nobody would have objected. Jews previously naturalized, after taking the sacrament, were not profaning it, as they did not believe in it, but to Christians it was profanation, so it was good to have Jews naturalized without such profanation. But since people don't like the Act, I don't mind its being repealed either whole or in part:—'I shall not give myself the trouble to differ from any of your lordships on this head, because I do not think religion in anyway concerned in the question', just as the Occasional Conformity and Schism Acts of Anne's reign were both passed and then repealed without any danger to the Protestant religion, though their repeal 'I believe was a very great advantage to our established Church...'. In Turkey the bishops are appointed by the Moslem Sultan, and Christians seldom complain that they are unfit: 'on the contrary they are generally better qualified than the bishop appointed by the Roman Pontiff'. But on one point at any rate he was clear: that the naturalization allowed by the Act of 1740 to Jews going to our colonies must not be tampered with, as such Jews put down money on the understanding from the government that they would be naturalized.[1]

By this time Newcastle was supreme in foreign policy, and practically free to pursue his absurd scheme of subsidizing German Electors to induce them to elect a Habsburg as King of the Romans, a scheme in which the court of Vienna itself took so little interest. Even Granville made no opposition to his proceedings: indeed in a great debate inaugurated in 1752 by the Duke of Bedford to protest against the subsidy promised to Saxony for that purpose Granville made the only effective speech on behalf of the ministry. Newcastle, according to Horace Walpole, had replied to Bedford 'in a wild, incoherent and incomprehensible speech of an hour and a quarter', whereas Granville, as Newcastle admitted, 'spoke a short speech for us, and, as you may imagine, with his usual vivacity set the House a-laughing'. His main argument was that France was offering subsidies right and left to secure allies for another war against England, and that, by counterbidding her at less cost, we might avoid that other war, which would cost millions. It is true, he added, that we do not keep up great armies in peace-time, yet all know that we can do so in war, and so, as long as our constitution is preserved, we are respected by friend and foe: and he added a characteristic reminiscence of his embassy to Copenhagen in 1720, when he was 'asked by a great prince [the King of Denmark] what we meant by that

[1] *P.H.* xv, 110.

magnificent bravado in the Preamble to our Mutiny Bill, where we say that we keep up 18,000 men to maintain the balance of Europe. "I told him", my Lords, "One day can make those eighteen fifty thousand...by a vote in Parliament...." This was not a Dutch commentary: it did not obscure the text it was meant to explain: he presently understood it, and he acknowledged what I said to be true.'[1] Largely as a result of Granville's speech Bedford's motion was rejected without a division. Nevertheless Pelham continued his protests against the waste of money and energy on a scheme which few wanted, and which ultimately proved useless for any purpose.

Fortunately Pelham devoted most of his energies to establishing the finances of the country on so sound a basis that we were able to stand the expense, vast for those days, of Pitt's glorious victories. But worn out by his exertions and also, it may be suspected, by the constant difficulties with his brother, he died almost suddenly on 6 March 1754. 'Now I shall have no more peace' exclaimed his sorrowing master, the King. His brother, the Duke, who, in spite of their frequent disagreements, loved him dearly, shut himself up, and for the next few days would take no comfort.

---

[1] *P.H.* 1179, 1184; supplemented by Horace Walpole's account in *Memoirs of George II*, I, 247–53; and *H. MSS. Mrs Stopford Sackville*, IX, ii, 181.

Chapter X

NEWCASTLE, GRANVILLE & PITT, 1754-61

On Pelham's death, reports H. Digby, the Duke of Newcastle, 'would not hear of business...he was... in violent passions of grief and said he would give up everything, and have nothing more to do with business, but as he can't do that I conclude he will alter his mind.'[1] Though he did in fact alter his mind, he left the rearrangement of the ministry entirely in the capable hands of his friend Hardwicke. No other intermediary could have served him so well, as the Chancellor could be trusted to further the Duke's claim to succeed his brother as First Lord of the Treasury and virtual head of the ministry. The only other politician with pretensions to this post was Henry Fox, especially obnoxious to Newcastle as an adherent of Cumberland, with whom Newcastle had now quarrelled, and also to Hardwicke, whom he had grossly insulted in the debate on the marriage bill. Nor did Fox's belated attempts to propitiate former enemies and possible rivals, such as Pitt, by ceremonious visits prove availing. In fact the King, agreeing with Hardwicke and Newcastle himself, had already decided that Newcastle should succeed his brother as First Lord. Accordingly the Cabinet Council held at the Chancellor's house on 12 March 1754, but not attended by Newcastle, resolved formally to advise the appointment of the Duke to the Treasury, and of Legge, a friend of Pitt's, to Pelham's other post as Chancellor of the Exchequer. For Secretary of State to succeed Newcastle 'His Majesty', it was stated, 'had cast his eyes on Mr Fox', but, disliking the man personally, stipulated that Newcastle's Northern province, in which he was chiefly interested, should be taken over by Holderness and Fox relegated to the Southern province. Two days later, however, Fox, finding he was to have no share in patronage and was not even to act as leader of the Commons, threw up his office; whereupon Newcastle chose as second secretary Sir Thomas Robinson, former ambassador in Vienna, a pompous nonentity with no administrative experience or knowledge of the Commons, but a docile follower of the Duke. Thus Newcastle secured an administration subservient to himself, and was only too glad to be spared two such masterful colleagues as Fox and Pitt. Neither he nor Hardwicke,

[1] *H. MSS.* VIII, App. Part i, 121.

indeed, had made any attempt to overcome the King's objection to Pitt, whom they dreaded as a rival even more than Fox.[1]

In the ministry so re-constituted the only man of real capacity and weight in foreign policy was Granville, who through all the changes of administration from 1751 until his death in 1763, remained in the same post as Lord President of the Council. He had long given up all ambition to be '*the* minister', but his vast knowledge of European politics and statesmanlike outlook always carried the greatest weight with his colleagues. The soul of magnanimity, and too proud to cherish a grudge, he had long forgiven Newcastle his intrigues of 1724 and 1744 and became his most trusted counsellor in the cabinet, especially on foreign policy. It is true he increasingly relied on deep potations of burgundy to stimulate his faculties, sometimes with excellent results, as on the occasion of which Holderness remarked: 'Our friend Granville was fine...wine had heightened his zeal and eloquence.'[2] But quite as often he was apt in his cups to make his colleagues supremely uncomfortable by the pungency of his remarks about them, especially the Chancellor, of whom he always thought meanly. Of such criticisms perhaps the most devastating was that reported by his future son-in-law Shelburne: 'At the commencement of the [Seven Years'] War Lord Granville, who had generally dined, turned round to say: "I am thinking that all over Europe they are waiting our determination and canvassing our characters. The Duke of Newcastle, they'll say, is a man of great fortune, who has spent a great deal of it in support of the present family; Fox, they'll say, is an impudent fellow who has fought his way here through the House of Commons; as for me they know me throughout Europe, they know my talents and my character, but I am thinking they will all be asking, 'Qui est ce —— de Chancelier, How came he there?'"'[3]

There is an illuminating comparison between the business methods of Newcastle and Granville in the correspondence of the Dutch statesman, Count William Bentinck, a lively and shrewd observer of our ministers' methods. He had been sent over in 1753, the year before Pelham's death, while Newcastle was still Secretary of State, to persuade England to contribute to the expense of strengthening the Barrier fortresses, as a defence against France. He found nobody prepared to waste money on such a scheme after the feeble spirit

---

[1] The ministerial reconstruction can best be followed in Yorke, *Hardwicke*, II, 187–94, 201–16.

[2] Yorke, *Hardwicke*, II, 34.   [3] Fitzmaurice, *Shelburne*, I, 66–7.

shown by the Dutch in the recent war; but there was a world of difference in the two ministers' methods of conveying this refusal. When Bentinck went to see Newcastle, 'he made me wait very long, sending word that he was dressing; and when he came in he gave me some papers to read which I put in my pocket and asked him if I might go with him to Kensington [to see the King]; no, because he was taking Pelham with him; and so we parted. However I met him at Court and afterwards at Lady Yarmouth's. On the same day I was to dine with him and arrived early to talk with him alone, but he did not want to talk...and made me go to his study where I found Holderness and Lincoln....When the Duke came in he was very friendly, but when dinner was announced he sent us in to dine with the Duchess, while he wrote a letter, but later came in to find the soup eaten. He asked me twenty times how I did....I told him he owed me a letter; he said no; I said yes....Pelham came in at 7 o'clock when we had finished dinner, but we sat with him while he ate and went on drinking till 10 p.m.....when Holderness had gone. It was plain that the Duke wanted to avoid talking business, so I went on to Lady Holderness....Next day, Wednesday, I went to see Granville....We talked of Brussels and the Barrier. Granville spoke to me of his system in general...which he said was also George II's and the Duke of Newcastle's, but that Pelham and the Chancellor were not so clear on it.... *Inter alia* he remarked that some thought the increased power of Prussia and her connexions with France were a good reason against a liaison of the Maritime Powers [England and Holland] with Vienna, but that his own opinion was and always would be that this was all the more reason for the Maritime Powers to come to an understanding with Vienna to counterbalance this increase of power on the other side, "puisque rien n'était plus simple que ceci que, quand un poids l'emporte, ce n'est pas en ôtant mais en mettant du poids dans le bassin opposé qu'on remit l'équilibre". As to the Barrier we could not bind our hands beforehand. In Holland one had to deal with "100 têtes de travers", in England with 10,000: when he was the minister he recommended himself to the first man he met, for in England a minister is dependent on a cobbler [an interesting and by no means unique illustration of Granville's sympathy with the rising tide of a more democratic feeling in England]; and he told me many amusing anecdotes to show his meaning...[among others] the story of a man to whom James II sent his confessor to convert him. "Sir," said the confessor, "you believe in God?" to which the other answered, "What I believe has nothing to do with you, it's your business to prove it", in reference to my question whether he had read the treaties between Burgundy and then Spain and England to which he had replied, "It's not my business to read them, I'm not the minister".[1] "Well," I said, "what is the result of all this? do you want a breach with Vienna...would you help us to seize the *comptoirs* assigned to us to secure our Barrier Treaty?" To this he said quite clearly, "No, because neither both of us, still less one of us alone, are strong enough to seize or keep them."'[2]

A fortnight after these interviews with Newcastle and Granville Bentinck sums up the difference between the two men. 'All the Duke's attention', he notes, 'is taken up with preparations for the new Parliament [due for election in 1754], to the neglect of all other business....He is so much afraid of any pretext that can be taken from his despatches by the House of Commons or the freeholding electors to his discredit that he writes them on no plan, but simply with a view to the effect they will have at home....He has no courage and so gives strength to those he fears, e.g. to Vienna, against which he swears as is here the fashion, though he should see that this method is dangerous with the new minister Kaunitz. So with the Barrier question he knows well that England has no special rights and that the treaties prove nothing, but he has no time to read the treaties, still less to weigh their import; but since the manufacturers of Yorkshire are anxious that things should be left as they were between 1715 and 1744, the Duke does not dare to assert that black is black and white white....Yet he is in the strongest possible position, for Bedford and Sandwich have been disposed of, Pelham is "timide et mol", he himself is "moins mol, mais aussi timide que son frère"; but the only rival he has to fear is Fox, supported as he is by Cumberland with whom Newcastle has quarrelled. Granville on the other hand, who has his £5000 a year, enjoys the King's affection and wants to live at peace with the other ministers, being ready to second them as long as they follow their present plan. All the despatches with minutes of replies and of orders and expeditions are communicated to him, but he is not shown the *private* and *most private* letters, nor does he ask for them, since having been Secretary of State himself he knows all those rubrics. Perhaps he is shown what is shown to

---

[1] By 'the minister' Granville meant the Secretary of State responsible for foreign policy.
[2] *Archives de la Maison d'Orange-Nassau*, 4e Série, II, 279 sqq. Bentinck writes in French, of which I give a rough translation.

the King, but no more. "Il ne fait semblant de rien pourtant, et va son train", giving his opinion on what is shown to him in conformity with his own ideas. "Enfin il ne veut plus de bruit ni de noise, et il donne beaucoup de poids dans la Chambre haute."[1]

Torrens, with his remarkable knowledge of the MS. authorities of this period, completes the picture of Granville in his final stage of political activity, during Pitt's ministry. 'The Lord President having nothing departmental to do, and possessing beyond most other men the gifts and accomplishments that render versatility useful, had made for himself an undefinable, but not indistinct or unimportant, function—that of taking the measure and the mood of everyone politically worth asking to dinner. He loved wit, of which his own stock was varied, and wine, of which, when anyone fitly companionable would help him, he would sometimes take more than enough; but though still the delight of good society, from the death of his beautiful second wife he was insensible to female charms. Those who envied his personal popularity at Court or country house called his levity at small party perplexities want of patriotism; and the freedom with which he poked fun at some of the bishops, want of reverence for the Established Church: and many, who never sat late with him, affected to be able to tell how much he loved burgundy. We find even Newcastle carping at his unguarded freedom of speech in Council, after he had dined; but save the Chancellor and the new Secretary of State [Pitt], there was, after all, nobody in office comparable with him in sagacity, experience or mother wit, when called on at short notice to advise on public affairs; and as he disdained alike Party prejudices and private jobbing, men of all shades of opinion freely availed themselves of fitting opportunity to be his guests, or, when he chose, to make him theirs.'[2]

Since 1751 indeed a remarkable change had been apparent in the relations between Newcastle and Granville, especially in the early days of their renewed association. On his side Newcastle, having no further cause for jealousy or distrust, but recognizing his former rival's 'superior lights', leans more and more upon his counsel in foreign affairs and whenever, as frequently was the case, he was in a difficulty sends out urgent appeals for his attendance at cabinet councils, such as 'We are much in want of your advice and assistance',

[1] *Archives...Orange-Nassau*, 4e Série, II, 283.
[2] Torrens, *History of Cabinets*, II, 241–2. Unfortunately, Torrens died before this *History* could be published, and the references to original MSS., which he used freely, are missing.

or even 'Nothing can be done in your absence'. In his turn Granville, having shed all personal ambition but still deeply concerned with the country's best interests, tenders his advice in a strangely humble tone, best calculated to convince the Duke, such as 'I submit [this] to your better judgment', or 'pardon this hint from Ever Yours, Granville'. In suggesting a new paragraph to the secret instructions given to an envoy abroad, he adds 'if you don't like it be pleased to burn it'. Nor is he chary in his praise of the prickly Duke, always eager to be applauded by his colleagues. 'I think', writes Granville on another occasion, 'you have done with all prudence as much as any man could do for ye success of ye great affaire, which I shall support you in, both in Publick, or Private, as occasions shall offer; and on my poor assistance your Grace may most securely reckon in all events'.[1] His few speeches in the House of Lords during his last years, mainly on foreign policy, were of invaluable assistance to the Duke, whose own utterances were apt to be fumbling and incoherent. In 1752, for example, when Bedford raised a debate on the Saxon treaty of subsidy, Bishop Thomas of Lincoln wrote that 'Lord Granville concluded the debate...with so much life and spirit as entertained the House', and no doubt contributed to the government majority. Again in 1755 a London correspondent writes 'Lord Granville is listened to in foreign affairs and *that* pushes them on with such vigour. I hear complaints that our *Home affairs* are executed with less vigour'.[2]

Besides his desire to avoid *toute noise* at this stage of his career, Granville was more disposed than Pelham had been to support Newcastle's policy of subsidizing, mainly at England's expense, a majority of the Electoral College for the election of the Archduke Joseph as King of the Romans and successor to the Imperial Crown, for he, no more than Newcastle, had divined the growing *rapprochement* between Paris and Vienna fostered by Kaunitz; and, until almost the outbreak of war, Newcastle's policy was based on the Old System of alliance between the Maritime Powers and Vienna. Cologne, the first elector to be subsidized, had soon changed sides to France, but Bavaria and Saxony had accepted English subsidies, and in 1755 a subsidy was promised to Hesse, mainly with a view to the defence of Hanover. But Granville, at any rate, recognized that it would be foolish to plan any general system without taking account of Frederic of Prussia. Unfortunately George II's antipathy to his nephew was

[1] Add. MSS. 32725, f. 237; 32730, ff. 205, 403; 32736, f. 422; 32859, f. 153.
[2] H. MSS. *Weston Underwood*, p. 307; H. MSS. IX, App. p. 241 a.

for the time being an almost insuperable bar to a close alliance between the two Kings; so, as a *pis-aller*, Granville argued that, 'if we could keep the King of Prussia quiet for one year only, it would be worth everything to us'.[1] To effect this he had always urged an alliance with Russia, both when he was 'the minister' and now as Newcastle's mentor: 'Your Grace knows', he wrote, 'I was long for that measure, as the only means to preserve the peace by keeping the King of Prussia in awe; who, if he was not free from the apprehension of being attacked by Russia, would know no bounds. If he is quiet, in all probability France would be quiet.'[2] In fact during his previous term of office, in December 1742, he had succeeded in making the first treaty of mutual guarantee with Russia, followed as it was by the more explicit treaty of November 1747, which had resulted in the actual despatch of Russian troops to the Rhine, though too late to have any influence on the war.[3] Since then persistent attempts had been made by Newcastle to persuade Russia to fall on Frederic's rear, if he attacked Hanover, all in vain until Hanbury Williams was sent to St Petersburg in 1755. Then at last a treaty was secured whereby Russia agreed, for a subsidy from England, to maintain a force on the Livonian border, ready to fall on Frederic if he attacked Hanover.[4]

Meanwhile troubles both at home and abroad were accumulating far beyond Newcastle's capacity to cope with. At home, indeed, he had, as usual, secured a fairly docile House of Commons by the elections of 1754; but even the most docile House needed a leader capable of guiding it with authority and with full knowledge of the ministry's own policy. There were two men in the Commons, Pitt and Fox, each eminently fitted for this task, but both were left out in the cold of minor offices with no voice in the government's decisions or even knowledge of them till they were presented for approval. Fox, indeed, as we have seen, had been offered a secretary-ship of state but with so little voice in policy or patronage that he had declined the office. Pitt, far the greater man of the two, had not even been seriously considered, on the plea that the King had not forgiven his former attacks on Hanover and the Hanover troops: but he had served the government well as Paymaster for eight years, and New-castle must have known from his own experience in 1746 that the King was bound to give way if enough pressure was brought upon

[1] Add. MSS. 32857, ff. 359, 506.
[2] Add. MSS. 32846, f. 277.   [3] See above, ch. VII, p. 129.
[4] F. de Martens, *Recueil des Traités, Russie*, IX (X), 134 sqq.

him. The fact was that Newcastle himself much preferred docile nonentities to troublesome geniuses such as Pitt, who might insist on a line of their own. At any rate in the Commons, besides the new Secretary Robinson, who was a mere butt to his opponents, he could rely only on the Attorney-General, Murray, a great lawyer and an able debater, but determined to quit as soon as the object of his ambition, the post of Lord Chief Justice, fell vacant. Newcastle himself, indeed, was quite satisfied with his team. In a letter to old Horace Walpole he wrote: 'Some great persons in the House of Commons don't think their merit rewarded, and therefore endeavour to have it thought that there is a necessity of having a minister, or the ministers, in the House of Commons....I am persuaded that the majority of this House of Commons will not enter into any scheme of this kind....I have now told you the whole grievance.'[1] But the good Duke's complacency was short-lived. For Pitt and Fox, being left out in the cold, entered into an alliance to show up the weakness of Newcastle's system of government. Pitt, on an election petition for bribery, always a matter of concern to the Duke, called on all good Whigs to defend their 'attacked and expiring liberty...unless you will degenerate into a little assembly, serving no other purpose than to register the decrees of *one* too powerful a subject [i.e. Newcastle]'. Fox on another such petition, taking occasion from Robinson's remark, even before the case had been considered, that the petitioner had a poor case, ironically called on the House to remember that Robinson had been twenty years abroad and not to be too hard on him for his irregular and blamable expression, or for the total inexperience he showed in matters before the House. Next Pitt turned his attention to Murray, bringing up his former Jacobite associations at Oxford, 'torturing' him for his 'distinctions and refinements and legal quibbles'; and declaring that 'arbitrary power was more detestable when dressed in the long robe than in all the panoply of war....If we must go for precedents, let them not be sought in the diabolic divans of Charles and James'.

Such an alliance was too strong even for Newcastle with his docile 'myrmidons' in the House of Commons, especially after the bad news, which reached London in September 1754, of a border affray in America, when Colonel Washington's colonial levies had been defeated and taken prisoner by a superior French force at Fort Necessity. On hearing the news Newcastle wrote in a panic to Hardwicke and Granville: 'Everybody', he writes to the latter, 'is

[1] Coxe, *Memoirs of Horatio Lord Walpole*, II, 370.

full of North America and our defeat there; the Opposers, I hear,
will endeavour to make some attack upon it, the King is in haste
to have something done, His Royal Highness [Cumberland]—you
will see by the enclosed letter—doubts, won't yet determine any
Thing, and it is so difficult to know what to do that I am sure your
Lordship will think we cannot be too cautious, nor too expeditious
in determining something...in short something must be resolv'd
and *that something* must be (if possible) Effectual': he goes on to
relate a 'disagreeable' talk he had with the King about the need of
a strong leader to conduct the business in the House of Commons,
and concludes with the inept plan of keeping Robinson as his own
mouthpiece, while merely telling Fox of the general programme
so as not to 'disoblige him'. Granville in his reply tries to put some
backbone into the Duke, suggesting that 'if proper measures are
taken and put in execution next spring and proper officers sent there
now with arms and clothes and money to raise what they can this
winter.... When that is done, it will give great spirit in the colonys,
forward the design of a general concert, show you what you may
depend on from them, and so know how to estimate what force
you must send.' A regular force should be sent from England in
time for the spring campaigning season, but meantime fix on your
officers 'with as little noise as possible', use all means, by presents
and assurances of protection, to gain the confidence of the Indian
tribes, 'demonstrating to them, that you intend to protect both
them and yourselves by the measures that you actually take in their
sight, by raising recruits in the proper season, to be followed by a
sufficient force in the spring. If this had been done, or even less than
this as a result of our meeting this time twelvemonth...much
expense had been saved which must now be incurred; and Mr Hanbury told us then, at the meeting, that it was too late to do anything
of consequence that year, except putting our colonies, during the
winter, in a condition to act in the spring.'[1] But Granville himself
had no longer any executive authority to see that his proposals were
carried out; and Newcastle for his part complained that 'Our friend,
Lord Granville, is always talking about our strength in North
America, and I don't see we are able to do anything'.[2] In fact the
only result of the scare was the despatch of a couple of ill-trained
regiments, under a barrack-yard general, Braddock, totally inexperienced in colonial warfare, and of whom the Chancellor's son,

[1] Add. MSS. 32736, ff. 554, 567.
[2] Add. MSS. 32706, f. 424.

Joseph Yorke, said that 'he never knew him do anything but swear',[1] to meet annihilation on the Monangahela in the following July.

Even more serious in Newcastle's eyes was the weakness of the government in the House of Commons through the dangerous alliance of Pitt and Fox. He would have preferred to secure Pitt, not only as the abler man, but because Fox was closely associated with his present *bête noire* Cumberland. But Pitt had been so often lured by Newcastle with false hopes of promotion that he had withered up his last advances with the devastating answer: 'Fewer words, if you please, my Lord, for your words have long lost all weight with me.' So Fox it had to be, especially as he could be had on cheaper terms than Pitt, merely for a place in the cabinet, without any executive function, while the absurd Robinson still remained the chief government spokesman in the Commons.[2] All the same Fox proved useful to Newcastle by 'talking' to members with persuasive inducements to vote for the government. As he admitted himself, 'Friend Pitt is as warm as I am—he is a much better speaker than I—that is the truth of it, I assure you. But tickling the palm, not the ear, is the business now, and he that can do that first is the best orator, speak he never so ill';[3] a disappointing attitude as compared with the ideal set before him by his patron, the old war-horse Granville: 'I want to instil a nobler ambition into you, to make you knock the heads of the Kings of Europe together, and jumble something out of it that may be of service to this country.'

To add to the difficulties of government and country on the eve of war, in the spring of 1755 the King must needs make his journey to Hanover, with all that it meant in the dislocation of state business and delay in executive action. Indeed, though war was not actually declared till 1756, we were actually carrying on hostilities with the French in America, India and the high seas. In April Boscawen, who had been sent to intercept French reinforcements to America, captured two small vessels, the *Alcide* and the *Lys*, but failed to engage the main body of their fleet. When the news came to London in July, Newcastle was all in a twitter as to the course to be adopted, and at the cabinet council that ensued proposed that another fleet under Boscawen should be despatched to prey upon French commerce wherever he found it. Granville at this stage, before we were assured of the Russian treaty or of what would be the attitude of Spain, Prussia and Holland at such piratical proceedings, strongly opposed

[1] Yorke, *Hardwicke*, II, 257.
[2] Ilchester, *Henry Fox*, I, 231 sqq.   [3] *Ib.* I, 245.

what he called 'vexing your neighbours for a little muck'; whereas, 'if we waited but a very short time, France in all probability will put us under the necessity of falling upon their trade in Europe, so as that no Power can blame us.... It may be wise and honest', he concluded, 'to postpone for a time the executing a measure, which once done admits of no conciliation but by dint of war; and the measure itself, if executed, may be attended with very little profit or advantage.... But I leave all to your better judgment', a judgment which produced the inept conclusion that Boscawen should still be sent out, but without any orders at all to guide him.[1]

Newcastle's difficulties indeed were mounting up. For some time he had been uneasy about the 'Closet', meaning thereby the King and his Egeria, Lady Yarmouth, and complaining to Hardwicke that 'the plan of the Closet is to stand by and look on, and if we can support ourselves to be pleased with it, but to avoid as much as possible to make our cause their own'. Worse still, the King had told him in so many words that 'there is no such thing as first minister in England, and therefore you should not seem to be so'; and he had spoken to the same effect to Fox, telling him that Newcastle was not sole minister, and should confine himself to the Treasury. Then there was 'a meeting of the Cabinet when my Lord President had dined and talked very unguardedly; I was frightened the whole time'. It may have been on this occasion that Granville, according to Dodington, told Newcastle that 'he would be served himself as he and his brother had served him'. Newcastle finally came to the conclusion that 'we must get help in the Commons to support me, who am the Butt of everybody'.[2] For months during the King's absence in Hanover he had been exchanging letters with Hardwicke as to the best means of securing that help, Robinson, as even Newcastle realized at last, being hopeless as leader. So, after a month of dithering correspondence with Hardwicke, Newcastle brought himself, though 'without much glee', to the point of asking Pitt to come and discuss the whole position. Pitt told him some home-truths: 'the House of Commons was now an assembly of atoms; the great wheels of the machine were stop'd', and Newcastle's tentative offer of a place in the cabinet council without executive authority 'was not sufficient to put them in motion: if the duke could be induced to part with some of his *sole power*... and offer

[1] Add. MSS. 93857, ff. 111, 266; Dodington, *Diary*, pp. 344-5.
[2] Add. MSS. 32737, f. 196; 35414, f. 259; 32858, f. 241; 32857, f. 53; Dodington, p. 361.

him an office of advice as well as execution...he would support measures which *he had himself advised* but would not like a lawyer speak from a brief': and he ended by expressing his objection to the Duke's treaties with German princelings, 'a mean and subsidiary system'. Even Newcastle himself was fain to confess to Hardwicke that 'we have ourselves given handle for proposals for little treaties with little princes for little bodies of troops'; but he had not yet come to the pass of giving up his own authority or his policy of subsidies; and still found an excuse for rejecting Pitt's claim to responsible office in the King's sullen dislike of Pitt.[1] So the leader of the Commons had to be Fox, in spite of his alliance with Cumberland and his comparative ignorance of foreign politics, an objection which had small weight with Newcastle. At any rate he was more accommodating than Pitt, had the strong backing of Granville, still in high favour with Newcastle, and was willing to accept on the distinct understanding, as Newcastle put it, that he was not to do anything, *even in the House of Commons*, without consulting me'.[2] Fox accordingly was promoted to Robinson's place, as Secretary of State and chief spokesman for the ministry in the Commons. At the beginning of the next session came the final breach with Pitt, who was summarily dismissed from his post of Paymaster for opposition to the Duke's European policy, and with him his friend Legge, for refusing to pay the Hessian subsidy till it had been approved by Parliament. Thus the only effective ministers left in the Commons were Fox and Murray, already half-hearted in their allegiance to the Duke, and soon to leave the sinking ship.

For in 1756 came the famous *renversement des alliances*, bringing to the ground all Newcastle's carefully planned schemes. In January Frederic of Prussia, alarmed at the Russian menace on his border, abandoned his alliance with France, and signed the Westminster Convention with George II, whereby both Kings agreed to resist the entry of foreign troops into the Empire. Since such an entry by Russian troops was the sole object of Newcastle's treaty with Russia, the Tsaritsa, not unnaturally, repudiated it and soon came to an understanding with France. Worse was to follow, for in May Louis XV, deserted by Prussia, at last consented to the alliance with Maria Theresa, for which her minister Kaunitz had long been angling. Nobody, probably, more than Granville, the great upholder of the Austrian alliance, felt so bitterly this desertion. When Colloredo,

---

[1] Yorke, *Hardwicke*, II, 237 sqq.; Add. MSS. 32858, f. 114.
[2] Tunstall, *William Pitt*, p. 142.

Maria Theresa's ambassador, came to make his excuses to Granville for this change in Austrian policy, 'Granville interrupted him and said, "Sir, this is not necessary; I understand that the treaty is only one of neutrality; but what grieves me is that our people will not understand it so; and the prejudice will be so great, that when it shall become necessary again, as it will do, for us to support your mistress, nobody will then dare to be a Lord Granville".'[1]

The stage was now set for the Seven Years' War. In fact hostilities in Europe had actually begun. In January news had reached London that Marshal Bellisle, counting on the notorious weakness of the country's defences, was planning an invasion of England itself. In a panic the ministers were reduced to the ignominious and highly unpopular expedient of bringing over hired Hessian and Hanoverian troops to guard our shores. This alarm passed off, but in February Newcastle was warned of an impending attack by the French on Minorca, then regarded as an even more important Mediterranean base than Gibraltar. The governor of the island and most of the officers of the garrison were actually absent from their posts at the time; and it was not till April that a small squadron under Byng was sent to relieve the island. Byng was of quite another kidney from his father, the victor at Passaro, and, after a half-hearted engagement with La Galissonière's investing fleet, retired to Gibraltar, leaving Minorca to its fate. In September Frederic II, by his sudden invasion of Saxony, started the Seven Years' War in earnest; and now more bad news was to come of French successes in America and India.

These mounting disasters, culminating in the loss of Minorca, roused a feeling in the country before which even Newcastle had to quail. Already he had been moaning to Hardwicke that 'the occasion of all our misfortunes, and that will increase every day, is that we are not equal to the work we have undertaken. We are not singly a match for France'; and his first reaction to the loss of Minorca was that it might incline the King to peace; 'that this war is hopeless and may be ruinous I have been for some time convinced'; and even a month earlier he had been writing to the same confidant: 'the Attorney-General out of the House of Commons, Fox disobliged, the possibility (I wish I could not say the probability) of a breach in the royal family, an alliance between the House of Austria and France—Four terrible events'.[2] Now, faced with the loss of Minorca, he characteristically tried to stem the popular

---

[1] H. Walpole, *Letters*, 24 July 1756.
[2] Add. MSS. 32864, f. 478; 32865, f. 193; 32866, f. 49.

indignation by ordering 'the immediate trial and condemnation of
Byng', and promising to a City deputation that 'he shall be tried
immediately, he shall be hanged directly'.

But even more ominous to him, 'in this time of difficulty, danger
and almost universal uneasiness and discontent thro'out the whole
kingdom, of which', as he confessed, 'I receive fresh accounts from
all quarters',[1] was the almost unanimous demand for 'justice against
persons however dignified or distinguished', persons whom he took
to mean Anson at the Admiralty, Anson's father-in-law Hardwicke
and the Duke himself. As further bad news filtered in from all parts
of the world, he may well have exclaimed—'Quae regio in terris
nostri non plena doloris?' Then, to cap all, the rats had begun to
leave the sinking ship of state. For no foreign disaster, perhaps,
loomed so large in Newcastle's eyes as the sudden desertion of his
only two capable ministers in the Commons. The post of Lord Chief
Justice had become vacant, and Murray as Attorney-General claimed
it as of right and would take no denial; then, as a culmination just
on the eve of the session, Fox handed in his resignation to the King,
putting it on the ground that 'tho' I have behaved in the best manner
I have been able to the Duke of Newcastle, yet I find that my credit
in the House of Commons diminishes for want of support and think
it impracticable for me to carry on His Majesty's affairs there, as
they ought to be carried on'. Newcastle indeed asserted that he
had done everything possible to support Fox, but it appears that ten
days previously he had in fact sent him a message that 'if he was sure
it would not offend him, his Grace would offer his place to Mr Pitt
the next day'. Even the King had at last come to the conclusion
that Pitt must be sounded, but, said he to the Duke, 'Suppose Pitt
will not serve with you'—'Then, Sir, I must go'—to which the
King replied 'most graciously and good-humouredly, "My Lord,
I know your faults, but I know also your integrity and zeal for
me"'—a charming and not wholly undeserved testimony to the
services of the now somewhat forlorn old statesman. Accordingly,
having at last made up his mind to take the plunge for Pitt, the
Duke, all of a twitter lest Granville should persuade Fox to make
his peace with the King and stay on 'as long as his Majesty thinks
it for his service', urges Hardwicke to summon Pitt at once, 'before
Lord Granville returns to court tomorrow'.[2]

Accordingly Hardwicke saw Pitt on 19 October, heard his terms
for accepting office, and a week later reported to him the King's

[1] Add. MSS. 32867, f. 175.   [2] Yorke, *Hardwicke*, II, 319-24.

answer. Pitt's terms were: an enquiry into the measures which had brought the country to so low a state; a militia bill, rejected that year, to be reintroduced and allowed to pass; Hanoverians and Hessians quartered in the country to be subject to the law of the land for civil offences; and above all that he would not serve with the Duke of Newcastle as a colleague and that he should have free access to the King and recommend to him any measure he thought necessary 'without going through the channel of any other minister'. The King's answer was that 'what has been suggested is not for his or the public service'. Nevertheless Newcastle and Hardwicke resigned on 26 October, on the same day that this answer was returned. On the 27th Fox was ordered to form a ministry. But without Pitt he would not undertake the ungrateful task: and Pitt, betrayed, as he believed, in the past, and conscious, as he proudly asserted, that 'I can save the country and nobody else can', refused to have anything to do with him. At last the only course left open to the King was to admit Pitt on his own terms. A ministry was formed with the Duke of Devonshire as First Lord of the Treasury and Pitt as Secretary of State for the South and virtual Prime Minister; Granville as Lord President was one of the very few of the old ministry left in office.

Thus for the first time since 1717, when he became Lord Chamberlain, Newcastle was no longer in the service of the Crown. It is to his credit that this unblushing dispenser of patronage to others, and now a relatively poor man, 'retired', as Fox wrote to a friend, 'from the King's service without either place or pension. He might, you may believe, have had either.'[1] But even then Newcastle could not disabuse himself of the belief that without him the country would go to the dogs. It is true that his creature Holderness was still left in the cabinet to report to him on its proceedings. But he lamented to Hardwicke that they had not a stronger man 'behind the curtain' to prevent bad appointments; to which his friend sensibly answered: 'We must not be ministers behind the curtain.'[2] But no advice could cure the Duke of his belief that he was indispensable.

Pitt had just time, before the new session, to compose a King's Speech 'captivating the people' and calling on all to exert themselves in the dangerous state of the country, and to prepare his own plans for the next campaign. These plans were conceived in a different spirit from Newcastle's. Scorning to rely on hireling troops from Germany, he raised fresh troops at home, including the famous

[1] H. MSS. Stopford Sackville, I, 50.   [2] Add. MSS. 32869, ff. 69, 76, 187.

Highland regiments, drafted a militia bill to put home defence on a national basis, and saw to it that his fleets were fully equipped to deal with the French in all parts of the world. When he appeared in Council, says Horace Walpole, he 'was haughty and visionary; so much that after one of their meetings Lord Granville said "Pitt used to call me a madman, but I never was half so mad as he is".'[1] It was evidently the same sort of madness of which Wolfe was accused before George II, who replied that 'if he is mad it were to be wished Wolfe would bite some of his other generals.' By his courage in standing up against the execution of Byng, Pitt had for the moment lost something of his popularity; but, when in April 1757 he was summarily dismissed by the King at Cumberland's request, the country realized what they were losing in him, and 'it rained gold boxes' on him with the freedom of London and eighteen other cities in the kingdom.[2]

For two months Granville and a skeleton ministry carried on the business of the country as best they could while the intrigues went on for setting up a new ministry. Cumberland and Granville wanted Fox to take the lead, but he was neither trusted enough, nor himself man enough, to take up the dangerous task. Finally approaches were made to Pitt by Hardwicke and Newcastle. Though it had become evident that without Newcastle's docile majority in the Commons it would be difficult to carry on, Pitt's terms of coalition were stiff and included, of course, control of the war policy and war operations by himself. But by the end of June the ministry was completed with Newcastle's return to the Treasury, Pitt's to the Secretaryship and Granville still Lord President. Newcastle returned in chastened mood, declaring that on his return to the Treasury, 'I intend to leave the ordinary business to the Chancellor of the Exchequer and the other Lords [of the Treasury], and, after having been for near forty years a daily attendant at Court, I shall desire the King to permit me to trouble him only twice a week, for I must have some ease and quiet for myself'. In the main he kept to this resolution, partly no doubt because Pitt would brook no interference in the general management of the war. What he required for war-expenses he called on Newcastle to provide, and saw that he got it. But he warned him that 'if he found the Duke of Newcastle whispered in the Closet or gave any disturbance in Parliament, or spread any-

---

[1] H. Walpole, *Memoirs of George II*, II, 284.
[2] For Pitt's achievements in his first ministry I may be allowed to refer to my *Chatham*, I, 287–316.

thing about, to the disadvantage of the administration, he might expect all kinds of hostilitys from Mr P.'[1]

During all this turmoil Granville had been his serene self, refusing to take any part in the hurly-burly of rival claims for place. Twice when Newcastle was finding his troubles thick upon him he had offered to give up his place as nominal head of the ministry to Granville, whose reply on the second occasion was, 'I thought I had cured you of such offers last year. I will be hanged a little before I take your place rather than a little after.'[2] He had no cause to love Pitt, the rival of his special protégé Fox, and by his attacks on the 'Hanoverian troop minister' one of the chief instruments of his own downfall in 1744; but as a colleague he always treated him with lofty politeness. During Pitt's first ministry, from which Newcastle was excluded, Holderness used to send the Duke reports of the cabinet proceedings and told him that at their first meeting 'the Lord President gave a good deal of flattery to Mr P., who from appearance thought the dose a little strong', but later that, though still friendly to Pitt and impressed by his 'great ideas', he thought him 'impracticable': to which Hardwicke, who hated Granville, adds the acid comment: 'As to my good friend, my Lord President, my rule is *nil admirari*. His fondness for the new minister is as inconsistent as his present conduct is with that of the last year. For what are *great ideas* that are *impracticable*?'[3] Pitt was, no doubt, occasionally tempted to harangue the cabinet as if it were the House of Commons and appealed habitually to even wider audiences by his King's Speeches, foreshadowings of President Roosevelt's 'fire-side chats' to his own people, but methods highly distasteful to Granville with his more aristocratic traditions. But when Pitt was more at ease in his second administration, with Newcastle's majority in the Commons to back him, he himself spoke of the cabinet discussions as 'the most agreeable conversations he ever experienced'. Shelburne's account of these discussions, derived partly from Chatham, partly from reports of his father-in-law Granville's table talk,[4] gives an amusing picture of this cabinet's proceedings: 'There were no party politics, and consequently no difference of opinion.... The Duke of Newcastle, a very good-humoured man, was abundantly content

---

[1] Add. MSS. 32870, f. 469.
[2] H. Walpole, *Memoirs of George II*, II, 87–8.
[3] Add. MSS. 32689, f. 79; 32870, f. 21; Yorke, *Hardwicke*, II, 383.
[4] It will be remembered that Shelburne met Granville only once, and before he married Granville's daughter.

with the whole patronage left to him.....Lord Hardwicke was kept in order by Lord Granville's wit, who took advantage of the meeting of the balance of all parties to pay off old scores, and to return all that he owed to the Pelhams and the Yorkes. He had a rooted aversion to Lord Hardwicke and to all his family, I don't precisely know for what reason, but he got the secret of cowing Lord Hardwicke, whose pretensions to classical learning gave Lord Granville, who was a very fine classical scholar, a great opportunity. To this was added his knowledge of civil law, in which Lord Hardwicke was deficient, and above all his wit; but whatever way he got the key, he used it on all occasions unmercifully.' [1]

During these last ten years of his life Granville appears to have made only two set speeches in the House of Lords. The first of these was on the Militia Bill passed by the House of Commons in May 1756 before its enthusiastic supporter Pitt had come to office. This speech was certainly not one of his best, showing him more inclined to trust to hireling Hessians and Hanoverians to defend the country than to a national uprising of the people. The bill, he said, was like 'throwing out a twig to a man in danger of drowning, by the grasping of which he is actually drowned, whereas by turning his eye another way, he might have caught hold of a rope, by which he might have been drawn to the shore'. He continued in cynical vein that the only way of securing a well-regulated militia was 'that of making it every man's immediate and apparent interest to breed himself to arms...it may be remarked of old scholars as well as young, that they never make great proficiency in any art or science they must be compelled to study'. Comparing the proposed scheme with that of Switzerland, 'where nearly every common man and gentleman has served in Swiss regiments in the pay of foreign powers and in return gets esteem and advancement in respect to the character he has attained on service'; and with the French system which 'makes it scandalous for the nobility not to fight and get credit accordingly', he denies that such good results will be attained 'by bluntly exacting that such a number of men in each parish or county shall be soldiers....In order to make men venturous and brave, the two chief qualities of a good soldier, you are going to starve those very passions, I mean ambition and avarice, which make men venturous and brave.' In the following year Pitt, now in office,

[1] Fitzmaurice, *Shelburne*, I, 66. The passage ends with Granville's thumb-nail sketches of Newcastle, Fox, himself and Hardwicke already quoted p. 190 above.

after sending back the Hessians and Hanoverians, re-introduced the bill himself and passed it again in the Commons: this time Granville made no protest and it was passed in the Lords. His last recorded speech, in May 1758, was on the more liberal side, though it also showed in its argument something of the old man's cynicism. It was on a bill, strongly supported by Pitt, for an amendment of the Habeas Corpus Act to cover the case of a man arrested by a press-gang and also to require the judges to consider such cases during the legal vacation. According to Hansard Granville's chief argument for the bill was 'its popularity, though he observed that he should scarcely be reproached with ever having been much biased by that consideration'. Since the nation was in great fermentation on the question, it would be 'better to pass the bill at first than at last, since it was likely to be sent up to them every year till they did so, and the approach of a new election of parliament would force them to do as they had done in the Jew Bill'.[1] The lawyers were all against the bill, Hardwicke remarking that Granville's speech seemed 'designed more for the diversion of the House than for delivering his own opinion, much less enforcing it'; while Mansfield showed great scorn for the bill brought in 'by those who knew no law, and who might as well write a history of Japan without knowing the Japanese'. As to Granville's disavowing popularity, 'his lordship would at last have it for his conduct in some points in which he had neglected it, as in his opposition to the Militia Act, which had only caused riots in the country'. It may, however, be suspected that there was more in Granville's speech than as reported by Hansard, since Pitt said of it that 'he had eternized his name with the nation, the city and the constitution' by the part he had taken on this Habeas Corpus amendment bill. George II, on the other hand, was so much annoyed by Granville's speech that he even thought of removing him from office, but was prevented by the cautious Hardwicke who thought such action would do 'infinite prejudice to the King's service'.[2]

Newcastle's relations with Pitt were wittily compared by Chesterfield to those of 'a man and wife, who jog on, seldom agreeing, often quarrelling, but by mutual interest upon the whole, not parting'. Newcastle was happy enough dispensing patronage, lay and clerical, as of old, and finding, as a rule, no great difficulty in raising the money for Pitt's widespread activities on land and sea against France.

[1] See above, for the Jew Bill, ch. ix, pp. 186–7.
[2] *P.H.* xv, 714, 900; Yorke, *Hardwicke*, iii, 46–49.

As Horace Walpole put it: 'Pitt *does* everything, the Duke of New-castle *gives* everything.' There is a pleasant picture of Newcastle once coming to consult Pitt when he was ill in bed: the Duke, finding the room chilly and spying another bed in the room, crept into it: and the two ministers were discovered arguing and gesticu-lating at one another from their respective beds. It was said of him before he had Pitt as a colleague that he lost an hour every morning and spent the rest of the day trying to catch up with it; but Pitt saw to it that in this respect he mended his ways, telling him on one occasion that 'the present moment *is decisive*, and *that moment, so seldom seized, is seldom offered twice*'. Every week, for example, Pitt insisted on having a meeting with him and the Secretary to the Treasury to make sure that the contracts for supplying his armies were being duly carried out. Once, but probably only once, New-castle excused himself from attending a cabinet meeting on the plea that he was entertaining a bishop at his country house: Pitt replied that he had hoped for the Duke's advice on 'so important and extensive a scene as the campaign in America, where England and Europe are to be fought for', but loftily excused him 'after the desire your Grace has expressed not to break the agreeable engagements at Claremont'. We hear of no further excuses of the Duke from ministerial meetings. Although, too, Pitt recognized as Newcastle's special sphere the raising of ways and means to carry out his own great schemes for attacking France at sea and on land in Europe, America, Africa and even India, he had no hesitation in expressing disapproval at the least sign of careless or extravagant methods of finance. Newcastle's budgets for both the years 1758 and 1759 aroused loud complaints from Pitt for their extravagance; complaints justified by the fact that Pitt was chiefly responsible for carrying them in the Commons: 'I would to God', he writes, 'I could see my way through this mountain of expense, but I confess I cannot, unless your Grace can prevail to reduce things to a reasonable bulk— this is peculiarly your Grace's province—and to so much precision at least as would enable me to deal openly and fairly with the House.' Pitt's protests were of avail, for in one case at least, Newcastle by more careful scrutiny of the items was able to reduce a demand for £1,866,419 by £600,000, no small reduction for those days. But though the Duke had perforce to give in, he was shrill in his com-plaints to Hardwicke: 'such treatment', he wrote, 'from one whom I have nourished and served is not and cannot be borne...he will be Treasurer, Secretary, General and Admiral'. The fact was that

Newcastle, whose whole upbringing had been confined to the 'meridian of Germany', was aghast at Pitt's world-wide schemes: 'To think', he exclaimed, 'of being able to extirpate the French from North America [as Pitt in fact did], or to think that such a nation as France would sit down tamely under it, is to me the idlest of all imaginings.'

But, when Pitt discovered that negotiations for peace were being carried on behind his back, his wrath was majestic and decisive. Hardwicke's son Joseph Yorke, ambassador at the Hague, had received some letters from a lady, believed to be the Princess of Anhalt-Zerbst, suggesting terms that might be acceptable to France; and, without informing either of the Secretaries of State, he had sent them to his father and Newcastle, who had shown them to the King. Pitt, on discovering this 'clandestine proceeding', as he called it, 'relating to certain dapplings for peace on the part of some lady', wrote that if the Duke had the King's orders to carry on such a correspondence, he himself must find himself 'thereby deprived of the means of doing His Majesty any service'; and when Newcastle answered airily that 'these cursed female letters were a matter purely for amusement', Pitt responded with the crushing answer: 'I trust it is not presumption to lay myself at His Majesty's feet and most humbly request his gracious permission to retire whenever his Majesty thinks it for his service to treat for a peace in the vehicle of letters for amusement, and to order his servants to conceal, under so thin a covering, the first dawnings of information relative to so high and delicate an object.' The poor old Duke was all of a twitter when he received this haughty rebuke, and tried to get out of his scrape by pretending he was 'sorry when the letters were sent to me'—whereas in fact he had originally received them with much glee—and ordering that for the future any approaches from the Hague to Vienna and Versailles should be 'kept a secret from Yorke'. This evasion and the implied rebuke to Yorke naturally aroused his old friend Hardwicke's resentment and for the time being there was a little coolness in their relations; but by the end of the year the two cronies had returned to their old affectionate intercourse. Pitt too, pacified by the Duke's fumbling apologies and also by the Garter bestowed on his brother-in-law Temple, had forgiven the Duke for his *gaucheries*; indeed in the following July he paid a visit to Claremont. Of the great man's visit Newcastle writes ecstatically to Temple: 'We were very lucky in the weather, and, without a compliment, wanted nothing but your good company.... With my lord Lincoln and Mr Pitt...I had the pleasure to drink your Lordship's health. Mr Pitt was extremely good and agreeable and was here by twelve o'clock. Claremont put on its best looks.'[1]

But with the death of George II on 25 October 1760 this idyllic harmony came to an end. At the outset of the new reign both Pitt and Newcastle were made to feel that the only man in George III's confidence was his Groom of the Stole, Lord Bute. With Bute's help the King hoped to destroy the Whig oligarchy's power, based largely on Newcastle's electoral influence, but, before that could be brought about, the war, of which Pitt was the guiding spirit, must be brought to an end. Pitt, once allied with Bute, had come to distrust him: Newcastle characteristically veered towards the rising sun, and, while at first expressing a desire to quit office, was easily persuaded to stay on in spite of Hardwicke's warning that 'it was not consistent either with his Grace's honour or personal satisfaction to remain on that foot, upon which alone he could expect to remain'.[2] Pitt, in the eyes of Bute and the King, was obviously the more dangerous, and had already, in the first week of the new reign, protested successfully against the King's description of *his* war as 'bloody and expensive': Newcastle meekly accepted the King's refusal to grant any money from the Secret Service Fund, on which he had relied in the past, for the general election due in 1761, and even struck up an alliance with Bute. Early in 1761 the first rift in the Pitt administration was made by the substitution of Bute, as Pitt's co-Secretary, for Holderness who, in George II's contemptuous phrase, had by this time become 'Pitt's footman' and completely deserted his original patron Newcastle.

By Bute's accession to the ministry the way was prepared for the resignation of Pitt, who found himself without a whole-hearted supporter among his colleagues except his unpopular brother-in-law, Temple. But in June 1761 it looked as if peace might be concluded with France through the negotiations then beginning between Pitt himself and Choiseul's envoy Bussy. Granville at first thought Pitt was proceeding on the right lines and expressed his unstinted approval of Pitt's answer to Choiseul's approaches: 'Lord Granville presents his compliments to Mr Pitt and thanks him for the communication of his answer to the Duc de Choiseul together with the draught of the Memorial. Neither of these draughts can in my

[1] See my *Chatham*, II, 74–6; Yorke, *Hardwicke*, III, 20–7, 65–87; *Grenville Papers*, I, 346.

[2] Yorke, *Hardwicke*, III, 307.

judgment be mended; and when this great affair comes out into
the world every person of candour will agree to impute the happy
setting out of this great affair, as well as the success of it, which
God grant, to the right author; whose spirit and perseverance and
judgment, under some discouragements, to my own knowledge,
have produced this salutary result. Ever yours Granville.' Towards
the end of July, when the negotiations seemed on the eve of
conclusion, the terms to which France seemed prepared to agree
were declared by Granville to be 'more advantageous to England
than any ever concluded since King Henry V's time'. But when
the negotiations still hung fire as Choiseul began to hope for an
offensive alliance with Spain, Granville began to have doubts about
Pitt's forthright method of carrying them on. Thus of Pitt's draught
reply to new demands from Choiseul he said 'it deserved to be
inserted in the Acta Regni; but for his part he did not love fine
letters on business. He thought even bad Latin preferable to good
in negotiations.'[1] But it was not till Pitt, convinced by irrefutable
evidence that Spain was on the point of joining France against us,
proposed at once declaring war on her before the two Bourbon
fleets could unite, that Granville definitely parted company with
him. Bute, representing the King's wishes, was anxious for peace
at almost any price, and Newcastle with the rest of the council,
except only Temple, were for a temporizing policy. Three meetings
in quick succession were held before the decisive vote was taken.
Even then Pitt's opponents, much as his dictatorial tone in council
irked them, were anxious, if possible, to avert his threatened resignation if his views were not accepted; especially as he might prove to
be right in the junction of the two Bourbon powers. For, as Newcastle said, 'We should then have given Mr Pitt such a handle against
us as might have very bad consequences'. In the last of these three
momentous councils, on 2 October 1761, the discussion was opened
by Granville in a temporizing strain, a strange contrast to his former
impetuous self-assurance: 'I would be behind-hand in nothing but
in the actual striking of the blow.... But consider your strength.
My opinion is to give no hostile answer to Spain; for what hostilities
can you begin with advantage.' Newcastle and the rest followed on
the same lines, except Temple, who, after a few scornful words at
his colleagues' timidity, left the council room, and Pitt, who after
repeating his well-founded argument for immediate action instead

---

[1] *Chatham Correspondence*, II, 113–14; *Bedford Correspondence*, I, 26; H. Walpole,
Memoirs of George III, I, 68–9.

of waiting for Spain to strike first, ended up with his famous declaration: 'I will go on no longer, since my advice is not taken. Being responsible I will direct, and will be responsible for nothing that I do not direct.' The proceedings were concluded by Granville who '(in his own nervous and manly eloquence) expressed his high opinion of Mr Pitt's wisdom, penetration, abilities, honour, and integrity, and in a very particular and most emphatical manner spoke of the innumerable and almost insurmountable difficulties which Mr Pitt and Lord Temple had had to struggle with'. This is Lord Granville's last recorded speech.[1]

[1] The somewhat depreciatory speech on Pitt attributed to Granville on this occasion in the *Annual Register* for 1761 appears to be entirely apocryphal. According to Almon, in his *Review of Lord Bute's Administration*, Granville declared that 'there was not even *one* word of truth in that spurious production, that so far from its containing *any* of *his* sentiments it was just the contrary'. I regret that in my *Chatham*, II, 113, I quoted the *Annual Register* version, overlooking Almon's more probable version, which is confirmed in Newcastle's account of this cabinet meeting in Yorke, *Hardwicke*, III, 280.

Chapter XI

GRANVILLE & NEWCASTLE: LAST SURVIVORS OF A REGIME

§ I

Pitt's resignation affected Granville less than Newcastle. Bute indeed, at the beginning of the new reign, had suggested that Hardwicke should replace Granville as Lord President; but Hardwicke, though willing still, as a Privy Councillor, to attend cabinet meetings, had put aside the suggestion.[1] Again, in November 1762, George III, among his numerous suggestions to Bute for changes in the cabinet, suggested that Granville should be pensioned off and his place given to the Duke of Bedford, but finally decided that he should continue as President for the short time he was likely to live, adding that on his death Hardwicke might succeed him, 'if he behaves as he ought'.[2] In fact, almost to the end of his life, Granville, though 'much broken', as Horace Walpole had noted in April 1762, attended cabinet councils, which, no doubt owing to his infirmities, were generally held at his own house in Arlington Street. Count Bentinck, writing in August 1761, states that 'Granville étoit toujours appelé au Conseil, mais que c'étoit à son désavantage à présent, pour ce que le Conseil se tenoit à midi, et qu'alors Granville n'avoit pas encore eu sa bouteille; que l'on avoit de tous côtés beaucoup de déférence tant pour sa capacité que pour sa connection avec les Finches [Lord Winchilsea's relations]...'. Even without his bottle, too, much of his old fire remained. When, in May 1762, after Pitt's resignation, negotiations were resumed with France, he supported, against Newcastle, Hardwicke and Devonshire, Bute's proposal to cease paying the subsidy to Frederic II, whom he called 'the greatest enemy the King had': on the other hand, at another council in August, when Bute, in spite of our continued successes, proposed terms of peace with France even less favourable than in 1761, Granville took the Council with him in refusing to conclude any treaty with France 'without proper security should be given that the French would not take part with Spain in their war with us'.[3]

[1] Yorke, *Hardwicke*, III, 259.
[2] R. Sedgwick, *Letters from George III to Lord Bute*, pp. 159, 165–6.
[3] Yorke, *Hardwicke*, III, 355, 406.

But, though crippled in his limbs, impoverished, by careless management, in his means, and, as Bentinck had said, 'ne voulant plus de bruit ni de noise', he still, in the evening of his days, retained all his zest and interest in life. The Hon. Thomas Robinson, son of Newcastle's pompous Secretary of State, recorded memoranda of Granville at this period of his life.[1] 'Lord Granville', he writes, 'in those days used in general to set at home and receive such visitors as his high station and lively conversation attracted at all hours of the day...and by thus staying at home saw the ministers that were out as well as those that were in.' Among others came the great Mr Pitt himself, to tell him about the unpopularity he had acquired by accepting a pension on resigning office, well knowing, as he told Granville, that 'his acceptance of a reward, which bore the name of a pension, would create much clamour among his friends and much triumph among his enemies; but', he added, 'he had just come from a meeting with these old city friends, and, by a speech he had made begging them not to be too hasty in their judgment, had entirely regained their affection'.

How gallantly the old statesman stood up against growing misfortunes and infirmities is shown in the two accounts left of his last days. One is in a letter written eight months after his death by an old friend, A. Forrester, to Sir Andrew Mitchell in Berlin. After painting the chaotic state of affairs left by Bute on the eve of his resignation in September 1763, Forrester continues: 'As to our deceased friend Lord Granville, he spun out life to the very last quarter inch. He had been gradually, but visibly, declining these four years, and was so far gone during the course of the last that even I could not wish his continuance in the world. He was almost bent double, worn to a skeleton, quite lost the use of his legs, and spent the best part of the day in dozing. Thus were we all deceived in our expectation of the manner of his death. He was most likely from his make to die suddenly, whereas he was at least one whole year about it. But the disorder of his affairs will surprise you. He has left debts not much short of £60,000. Furniture, plate, and the house in Arlington Street are all sold: the latter was bought, I think, for £15,000 by Sir Laurence Dundas, of whose second immense fortune you must, even at your distance, have hear'd. The curiously well chosen library at Hawnes must, I fear, go too: but I know not whether that be determined, being an utter stranger to the successor. As to his L[p]'s conduct during our various revolutions, his chief aim,

[1] Robinson's memorandum book is, or was in 1913, among the Wrest Park MSS.

I believe from a consciousness of the bad state of his affairs, was to keep his employment, wherein he succeeded by taking no share in the broils, and by a readiness to give his best advice, while he continued able, to each set that was in.'[1]

The other account, of his last public duty performed, is even more moving. It is given by Robert Wood, who was Under-Secretary of State from 1756 to 1763 and again from 1768 to 1770. He was also the author of an *Essay on the Original Genius of Homer*, in the preface of which he relates that 'being directed to call upon his lordship [Granville] a few days before he died, with the Preliminary Articles of the Treaty of Paris [of 1763], I found him so languid that I proposed postponing the business for another time; but he insisted that I should stay, saying, it could not prolong his life to neglect his duty; and, repeating the following passage out of Sarpedon's speech, he dwelled with particular emphasis on the third line, which recalled to his mind the distinguishing part he had taken in public affairs:

ὦ πέπον, εἰ μὲν γὰρ πόλεμον περὶ τόνδε φυγόντε
αἰεὶ δὴ μέλλοιμεν ἀγήρω τ᾽ ἀθανάτω τε
ἔσσεσθ᾽, οὔτε κεν αὐτὸς ἐνὶ πρώτοισι μαχοίμην
οὔτε κε σὲ στέλλοιμι μάχην ἐς κυδιάνειραν·
νῦν δ᾽ ἔμπης γὰρ κῆρες ἐφεστᾶσιν θανάτοιο
μυρίαι, ἃς οὐκ ἔστι φυγεῖν βροτὸν οὐδ᾽ ὑπαλύξαι,
ἴομεν.[2]

On 2 January 1763, a few days after this last public duty performed, Granville died at Bath, and on the 11th found his last resting place, by the side of his two wives, in Westminster Abbey.

§ II

Newcastle, unfortunately for himself, survived Granville by over five years, years of almost continuous disappointment and disillusion. Even before the accession of George III, Holderness, of whom, it may be recalled, he had once said, 'Though a d'Arcy he is not proud, you can tell him his faults and he will mend them', that same

---

[1] Add. MSS. 30999, f. 16.

[2] *Iliad*, XII, 322-8: 'Ah friend, if once escaped from this battle we were for ever to be ageless and immortal, *neither should I fight myself amid the foremost*, nor should I send thee into battle where men win glory; but now—for in any case fates of death beset us, fates past counting, which no mortal may escape or avoid— now let us go forward!' (trans. by A. T. Murray in *Loeb Classical Library*).

Holderness, his special protégé, had deserted him and become 'that poor wretch Holderness...the most *double* man that I ever knew in my life'.[1] Even more galling must have been the desertion of his once faithful secretary Andrew Stone, the recipient of all his most secret confidences, on whom he had heaped benefits, and who now transferred his allegiance to the new favourite Bute. True that, as an offset to these desertions, Pitt, though occasionally treating him with the rough side of his tongue if the Duke was obstructive to his military measures, had on the whole worked well and loyally with him, and at the beginning of the new reign had assured Hardwicke, who passed it on to Newcastle, that 'your Grace was indispensably necessary to be part of the administration; and he had most fully and expressly declared to my Lord Bute...how sincerely he wished to continue to act with you, upon whom he could depend'.[2] But Bute and the new King had made up their minds to get rid of both Pitt and Newcastle, the first in order to obtain an early peace, if need be on such terms as Pitt would not consent to, and Newcastle as the fugleman of the old electoral and patronage systems, for which they proposed to substitute more direct royal action. The dismissal of Newcastle could well wait, for, as Devonshire explained to the King, 'the D. of N——e was easily managed, for that trifles pleas'd him; a little seeming good humour from me [i.e. George III] and your [Bute] telling him things before he hears them from others are the sure maxims to keep him in order, for nothing is so hateful to him as the thought of retiring'.[3] Accordingly the first to go had been Pitt, with' the help, among others, of Newcastle, who had already hitched his wagon to the rising star of Bute.

Pitt had hardly gone a fortnight before Newcastle was beginning to complain that, being no longer so necessary to Bute and the King, he was being treated 'as subservient to and dependent upon and, in short, to use my own word, aide-de-camp to my Lord Bute...not consistent to my rank, age and honour'.[4] What perhaps touched him most nearly was Bute's interference with ecclesiastical patronage which, since 1736, he had always regarded as his special province. When the important see of London fell vacant, Bute appointed Hayter of Norwich instead of Newcastle's nominee Thomas of Lincoln, and, on Newcastle protesting, told him roughly: 'If Thomas is such a favourite of yours, why did you not promote him when you had the power?'[5] A succession of such rebuffs brought him at

[1] Yorke, *Hardwicke*, III, 98–9.   [2] *Ib.* III, 308.   [3] Sedgwick, *l.c.* p. 70.
[4] Yorke, *Hardwicke*, III, 335.   [5] Walpole, *George III*, I, 74.

last to serious thoughts of resigning. Already in August 1761 he was writing to Hardwicke, 'it is probable that the party is taken to have no regard for my situation, to any recommendations that may come from me, and to leave me to take such resolutions as I may think proper; either to swallow it, and thereby make the most contemptible figure that ever man did, or to resign my employment, in which case my Lord Bute is ready and desirous to undertake it'. But it was only after endless letters and confabulations between him and Hardwicke, and others taken into counsel, and when, as a last straw, he was overruled by his own Treasury Board, being treated, as he complained, 'as an old piece of household stuff that they may do what they please with',[1] that in May 1762 he finally brought himself to the pitch of resigning. Even then the poor old man alternated between hopes that Bute would urge him to stay on and complaints that Bute was 'determined not to give the least handle' to such a proposal, 'showing plainly that it had been his determination for some time and to use me so as to make it impossible for me to continue in employment with ease or honour, or with any utility to the public'—by 'setting up my own Board of Treasury against me, not allowing me the common power and credit belonging to my office or in the general conduct of the affairs of the kingdom'.[2] Even when he went to take his leave of the King, George III 'did not drop one word of concern at my leaving him, nor even made me a polite compliment after nearly fifty years service and devotion to the interest of his Royal family. I will say nothing more of myself, but that I believe never any man was so dismissed.'[3] He was indeed offered a pension on retiring, to which, according to the standards of the time, he was fully entitled; for his income, originally reckoned at £40,000 from land and £11,000 from public employments, was now reduced to scarcely £6000 a year, largely owing to his vast expenses in hospitality and electioneering, which he had always regarded as a public duty. Nevertheless, prompted, it was said, by the Duke of Cumberland in order to distinguish him from Pitt, he refused to accept anything. In this respect, as Cumberland told him, 'The manner of your going out has more decency and dignity than I have seen in my period'.[4]

But worse indignities were to follow. When the Preliminaries for

---

[1] Yorke, *Hardwicke*, III, 420.   [2] *H. MSS. Rutland*, II, 276.

[3] Rockingham, *Memoirs*, I, 112. But in his account to Hardwicke (Yorke, *Hardwicke*, III, 357) Newcastle says that the 'King was extremely civil and gracious'.

[4] See Yorke, *Hardwicke*, III, 302 and the references there quoted.

the Peace of Paris came to be debated in Parliament in 1762 New-castle joined Pitt in criticizing some of the terms as far too favourable to France, and an inadequate return either for the resounding victories of Pitt's ministry or for the further successes against Spain and France achieved since his resignation. But by this time Bute had strengthened himself by installing Fox as chief bribe-master and disciplinarian of awkward minorities; and under his ruthless regime no quarter was given to opponents of the royal will, however highly they might be placed. Not least, Newcastle's influence in Parliament and in the country was to be finally broken, and such an example made that Parliament and its electors should be led to understand that for the future the King himself, and Newcastle no longer, was to be the chief dispenser of favours. Accordingly Newcastle was summarily dismissed from his three lord-lieutenancies of Middlesex, Sussex and Nottinghamshire,[1] and from the stewardship of Sherwood Forest; and the government stooped even so low as to hunt out and deprive of their subsistence clerks, schoolboys, widows, servants and old pensioners, provided for by the Duke, and give their places to Fox's relations and dependents: as a wag remarked at the time, 'everybody was to be turned out that the Duke of Newcastle had brought in, save the King himself'. On Christmas Day 1762 Newcastle wrote complaining bitterly to his friend Hardwicke that the King had ministers capable of thus depriving 'an old and faithful servant and subject of his royal family [of honours] which he has enjoyed from the hour this royal family came to the crown, now near fifty years'. Hardwicke, replying on the same day, gave him the bracing advice 'not to talk too much in a plaintive style, but in a style of disregard and defiance as to ministers, and hold up your head higher', an answer which gave the Duke fresh courage: 'I was so happy', he wrote, '... with your most affectionate, most wise and most spirited letter. I sent it immediately to the Duchess of Newcastle, who is greatly relieved by it.... The spirit of it and the solidity of the advice charms the Duchess.' An even more grievous blow, however, befell him in March 1764, by the death of his faithful old friend and mentor Hardwicke himself, the friend in whom for over thirty years he had reposed implicit confidence, and on whose prudent advice, however much it erred on the side of excessive caution, he absolutely depended. This loss was all the sadder, since the Chancellor's

---

[1] He had held the Lord-Lieutenancies of Middlesex and Notts since 1714, that of Sussex since 1761. The Lord-Lieutenancy of Notts was restored to him in 1765 when he once more became a minister.

sons, who at one time were very near to him, grown tired of the old man's fussy ways, had become more or less estranged. Charles Yorke, for example, writing to his eldest brother Royston, begs him, after an irksome visit to Claremont, 'to have weight and decision enough to deliver me from the slavery of eating a neck of roasted mutton with the Duchess of Newcastle at one o'clock in the morning'.[1]

Even at Cambridge, where Newcastle, as Chancellor, had seemed to be in an impregnable position, there were signs that his influence was waning. Clare, his own beloved college, the recipient of his benefactions and always one of the first to be visited in his frequent journeys to Cambridge, had in 1762 gone over to the enemy in electing as Master his personal and political opponent Goddard. Next year it was worse, for Goddard had become Vice-Chancellor and, having drawn up a fulsome address to the King on the Peace of Paris, had the face to ask Newcastle as Chancellor to present it, in spite of his known opposition to many of its terms: a request which Newcastle naturally refused. He never again set foot in Clare. A year later, he had another disappointment in the rejection of his own candidate for a professorship, in spite of all he could do for him. On this occasion he wrote more in sorrow than in anger: 'My friends at Cambridge are not so good managers at elections as I was formerly; and perhaps should be still if I knew as well how to go about getting an university (in which I have much miscarried) as in carrying a county.'[2] On the other hand in the election of High Steward of the University to fill the place of his friend Hardwicke he carried the day, though only by a narrow margin. Newcastle's candidate for the post was the Chancellor's eldest son and heir: against him stood Lord Sandwich, 'Jemmy Twitcher', who, in spite of his unsavoury reputation, had a strong backing from the ministry and the King himself, and consequently of all those who looked for favours from the court, while Newcastle was handicapped by the little interest in the contest evinced by the new Lord Hardwicke himself. At Cambridge both sides claimed the victory; but, on reference to the King's Bench, Newcastle's man was declared duly elected. To balance this slender success Hardwicke's brother, Charles Yorke, chose this moment to desert Newcastle's party in Parliament and make his peace with the court.[3]

---

[1] Yorke, *Hardwicke*, III, 367.
[2] D. A. Winstanley, *Cambridge in the 18th Century*, p. 264.
[3] *Ib.* pp. 55–139.

By this time Newcastle, after over fifty years of almost ceaseless political activity, might well have retired from the fray. Of his more immediate contemporaries Granville and his faithful confidant Hard-wicke were dead: the Whig governmental party, to which most of his energies had been devoted, had been defeated and scattered by the Patriot King, his minister Bute and their cynical *condottiere* Fox. Pitt, the only other notable survivor of the great ministry which had carried the Seven Years' War to resounding victory, stood proudly aloof from Bute's new dispensation; but he had never for-given Newcastle for deserting him in 1761; nor, with his motto 'measures not men', was he a comfortable member of any party. The only hope for a revival of the old Whig party, in which alone Newcastle could see any cheerful prospect for the future, appeared to be in untried men such as the Marquess of Rockingham and the Duke of Grafton, both almost young enough to be Newcastle's grandsons. So in his few remaining years, instead of enjoying a well-earned repose, he must needs turn to such as these, and was even willing to serve under them, in order to restore the old Whig supremacy. It is true he never forgot that he was the 'elder states-man' with an experience of half a century in office, but even so he put up with many rebuffs from his inexperienced juniors, as long as they upheld the banner, as he understood it, of true-blue Whiggery.

The Whigs had their chance again in 1765. After Bute's resigna-tion in 1763, George Grenville, who succeeded him, proved so dis-tasteful to George III by his hectoring ways, and dreary lectures in the Closet, that the King turned to Pitt again as less offensive and also as holding a view superficially the same as his own, that 'measures not men', i.e. a definite policy not necessarily depending on party ties, must be the acid test of an administration. Unfortunately Pitt had his difficulties and delicacies, especially in his inability to persuade his brother-in-law Temple to join him: so at last in despair George had to accept a purely Whig administration headed by the young Marquess of Rockingham in Newcastle's old post of First Lord of the Treasury, with Grafton and Conway as Secretaries of State, 'an administration of boys', as Newcastle called it.[1] Newcastle himself accepted the comparatively unimportant post of Lord Privy Seal, but was especially gratified by the King's command that he should undertake Church affairs and recommend to all Church preferments. With the assistance of the Archbishop of Canterbury, he replied, he would take care to recommend none but those with two qualifica-

[1] D. A. Winstanley, *Chatham and the Whig Opposition*, p. 38.

tions: '*First* that he should always be one of a good unblemished
life and character, and such as one of his profession ought to be:
second, that he should be, and should have always been, most
zealously attach'd to the protestant succession in his Royal Family.'[1]
And so it was settled.

Newcastle at first, according to his enemy, Lord George Sackville,
'began his old tricks by meddling with everything in every department, but the Duke of Grafton called him to order, and he promises
to behave better for the future'.[2] In fact Newcastle, with his vast
experience of administration, was occasionally very helpful in guiding
his colleagues round pitfalls in the path. But, almost from the start,
it was a ministry doomed to failure. It was accepted most unwillingly
by the King, after he had failed to secure Pitt as leader of a non-party
government, simply as a *pis-aller* to rescue him from the insufferable
pedant Grenville. Moreover, he had kept in it two critical observers,
the Chancellor Northington and Barrington the Secretary at War,
the former of whom used to report to him, with unfavourable
comments, the ministerial deliberations. They started indeed well
by repealing Grenville's Stamp Act and the unpopular cyder tax,
while general warrants, the main issue on which Wilkes, supported
by Pitt, had protested against Grenville's arbitrary policy, were
declared illegal. But after that they had little support in either House;
indeed Newcastle complained that 'my Lord Rockingham has not
so much as desired my assistance in the House of Lords; he depends
upon my Lord Chancellor and my Lord Egmont for his supports.
A strange phenomenon!' strange indeed, for they were at best luke-
warm supporters of the ministry. In consequence George III, prejudiced against the Rockingham administration from the start, and
increasingly aware of its ineffectiveness in Parliament, made another
attempt to secure Pitt. In this he finally succeeded; Pitt no longer
refused to take office without Temple, who had definitely gone over
to the Grenville camp, but stipulated that he 'could not sit at Council
with the Duke of Newcastle', an expression which rankled in the
Duke's mind almost to the end of his life.[3]

So this was the end of the Duke's long official career. In a series
of letters to an old friend, John White, M.P. for East Retford 1733–68,
he gives his own account of his troubles during this short-lived
Rockingham ministry and of his final interviews with the King.

[1] *Changes in the Ministry* (Mary Bateson, editor), p. 33.
[2] H. MSS. *Stopford-Sackville*, I, 101.
[3] *Changes in the Ministry*, pp. 42, 44, 54, 159.

Almost his last official act was to propose to the King a series of episcopal appointments, among others the translation of John Hume from Oxford to the more important see of Salisbury, to enforce which, he writes, 'I added one argument which I hoped might have weight with His Majesty, that the Dutchess of Newcastle, who has been the best friend, and best wife to me for forty-five, and I might have said forty-nine years, had this so much at heart, that I did not know how the disappointment might affect her health'. On 30 July 1766, when the Duke came to give up the seal of office, the King told him that 'he was extremely glad to do what he had done for the Bishop of Oxford [translated him to Salisbury], as it pleased me; but he owned he had another inducement to it, and that was, that he knew it would be agreeable to the Dutchess of Newcastle; and desired me to tell her so from him'. One further request the Duke made, in recommending his beloved 'University of Cambridge and the deserving men there...I observed how much the University would fear that they should be sufferers by my being out of His Majesty's service; that in order to give some consolation for them, at my going out, I hoped His Majesty would allow me to recommend to him my very deserving friend, Dr Powell, our present Vice-Chancellor...for the Archdeaconry of Colchester.... His Majesty, with the greatest readiness and pleasure, said he would do it....I then told the King that, as this would probably be the last time that I should come into His Majesty's closet, as one of his servants, (the King replied very graciously, "I hope you mean it in that sense only"), I would take the liberty to advise him to keep as many of *his servants as he could.*' 'I hear', he adds, 'that the *offer* or *no offer* of the pension [of £4000];[1] and *my certain refusal*, is much approved, and particularly by the Duke of Bedford, who told my Lord Albemarle, it was the greatest and noblest part that ever man acted, and *what he should have expected from me.*' Nothing indeed in Newcastle's long career became him more than this final parting with the King.[2]

But though Newcastle himself could hardly have expected to sit in another ministry, almost to the very last days of his life he was busy making plans for the return of his friends to power. In 1767 when, owing to Chatham's long illness and seclusion from public affairs, the dissolution of his ministry seemed imminent, the Duke was particularly active in trying to unite the various sections of the

[1] It was actually offered him, see *Grenville Correspondence*, III, 291.
[2] *Changes in the Ministry*, pp. 86-100.

opposition led by Bedford, Grenville and Rockingham respectively. But in spite of numerous meetings at Newcastle House and 'volumes of advice to my Lord Rockingham' from the Duke himself, no common ground for settling the political, and still less the personal differences of these sections could be found. None the less he was almost as active as ever in organizing the general election of 1768. He had some failures which he took greatly to heart: Grafton, for example, though 'quite defeated at Rye', had 'settled' Hastings, 'a town where ever since the year 1714, I have', said the Duke, 'constantly chose both the members to this very day', and, bitterest perhaps of all, 'that ungrateful town of Lewes', the capital of his own county, was captured by the enemy. Here, however, he was able to take signal vengeance, for he told his steward 'to give notice to such of my tenants at Lewes who did not vote for [his candidates]...to quit their several houses at Michmas next: also...to call in the bills of such tradesmen at Lewes, who have been usually employed by me, and did not vote as above, and not employ them again on my account'. But on the whole he lost little ground in the other constituencies where he had always taken a personal interest, though of course he no longer commanded the power of punishing or rewarding electors for their votes in the many constituencies amenable solely to government influence.[1]

When Newcastle died at his house in Lincoln's Inn Fields on 17 November 1768 he died an embittered, disappointed man. His electoral craft, the main source of his power, was no longer proof against the assaults of younger and even richer and more unscrupulous electioneers. His friends and many even of his own relatives were deserting him. In the last published letter addressed to his old friend John White,[2] his lifelong confidant, he unburdens the bitterness of his soul. He begins by owning that 'I was never so much hurt, mortified and disappointed in my whole life, as I was, last night, by the receipt of your short, cold, and I must say, unfriendly letter of the 10th, to the warmest, most confidential, and, I think, the most interesting letter I ever wrote in my life, wherein I pointed out to you my distress; I implored your advice and assistance; I called upon all my Whig friends for theirs....I can call God to witness that, during my whole life...ever since the year 1711, my whole study has been to show my love, affection, respect, and confidence to your good father and yourself, without any drawback for one moment.

[1] See D. A. Winstanley, *Chatham and the Whig Opposition*, pp. 213-17.
[2] *Changes in the Ministry*, pp. 166-9.

To you I apply for advice: it is from you I expect the first assistance.'
He then proceeds to complain of the Duke of Portland's 'most
extraordinary and amazing silence.... For it is my partiality... for
the Duke of Portland that has brought all these difficulties.' To that
'partiality' he goes on to attribute the 'cruel behaviour of my Lord
Lincoln', his own favourite nephew and heir, who,[1] taking offence
at Newcastle's favours to Portland, had set up anti-Newcastle candidates in Nottinghamshire, when it was known 'that it was myself,
and I may almost say, myself alone, who rescued the county of
Nottingham, and all the boroughs in it out of the hands of the
Tories.... What', he concludes, 'would all my old county friends
say if they were alive, to see me upon the point of being drove out
of the county by two such ungrateful young men?'

On his death, forlorn and almost alone, all that his discredited
enemy, Sackville, could find to say was: 'His death would occasion
distress in some of the Sussex elections; in all other lights it seems
an event of little consequence.'[2] A juster and more charitable verdict
was that of his contemporary Chesterfield: 'I own I feel for his
death, not because it will be my turn next, but because I knew him
to be very goodnatured, and his hands to be extremely clean.'

*   *

*

Both Carteret and Newcastle, at the outset of their careers, had the
advantages, great in an oligarchic age, of ample fortunes and widespread connexions with the ruling families of England. Newcastle
of the two was the more richly endowed. His family connexions,
besides his own immediate Pelham relations, included Cavendishes,
Churchills, Harleys, Godolphins, Spencers, Townshends, Shelleys,
Mannerses, Holleses, Pierreponts, Clintons, Talbots; and it was not
amiss that, at the beginning of the Hanoverian period, nearly all
these families were closely bound up with the Revolution settlement.
Also he had the great advantage of starting his career with a rent-

---

[1] In 1756, after the death without male heirs of his brother Henry Pelham,
on whom the succession to the dukedom of Newcastle-upon-Tyne would have
devolved, Newcastle was created Duke of Newcastle-under-Line, so Lyme was
spelt in the original patent, with special remainder to his nephew Henry, seventh
Earl of Lincoln, who had married a daughter of Henry Pelham. Lincoln, on succeeding to this dukedom, also obtained the old Duke's restored Lord-Lieutenancy
of Notts and his former post of Steward of Sherwood Forest.

[2] H. MSS. Stopford-Sackville, I, 126.

roll of some £40,000 a year, with properties in London and some half-dozen counties of England, and notably in Sussex and Nottinghamshire. Carteret was less well-endowed, it is true, with wealth and important family connexions, nor were those connexions so predominantly Whig as were Newcastle's; for both Carterets and Granvilles were largely tinged with Tory traditions; still both these families had for many generations produced statesmen and warriors of some eminence. Carteret was also allied, either by previous connexions or, later, by the marriages of his daughters, with Montagus, Tollemaches, Finches, Spencers and Cowpers, Pomfrets, Tweeddales and Shelburnes; but his territorial influence was not so widespread or important as Newcastle's, being entirely confined to the comparatively remote counties of Cornwall and Devon. Nor was he ever, except in his outlook on foreign politics, so full-blooded a Whig as Newcastle: indeed in his first years in Parliament it was still a moot point whether he could be reckoned as a Hanover Tory or a Whig; and even in later days he showed no insurmountable objection to using Tories for his purposes. Each, however, with these initial advantages, differed *toto caelo* from the other in the use to which they put them and in their outlook on life and politics generally: except that, unlike the general run of politicians of their time, both of them were moved, not by personal self-interest, but by what each—according to his lights—believed to be in the best interests of England.

If public honours were any indication of greatness Newcastle would count as one of the greatest in our annals. Succeeding to his father's barony before he was of age, when he was twenty-one he was created Viscount Haughton and Earl of Clare and next year Marquess of Clare and Duke of Newcastle-upon-Tyne. At various times he was appointed Lord-Lieutenant of Middlesex, Nottinghamshire and Sussex, Steward of Sherwood Forest and Vice-Admiral of Sussex, and in 1756 he obtained a second Dukedom. He was given the honorary degree of LL.D. at Cambridge many years before Carteret had his doctorate at Oxford; became High Steward and then Chancellor of Cambridge University, and, oddly enough, a Fellow of the Royal Society, at a period indeed when such a distinction in no way testified to scientific attainments: he was enrolled among the Knights of the Garter at the age of twenty-five, more than thirty years before Carteret, his senior, was raised to that order. Above all for nearly fifty years he was a minister of the Crown.

The reason for all these honours and for his long service in the political world was originally that he had, at a critical time in our annals, made himself indispensable as a manager of elections in the interest of the new dynasty; and later he had so strongly entrenched himself as the chief dispenser of patronage in Church and State, that no ministry, not even Pitt's, up to the end of George II's reign could afford to be bereft of his services.

In the course of this sketch full expression has been given to the Duke's tiresome and often ridiculous idiosyncrasies. Fully conscious of his own weaknesses—want of decision and inability to enforce his views on colleagues abler than himself—he was always seeking balm for his wounded vanity from passing confidants, Craggs, old Horace Walpole, Chesterfield, Sandwich, Holderness and countless others such as even Carteret, Townshend, Walpole himself, the royal Duke of Cumberland and his sister the Princess Amelia, with whom he at one time was delighted to be accused of carrying on a mild flirtation; and especially from his trusty mentor Lord Chancellor Hardwicke. But above all these personal, and often ridiculous, idiosyncrasies was his firm belief, justified at any rate in the early years of his career, that England was to be saved from a return to Jacobitism and a general revolution only by his unwearying support of the Revolution settlement, by his personal attention to elections and his careful exercise of patronage in the Whig interest.

In spite of his eccentricities, pilloried by Hervey and Horace Walpole and ridiculed by Smollett in his account of one of the Duke's levies in *Humphrey Clinker*, in spite too of his recurring complaints that he was not sufficiently considered by his constantly changing colleagues, he had a fund of real affection for those with whom he was brought into closest contact. His 'dearest' Duchess, of whom we know little except by his constant letters to her and by the loving care they lavished on one another, was a faithful mentor and helpmeet to him in all those little, important affairs of life, such as his health or her use as his secretary to transcribe his almost illegible epistles on his most secret concerns; and perhaps among the bitterest disappointments of his old age, when, with the accession of George III, the tide had turned against him, was the desertion of him by his former, most trusted secretary Andrew Stone, and by John White his Nottingham correspondent for fifty years. Above all, his single-minded devotion to what he considered the best interests of the country is attested by the fact that he three times refused a pension, justly earned by every standard of his age, offered to him when he had reduced his original income of £40,000 to a mere £6000, almost entirely by his electoral activities in the Whig interest.

With all his absurdities he was a public-spirited servant of the state, and, at least in the early years of his career, valuable for his public services in helping to establish a stable system of Whig government when it was most needed.

To Carteret the amenities of polite civilization were at least as important, if not more so, than the hurly-burly of domestic politics. He was a real scholar all his life, not only in Latin and Greek, but also as a voracious reader in German, French, Spanish, Portuguese and possibly other languages—in Sweden, for example, he made a point of making acquaintance with the scholars of Upsala University. Nor was he influenced by any political bias in his discriminating patronage of literature and scholarship. In politics he cared little for the minor business of rewarding party fidelity, and undoubtedly lost much by his Olympian contempt for that side of politics. In domestic affairs he showed for his time a precocious appreciation of the hardships and rights of the underdog, especially in some of his speeches during the years of opposition to Walpole's government. He protested, it will be remembered, against the revival of the Salt Tax because, though 'the rich generally live upon fresh provisions, a poor man will live upon salt meat'; he objected to the raid on the Sinking Fund, because that would mean additional taxes which 'lie heavy on the poor'; he urged reform of iniquitous laws rather than repression by the soldiery, for 'the people seldom or ever assemble in any riotous or tumultuous manner unless they are oppressed.... You may shoot them, you may hang them, but till the oppression is removed there will never be quiet.... [If injustice is found to be done remove it:] this is the only human method of preventing riots or tumults...nor should you, if the magistrate cannot execute the law, agree to erect a barrack at every turnpike.'[1]

But his main interest was in the wider aspects of foreign policy. He was the only statesman of his day familiar with the complicated but important constitutional system of the Empire, which then concerned, either directly or indirectly, about half the population of Europe. In his conception of England's foreign policy he was the pupil of that great foreign minister Stanhope, and for a time had as his own pupil, 'in the upper parts of government', that greater

[1] See above, ch. VI.

genius Pitt, on Pitt's own admission; though with this difference that, whereas Carteret's vision hardly penetrated beyond Europe, Pitt comprehended the whole of both continents as the concern of this island nation.

Carteret's political career is marked by three clearly defined periods: first his brilliant youth, distinguished by his successful embassy to Sweden and his vice-royalty of Ireland, unsurpassed for tact and efficiency by that of any other Lord-Lieutenant of the century; secondly the full flowering of his flamboyant power in his great speeches against Walpole's government and his masterful direction of foreign politics during his second tenure of the Secretary's seals; and lastly his period of tactful acquiescence combined with practical wisdom as Lord President, in the evening of his days.

And yet at best he can only be assigned the place of a brilliant failure, for which there are three reasons. First—and this was through no fault of his own—he was handicapped by never having to take his part in the hurly-burly of the House of Commons at the very time when Walpole was establishing that House as the decisive arbiter of national policy. Secondly, he did not take account, as Pitt did, of the dependence of foreign policy on parliamentary strength in internal politics, and was apt to treat colleagues like Newcastle, immersed in the details of building up parliamentary support, with a contempt which led to their revolt and his own downfall. Thirdly, though Newcastle's remark, that 'Carteret was a man who never doubted', is true enough, he never faced up to rebuffs with Pitt's sublime self-assurance—'I know that I can save the country, and that I alone can'; which meant that Pitt not only knew he could save the country but was determined to do so. Pitt, even in his most masterful moods, always recognized that his colleagues' and Parliament's assent was essential for carrying out his plans and always, till the very end of his great ministry, succeeded in obtaining their support either by persuasion or by threats of worse alternatives. Carteret, faced with serious opposition in 1724 and 1744—perhaps too proud to assert himself against intriguers he despised—simply threw up the sponge, and ended his days, giving indeed the best advice he could—and that was generally the best possible—but never pressing the point against strong opposition in his desire 'd'éviter toute noise'. As Horace Walpole said of him: 'Carteret was at once the victim, the creature and the scourge of the Duke of Newcastle.'

This view of Carteret as a great man *manqué* could not be better expressed than in Horace Walpole's epitaph:

Commanding beauty, smooth'd by chearful grace,
Sat on the open features of his face.
Bold was his language, rapid, glowing, strong,
And science flow'd spontaneous from his tongue.
A genius, seizing systems, slighting rules,
And void of gall, with boundless scorn of fools.
Ambition dealt her flambeau to his hand,
And Bacchus sprinkled fuel on the brand.
His wish—to counsel Monarchs, or controul,
His means—the impetuous ardours of his soul:
For while his views outstript a mortal span,
Nor prudence drew, nor craft pursu'd the plan.
Swift fell the scaffold of his airy pride,
But, slightly built, diffus'd no ruin wide.
Unhurt, undaunted, undisturb'd he fell,
Could laugh the same, and the same stories tell:
And, more a sage than he, who bade await
His revels, till his conquests were complete,
Our jovial statesman either sail unfurl'd,
And drank his bottle, tho' he miss'd the world.

And yet this noble tribute by a greater than Horace Walpole is
perhaps the truer account of Carteret's service to his country.
Chatham, in lofty words of gratitude, forty years after he had sat
at Carteret's feet,[1] told the House of Lords what he owed him:
"In the upper departments of government Lord Granville had
not his equal. I feel a pride in declaring that to his patronage, to
his friendship and instruction I owe whatever I am."

[1] See above, p. 106.

INDEX[1]

[1] Throughout the index the Duke of Newcastle is referred to as 'D. of N.' and Carteret, Lord Granville, as 'Cart.'

e Poitiers 1356) of Pelham in Herts.

ettled in Sussex, Constable of Pevensey Castle

amberlain to Henry V's wife Katharine)

n. Pelham of Laughton = (2) Mary d. of Lord Sands
d. 1539

II = Anne Sackville of Buckhurst

Sir William Pelham, soldier, and Ld. Justice in Ireland, d. 1587, ancestor of Pelhams of Brocklesbury Lincs. | Sir Edmund Pelham Chief Baron in Ireland d. 1606

mas Pelham = Mary Walsingham
: Barr.
40-1624

(2) Judith Shirley, (3) Mary Fane
s.p.   s.p.

Judith = E. of Rochford

Henry Pelham = Frances Brynde of Sussex

Annette Bridges = Thos. Pelham of Stanmer

hy sister of Walpole

nd = Sir Thos. Pelham Bart.

Baron Pelham of Stanmer 1768 E. of Chichester 1805

3. of Chichester = Lady Mary Osborne 756-1826

II = Hy. Thos. E. of Chichester 1804-86

=J. Naylor of Sussex | Frances = Ld. Castlecomer 1688-1756 1684-1719 | Lucy 1692-1736 = Hy. Fiennes-Clinton E. of Lincoln 1693-1728 | Margaret = Sir John Shelley 1696-1758 1692-1771 | Henrietta = E. of Onslow 1730-1809 1731-1814

Catherine = H. F.-Clinton E. of Lincoln, 1727-60 D. of Newcastle-under-Line 1768 | Henry D. of Newcastle 1720-94

Henry D. of Newcastle 1785-1851

Hy D. of Newcastle 1811-64

ıy Seal.
utenancies;
Cambridge
1st Lord of
1718 K.G.;
emander to
and Notts.;
e in Suffolk,
astle-under-

* Baron Pelham of Laughton Feb. 1711-12; Viscount Haughton of Notts, E. of Cla[re]
2 Aug. 1714; Marquess of Clare, 4th D. of Newcastle-on-Tyne, 2 Aug. 1715; D. of New[castle]
Line, with remainder to E. of Lincoln, 13 Nov. 1756; Baron Pelham of Stanmer with
Thos. Pelham of Stanmer, May 1762. 10 Oct. 1714, Ld. Lt. of Middx., Westminster
22 Oct. 1714, Warden of Sherwood Forest, etc.; 15 Ap. 1717, Ld. Chamberlain; 31 Marc[h]
2 April 1724, S. of S.; July 1737, High Steward of Cambridge; 14 Dec. 1748, Chancellor o[f]
Univ.; 6 March 1754, 1st Lord of Treasury; Nov. 1756, resigned Treasury; 2 July 1757
Treasury; 1761, Ld. Lt. of Sussex; May 1762, resigned Treasury; 1763, deprived of Ld. Li[eut]
July 1765, Lord Privy Seal; Sept. 1765, Ld. Lt. of Notts. again; Aug. 1766, R[e]signed Pr[ivy]

Grace = Lord Sondes

Grace
1687-1714

Catherine
Manners
1695?-1754

Henry Pelham = Lady Catherine

Lady Harriot Godolphin = Thomas Pelham-Holles
2 Ap. 1717
21 July/1 Aug. 1693-
17 Nov. 1768*

Lady Mary Bruden[ell]

Thos.

Ann Frankl[in]

Sir R.

Henrietta 1st dau. = 1st E. of Godolphin
1645-1712
and 2nd Duchess
of Marlborough
d. 1733

Mary 4th dau.
= 2nd D. of Montagu

(1) Elizabeth = Chas. Viscount Townshend = (2) Doro[thy]
1653-23 Feb. 1711-2
1st Baron Pelham
of Laughton (1706)   Sir Wm. Jones

Lady Eliz. Holles = Chas. Vane,
Lord Barnard

(2) Lady Grace Holles = Sir Thomas Pelham = (1) Elizabeth d. of

Lady Lucy Sidney = Sir John Pelham
d. of 2nd E. of   c. 1624-1703
Leicester

(1) Mary Wilbraham = Sir Thomas Pelham =
1597-1654

Denzil Ld. Holles 1675-93

Francis Ld. Holles 1627-90

Denzil Holles 1599-1680
Ld. Holles of Ifield (1661)

John Holles c. 1564-1637
16 Baron Laughton (Sussex)
1624 E. of Clare

Sir Wm. Holles

...Holles c. 1471-1572 of Stoke, Warwicks.
...of London, and property in 7 counties

John Pelham

Sir John Pelham fl. 1368,

Sir John Pelham (C...)

(1) Mary Carew = Sir W...
of Sussex

Sir Nicholas Pelha[m]
1515-60

Sir Th...

c. 1...

is...

Argent (Pelham)
...int Sable (Holles)

Argent
...his pride Argent
...gent

...er a bear proper, each gorged
...ent, buckle and studs Or

...e of Newcastle

...of

Mary 4th dau.
= 2nd D. of Montagu

...f Portland
...9-62

...rd
...1741

B. of Clare
...-89

E. of Clare
...9996

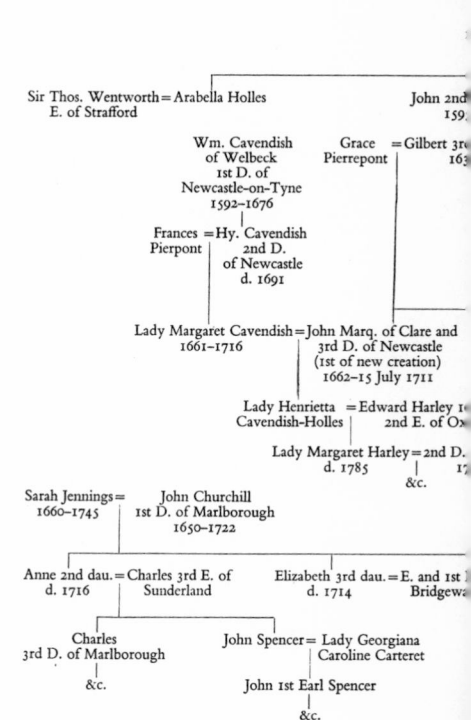

Sir William
Lord May...

Sir Thos. Wentworth = Arabella Holles   John 2nd
E. of Strafford   159.

Wm. Cavendish   Grace = Gilbert 3r...
of Welbeck   Pierrepont   163
1st D. of
Newcastle-on-Tyne
1592–1676

Frances = Hy. Cavendish
Pierpont   2nd D.
of Newcastle
d. 1691

Lady Margaret Cavendish = John Marq. of Clare and
1661–1716   3rd D. of Newcastle
(1st of new creation)
1662–15 July 1711

Lady Henrietta = Edward Harley 1...
Cavendish-Holles   2nd E. of Ox...

Lady Margaret Harley = 2nd D.
d. 1785 | 17
&c.

Sarah Jennings =   John Churchill
1660–1745   1st D. of Marlborough
1650–1722

Anne 2nd dau. = Charles 3rd E. of   Elizabeth 3rd dau. = E. 1st
d. 1716   Sunderland   d. 1714   Bridgewa...

Charles   John Spencer = Lady Georgiana
3rd D. of Marlborough | Caroline Carteret
| John 1st Earl Spencer
&c. |
&c.

Arms of Thomas Pelham-Holles,

Quarterly I and IV Azure 3 Pel...
   II and III Ermine 2 Piles

Crests (1) On a wreath a Peaco...
   (2) On a wreath a Buck...

Supporters Dexter a bay horse, ...
   with a belt Argent, strap...

Motto Vincit Amor Patriae